THE HON. MISS FERRARD

BY

MAY LAFFAN

AUTHOR OF THE FOLLOWING WORKS IN THE SEASIDE LIBRARY:

NO.		CTS.
681	A Singer's Story	10

ORDINARY EDITION:

NO.		CTS.
563	Flitters, Tatters, and the Counsellor	10
763	No Relations	20
1100	Weeds	10
1175	Hogan, M. P.	10

NEW YORK
GEORGE MUNRO, PUBLISHER
17 TO 27 VANDEWATER STREET

NOTE.—*The Author has consented to some modifications in this edition made by an American editor with reference to local tastes.*

THE HONORABLE MISS FERRARD.

CHAPTER I.

"Mon avis est, qu'on ne peut créer des personnages que lorsqu'on a beaucoup étudié les hommes, comme on ne peut parler une langue qu'à la condition de l'avoir sérieusement appris."—DUMAS.

THE mail from Ballycormack to Darraghstown, a rickety old outside-car, painted red, with her Majesty's initials interlaced in yellow paint on the back of the well, carried on the 18th of September, 187—, an unusual burden. A tourist on one side, and his luggage, which balanced him nicely, carefully fastened on the other seat. The tourist was a man of about thirty-five, dressed in a shooting-suit of heather mixture, with knickerbockers and stout buttoned boots, one of which dangled carelessly below the foot-board as he leaned back on the well. He was a strongly-built man, with a tanned face and bright English blue eyes, which roved over the landscape incessantly and intelligently. The driver's head was bent to one side, following with his eyes the outstretched hand of his fare, and answering the never-ceasing questions with which he plied him.

"That is Darraghmore—eh?" the tourist said.

"That's Darraghmore, your honor; I'll pull up one minute here at the gap in the hedge, and then you'll have a clane view of the front. All the land you can see now on the far side of the river was the estate, up over there to the foot of Tobergeen, an' the finest pasture ever you seen lies there beyond to the wood. The demesne was five miles long, and the river ran by the bounds of it; Jim Devereux's farm 'tis called now."

"What's that I see to the left? a ruin?"

"Yes, your honor, that's a ruin—one of the owld castles Cromwell tumbled down. What you see is the new castle, though it's owld enough too."

"It does not look very old."

"Not from this, sir. There's more than three miles between you and it, but if you were nearer there's not a windy, nor a chimney, nor, for the matter of that, a floor left in it—"

"A floor, do you say! What happened then?"

"Augh, sir, the old lord before he was bate up entirely was livin' in it, an' sure they didn't care what they done wid it. So they burned the flooring of all the rooms they didn't want, an' a part of the stairs an' the dures; just whatever come handy. Get along wid ye, Bess."

Then Bess, a wiry old gray mare, received a cut of the whip that made her start at a pace that soon left the great bleak house behind. Mr. Satterthwaite forgot his cigar and turned his head to watch, as long as the car kept the valley road, the beautiful view that lay beneath.

"They're a terrible crew, them Ferrards," the driver began again after awhile. "Like most of the rale owld stock, they were bad livers. Anyhow they're broke now, horse and foot."

"Are they? Who were they? Lord Darraghmore—I know that name. I've seen it beyond a doubt," he added to himself, "but I never heard it within my recollection—was Lord Darraghmore married? Tell me about the family."

The driver was only too happy to be allowed to do this; and his passenger, having rekindled his cigar, disposed himself comfortably to listen.

"Married? wisha! he was married twice itself, an' has

sons and daughters as old as what I am, an' that's forty odd. He wasn't more than eighteen when he ran away to the Continent with a Dublin lady. She was no match for him, an' when she died he married an Englishwoman; she'd a couple of thousand, I b'lieve—but that was a drop in the sea to me lord."

"Are there any children living?"

"There's children, sir, as I said, plenty; but whether they are all to the good or no, I can't say. The eldest son of all in the Austrian army, another's gone to the diggings, wan was shot, an' wan was drownded at sea, an' wan died—anyhow they say he died. Then there's three boys by the last mar'ge. I b'lieve they're wid him, wherever he is."

"No daughters?"

"Ay! wan married some fellow, an' she's livin' in Paris wid him—God forgive me if I'm tellin' a lie, but they do say he can't live in this country; an' wan married a sailor chap, a captain of some boat they were travelin' by. There's wan by the second wife, too."

"Were there no relatives? no friends?" asked the Englishman, thinking it strange that in this tuft-hunting age the Misses Ferrard could not have found mates more suitable to their rank in life than "the fellow in Paris" or the "sailor chap."

"I dunno, sir; 'tis twenty years nearly since they left this, an' I disremember; but my father—God ha' mercy on him—I mind him sayin' Ferrard o' Darraghmore was worth, once on a time, twenty thousand a year. Augh! they're a terrible lot. They'd go through the Bank, sir; not but what these never had so much. Claude Ferrard, that's the last lord, he kept race-horses an' a pack of hounds; a hogshead of whiskey stood in the hall; an' I believe, when this man got it, what wid Jews, an' lawyers, an' leases fallin', there wasn't more than three thousand a year left. He just came home here from abroad wid his wife, when Claude dropped, an' he brought a pack of furriners wid him; then they just lathered away till he had to run in the night!"

"Ah! indeed, the good old style of living, hey?"

"Bedad, yes, sir; rale old stock, them Ferrards, an' as handsome men and women as ever walked!"

"None of them ever did anything for themselves—anything for a living, I mean?"

"Is it gentry like them?" returned the driver, scornfully. "No Ferrard that ever stepped yet set hand to anything, if it wasn't the stock of a gun or may be a fishing-rod; I remember Claude, the lord that will be, the greatest shot ever I seen. Many a time when I was a boy I followed him into the bogs after the ducks an' snipe. Sure it was that way the second wan was killed."

"Ah! by accident?"

"Be accident," replied the driver, shutting up his lips tightly and nodding his head significantly, as if to give his listener to infer that there was a great deal more in it than he chose to tell.

Mr. Satterthwaite did not press him; from what he had said of the family in general it was easy to deduce that the "second one" had met with a violent death, deserved or not. He leaned his elbow on the well, and giving the Jarvey a cigar, lighted a fresh one for himself, and letting his eyes wander at pleasure over the wild vale of the Darragh river, amused himself conjuring up pictures of the savage tribe that had once peopled the desolate house of Darraghmore.

A mellow September sunset gilded the birch copses and lighted up the red trunks of the pines that crowned the hill; a light breeze, scented with the ripe autumn bouquet of the woods, swept the leaves, which were yet crisp and dry, in fantastic dances along the road. The river, a mere brook, but deep and swift, was now rushing angrily through a rocky channel below and sent up a hollow roar. The rooks were hovering over their nests in a black cloud, and their hoarse cawing was borne fitfully on the wind. A flock of wild geese, flying southward, passed overhead with their weird, clanging cry.

"That's for a hard winter," said the driver, pointing up to the emigrants with his whip; "an' the haws are thick an' early too."

The car was going down the hill now, and about a mile ahead could be seen the pale thin smoke of Darraghstown. It soon turned into a broad high-road running level with the river-side. Here the river joined its waters to those of a broader stream which, wide and smooth, was almost hidden from sight by the tall reeds which lined both banks and swung their tasseled heads with the wind.

"That's the Rack, sir; there it goes off by Lord Comerford's park. He holds the most of the old lord's ground now."

"Lord Comerford? Oh, yes, to be sure, he has a place here."

"He has a place here," continued the driver, "sure enough, your honor, but divvle a toe of the rackrentin' blackguard has been in it these two years. He have an agent, though, an', be jabers, he won't be left in it long."

The driver closed his sentence with an impressive snap of his jaws. He would have liked to entangle Mr. Satterthwaite in a discussion on Lord Comerford's doings, and to terrify him, as he loved to do all strangers, with a history of the vengeances planning for the absentee and his agents; but his listener was well up to that sort of thing, so turned a deaf ear to him.

"Whose house is that?" he asked, abruptly, indicating a handsome cottage in the Swiss style, situated on the brow of a hill.

"That's Really's, sir—Reilly he was in Cork before he got rich an' grand, an' madam they call his wife! Over there to the left of you, the brown house with the garden"—he pointed with his whip to a big straggling edifice—"that's Hoolahan's; he made all his money in the town; Strains has his shop now. There's another nice house an' place out on the Comerford road, it belongs to Tom Fair; he's a jah pea and a great man entirely."

"Jah pea, jah pea," repeated the Englishman to himself in a puzzled tone of voice. "Oh! I've got it now—Justice of the Peace, J.P. Well," he went on aloud, "you have a good sprinkling of respectable people. Darraghstown is not so badly off after all."

"No, bedad, as times goes," replied the carman, flinging away the ash of his cigar.

"Tell me, my man, which is the best hotel in the town?"

"Best! your honor? I'll take you to the best, never fear; 'twill be easy doin' that!" he added with a grin, "seein' there's only wan in the place. That's the weir, sir," said he, pointing to the left of the bridge by which the car was now passing; "an' do you see that big ash tree? just by the stump of that Mr. Hawtrey was shot dead. Poor Con O'Moore! he was a grand aim, to be sure."

"What had Mr. Hawtrey done?" asked the tourist in a dry tone, after a long look in the direction of the ash tree.

"Done, is it, your honor? raisin' the rints, an' harassin', an' parsecutin'. He was noticed to drop it a half dozen ov times. So, bedad, poor Con was brought down to him, an' then there it was."

"Con was hanged, eh?" said Mr. Satterthwaite, whose ear had detected a sorrowful tone in the pronunciation of Mr. O'Moore's first name.

"Ay, faith, sir! the poor boy, he earned his hangin' on that bit of wild justice."

"I think so, indeed. Wild justice!" repeated Mr. Satterthwaite to himself with a laugh. "I wonder has this gentleman any idea of the context of Lord Bacon's saying. Who first taught these wretches to abuse that expression, I wonder? and has my loquacious friend got wind of my intended purchase of Rosslyne estate in this district? if so, these delightful anecdotes may have a special meaning."

The car had crossed the river now by a broad, single-arched bridge, and Mr. Satterthwaite was busy looking at a double row of miserable cabins with sunk roofs and dreadfully dilapidated walls. These gave way soon to a row of plastered houses two stories high, the lower parts of which seemed to be occupied by shops; then they came to the market-place, an open square. At right angles with this ran a fine highway leading out across the country, and flanked for a short distance by houses of somewhat better appearance than those of the main street, but equally old and ill-kept externally. The river, which had taken a bend to the right after passing beneath the bridge, ran behind these houses.

"That's the chapel down there, your honor," said the driver; "and the red house with the white wall to the garden, that's the priest's house—'tis the biggest of them. Then Dr. Cartan's and the dispensary, and next to him—this one we're passin' now—is Lawyer Perry's."

The tourist looked up quickly at the name and glanced at the house indicated by his driver. It stood in a little way from the unpaved footpath, from which an ill-kept front garden divided it. The windows were dirty and some of them were without blinds; and the yellow plaster was discolored and in many places had fallen off. A number of faces, most of them young, presented themselves at the panes of the lower front windows as the mail passed.

"Them's the Miss Perrys," explained the driver; "'tis a wonder they're not out in the street; they mostly meets the mail-cart every night. Fine blossoms they are. Owld Perry can give every wan o' 'em twelve or fifteen hundred; small good that money'll do any one that gets it."

"How many of them are there?" asked his passenger, who seemed to make some mental calculation.

"How did he make it, is it, your honor?" replied the driver, purposely misunderstanding him. "Oh! how does all lawyers make their money? The Old Boy helps them. They say Perry was one ov them that helped to sell up owld Lord Darraghmore; but how do I know?" he added, cautiously. "He is an awful man hereabouts anyhow. He has a couple of farms there beyant Comerford Park he got from the poor men that had them, lending money to them and closin' on their leases. Oh! he's an owld rogue—a condemned owld villain!"

"Is that a mill?" asked Mr. Satterthwaite as they passed the corner house—a large, rambling old building, with latticed windows and with old gables to which the ivy formed a green frame-work, and no doubt helped to hold secure. The front was nearly hidden by rows of overgrown holly and poplar trees. Beside the house and separating it from the bridge was a high wall, over which appeared the slated roofs of outhouses which looked like stores.

"It was a mill, sir, but now the building is used for wool-stores—Milligan's 'tis called; there's no one in it but the old couple that owns it all. Sure if you wanted lodgings they'd take your honor and welcome—"

"No, no! take me to the hotel."

In a moment or two the car drew up at the post-office. This was a little crockery-shop, on one side of which was a wooden partition, dividing off a space of about four feet square, where the telegraphist, who was also post-mistress, fulfilled her joint avocations. There were two or three other mail-cars which had arrived some time before, and the bags were being made up for the seven o'clock mail train which was to be met at a station five miles away.

"Come on here, Batterstown mails," said a hanger-on; "ye're late a quarter of an hour already."

Mr. Satterthwaite had got down, and having taken his valise was counting out the fare to the driver.

"'Twas the stops as done it, captain dear," he said, with a sly, appealing look.

This was irresistible, so an extra two-shilling piece was forthcoming to mend matters, and with a grin that argued but scant reverence for outraged official punctilio, the driver disappeared into the murky shop, and the Englishman crossed the street to the Darraghmore Arms Hotel.

"Private rooms, sir, this way," said the landlord. "Dinner? yes, sir, directly; what would you like?"

"What would I like?" thought Mr. Satterthwaite, rather amused at the query, and divining by the light of experience what this apparently unlimited field of choice would resolve itself into.

He was not hungry, and having a mind to chaff the landlord, replied literally:

"Have you got a lobster? What soup have you?"

"No lobster, sir; we don't have fish unless specially ordered from Waterford."

"Well now, my good fellow," said the stranger with a smile, sitting down in an easy-chair, "to save trouble let's say at once bacon and cabbage, or rashers and eggs?"

Now it was the landlord's turn to smile.

"We can do better for you than that, sir; I've a good dish of river trout just come in, and there's a cold partridge. Could give you a fowl, sir."

"Thank you; I'll have the trout and the cold partridge. I'll go out for a stroll; you may have a fire lighted here when I return."

So Satterthwaite set out to stretch his legs for half an hour by a walk about the town; he had plenty of roads to choose from. The main street, and, at right angles with it, the Comerford road or the Dublin highway. They were all dry and inviting looking; there was nothing doing in the little town. A few country women stood at the corners with pails of milk, which they were selling to the towns-folk. A little crowd of loungers was gathered near the post-office, reading the Dublin papers which had just arrived by the mail. Flocks of geese, half-starved dogs, and lank-bodied pigs roamed the streets at their wills.

He walked up the town and passed the rows of cabins and the cemetery, and, ascending the slope on which lay this last, entered the parish chapel. It was a large limestone edifice, imposing enough outside. The interior was a fair specimen of the meretricious taste he had observed in all the chapels he had visited during his stay in the south. The limestone pillars, tolerably well-hewn square blocks, had all been plastered, as had also the solid mouldings, and the walls, which in addition were nearly covered with stenciled patterns in glaring pink, green, and yellow. Bands of hideous little wheels, meant to represent roses, and acorns growing upon nothing ran round and round, and up and down everywhere. The chapel was very large and lofty in proportion, and the effect of these stenciled wreathings in certain positions, such as over a lofty window, was simply that of a smear such as a gigantic dirty finger might make. The altar was of white Carrara marble—of the most approved style of confectioner's work. On it were placed pots of French india-rubber flowers, selected, as the tourist noted with a smile, without much regard to the "unities," if one may so express it, of season. Roses placed beside camellias, and white lilies and dahlias blooming simultaneously. The altar must have cost a large sum, to judge by the fineness of the carving, which was utterly lost owing to its comparatively small size.

Satterthwaite sat down on a bench to rest and leaned back, for he was a little weary after his long drive, and unused, moreover, to the jolting of the barbarous vehicle.

Above the high altar was a large stained-glass window. The evening sun shone on this, and the rays fell through, split into gorgeous rainbow-like bands of purple, crimson, and yellow, which streamed into the sanctuary and made the aisles and side-chapels look dark and shadowy. The lamp before the altar seemed dead; its little flame was so colorless in comparison.

The chief feature of the interior of the church was, however, the huge painted statues distributed about at the bases of the pillars; they were gorgeously colored—scarlet and sky-blue being the predominant tones of the drapery; even the eyes, hair, and cheeks were liberally tinted. St. John, the patron saint of the church, who was in the place of honor, looked like a typical South German with his turquoise blue eyes, long blonde ringlets, and vividly pink fingers, which the blue and gold garments set off to perfection.

"Who first conceived the design of such a creation?" thought Mr. Satterthwaite, staring at it in wonder. "After all," he continued to himself, "it may be some comfort to those poverty-stricken creatures who frequent the church to think that in heaven, which is specially reserved for poor people, they will be clothed like these saints."

Then a low muttering sound reached his ears. A couple of poor, barefooted old women had come in noiselessly and were praying; one with her arms uplifted in the form of a cross, under the lamp. The red glare of its flame was now apparent, for the sunbeams had vanished, and with them the glories of the "storied window richly dight." Wretchedly poor the old creatures looked; one, with a white, wrinkled face, had an air of quiet thoughtfulness, almost of refinement, about her as she prayed, the beads of her old black rosary slipping one by one through her fingers, and her eyes fixed immovably on the altar.

A window was open at the side, and the swallows, not yet away to their winter quarters beyond the sea, were flitting to and fro from their nests; there was a heavy odor of lime and paint, and Satterthwaite began to feel the place oppressive. He got up to go, and taking some small change from his pocket laid it on the ground beside the old women; they took it up gratefully with many muttered benedictions as he walked away, having evidently directed their orisons into a new channel.

"Now to the post," thought Mr. Satterthwaite; "the crowd will have dispersed by this. I hope to get letters and papers from Limerick; I hope they won't have forgotten them."

As he strolled back down the main street, the little shops beginning to light their lamps,—gas had not yet got to Darraghstown—cast a pale reflection on the cobblestone pavement. He found, as he anticipated, the place tolerably free from loungers; received the packet, and, bestowing it for the nonce in the pocket of his great-coat, on thoughts of dinner intent, sought the inn once more.

As he turned the corner he almost knocked against a trio of loud-voiced girls, advancing at a pace that was almost a run from the main street in the direction of the Comerford road. They all wore felt hats, flying off the backs of their heads, and their round, staring eyes looked out under "fringed" hair. One, who, from the fact of her wearing short skirts and a long yellow mane of ill-kempt hair down her back, seemed to be about fifteen or sixteen, turned and looked after the oddly-dressed stranger with a giggle. The others, who might have been any age from eighteen to twenty-five, walked on demurely enough. Satterthwaite remembered the eager faces he had seen looking out of Lawyer Perry's windows and the driver's comments.

"Poor girls," thought he, "shut up in such a place as Darraghstown. I don't wonder the coming and going of the mail should be the event of the day."

By this time he had reached his room. The fire was sparkling in the grate; a fire of sods, piled up evenly in the grate, and blazing intensely. No fire so picturesque—not even the split pine fires of Norway. The cloth had been laid on a round table at one side of the fire, a sofa drawn up to the other; altogether it looked very snug and inviting.

The river trout was capital, the partridge by no means to be despised; and the host uncorked a bottle of dry sherry which, considering where he was, fairly astonished the tourist. Dinner over, the landlord presented himself to remove the cloth and asked Satterthwaite if he would care for a cup of coffee. He declined this, however, and having ordered tea at nine o'clock and made the necessary inquiries about the morning mail train to Dublin, lay down on the sofa to read his correspondence.

Sir Frederick Redingham, whose shooting-box he had quitted that morning before post-hour, had promised to forward everything to Darraghmore. Nothing was there of importance; an invitation to go up to Banff for a fortnight's deer-stalking.

"It might not be a bad plan to go north," thought Mr. Satterthwaite, lazily.

Then he lighted a cheroot; the long drive in the cool mountain air had left a sort of drowsiness of mind and body. He tried to read the paper; there was nothing in the *Pall Mall Gazette*. A Dublin paper rolled out of the next wrapper torn open. What did he care about Dublin? To be sure there was the advertisement of that property he had been told about. Wherever are the

Landed Estates Court's advertisements? At last—"All that and those—hum—hum! Barony of Darragh—barony of Clonfislk—acreage—turbary—" Mr. Satterthwaite threw it away also and took up a tiny, ill-printed county paper—a weekly—issued that very morning.

Almost the first thing that caught his eye was the following paragraph:

"It may be of interest to some of our readers to learn that we have received intelligence of the death of Lady Darraghmore, which lamentable event took place in Galway on Thursday morning. Her ladyship was the second wife of Lord Darraghmore, and leaves three sons and one daughter to mourn her loss."

"Doesn't say whose daughter her ladyship was," noted he, laying down the paper and composing himself for a nap till tea-time; "nor how old either. I wonder if the peerage will ever hear of that lamentable demise?"

It seemed to him that he had only been asleep a few minutes when the landlord came in with tea.

"I say, what's this in the Darraghstown—*Ballynahinch Advertiser*, eh? I mean the death of Lady Darraghmore."

"Yes, sir. No one knew anything of it till that came out this afternoon. The family are quite broken up, sir—have left Darraghmore this twenty years or more."

"Who was the second Lady Darraghmore?" he asked.

"No one knows, sir, hereabouts; though she lived here for some time. An Englishwoman—she had money I believe, too."

"They were very extravagant?"

"Extravagance, sir, did all the mischief; and they are all as proud and fiery as can be. Lord Darraghmore must be seventy now—fully seventy, and a fine old family they are, too."

Satterthwaite dismissed his host and promised himself to make inquiries about this fine old Irish family as soon as he reached London. He meant to start next morning and counted upon arriving there the following day

CHAPTER II.

"Voir et peindre sont deux. Tout ce que l'artiste peut espérer de mieux, c'est d'engager ceux qui ont des yeux à regarder aussi."

ONE gusty evening, late in September, there might have been seen in the window of a house situated in one of the old narrow streets of Galway the face of a young girl pressed close against the dingy pane. The street led down to the Claddagh; and from her post of observation the watcher could see a narrow strip of Galway Bay and a part of the harbor wall. On this was gathered a number of people on the look-out for the fishing-boats, whose red sails were now rounding the headland into the bay. Up and down the street passed the fishers, male and female, to whom the Claddagh, of savory memory, is consecrated; and the shrill accents of the women as they hurried to and fro rose to the ears of the girl. She could not see the entry of the boats into the harbor, but she knew from the attitudes and motions of those on the pier wall that they were in sight; and also that, as soon as the first boat should reach the quay, the figures would disappear from her view, quitting their perch in eager haste to hail the fishers and learn their luck.

Nearly opposite to her window was one of the finest relics of Moorish architecture to be found in Galway—the horse-shoe arches of the doors, the rich tracery of the lintels, the ornaments, medallion-shaped, let into the walls and inscribed with some strange lettering, half defaced and nearly hid by the grasses and weeds that had taken root among the cracks—all formed a picture to delight the eye. A tall, handsome peasant girl, straight and lithe as a willow wand, dressed in a skirt of the madder red worn by the Galway women, with a snowy kerchief pinned across her shapely bust, halted for a moment in the archway, and, laying down her basket, looked down the street towards the sea. The exquisite grace and naturalness of her *pose*, the brilliant colors of her dress relieved against the gray stone framing, formed a picture that would have impressed itself indelibly on an artist's brain, until he reproduced it in tints as vivid on his canvas.

After a stay of a minute or two the girl was joined by a tall lad, whose leather boots reaching mid-leg showed him to belong to the folk of the Claddagh. The girl lifted her basket once more; he, with scant gallantry, trudged on beside her, his brawny fists buried in his pockets, and they disappeared from view.

The street seemed crowded now; nearly all the idlers thronged down to witness the arrival of the boats. The red skirts of the women formed picturesque bits of color among the crowd, and their shrill, quick speech rang above the muttered English of the black-coated townsfolk. The dusk was falling now; the Angelus had rung from the chapel bells some time before, and the girl's eyes were strained to see the figures on the pier wall. She turned her head peevishly to reply to some one who addressed her; when she looked again she uttered a cry as if of relief. The watchers were all gone. Mauriade Blake's red petticoat (she was the tallest woman in the Claddagh) had disappeared. The fishing-boats were in.

"They're in now," she said, swinging herself leisurely off the window-ledge and crossing the room to the fireplace.

"Hel, you can say so to Cawth, then," said some one from a dark corner by the fire.

The voice came from an old man who was stretched at full length on a sofa near the fire. As he spoke to the girl he raised his head, and the light from the turf fire fell on it. He must have been at one time a handsome man, tall and shapely, with a fine skin, and clearly cut, if somewhat weak, features. A quantity of white hair still curled about his temples, and the right hand, which hung listlessly down nearly touching the floor, was perfect in form. His attire consisted of a huge frieze great-coat wrapped over a double-breasted and tightly-buttoned frock-coat; neither collar nor shirt was to be seen, and an old greasy neck-tie covered the neck to the chin. He seemed feeble and weak, and spoke with a querulous, trembling voice. A clay pipe was beside him on a chair, with a sheet of the London *Times*. A huge old wolf-dog lay on the floor, every now and again opening his bleared, dull eyes and looking affectionately at his master.

The girl turned away and opening a door which led into a back room disappeared from sight. Presently she came back; in her hand an old branched candlestick, grimy and ill-kept, in which were a pair of candles lighted. She set this on the table near the old man, and then returned to her post by the window.

She was a slight, unformed creature, perhaps sixteen years old. Her hair, thick and black, was plaited in one rough, loose tail that hung nearly to her waist. It grew low on her forehead, but her temples were wide and clear; the eyebrows black, straight, and very close set; her eyes were a long almond shape, and their color was the rarest, sweetest color in the world, violet blue. The lashes were long and thick and turned up at the ends. For the rest, the profile was irregular, the nose the least bit *retroussé*, and the upper lip rather short; but the teeth were the most beautiful little pearls; when she smiled, which the Honorable Helena Ferrard did not often vouchsafe to do, the red lips parted, and they showed with a flash that was like a surprise. Her skin was pale, naturally pale—perhaps olive would describe her complexion best; and the expression of her face, grievous to relate, was ill-tempered in the extreme. The straight, fine brows were almost always puckered in a frown, and the pout of her under lip, though in part natural, was also in great part acquired. It was a troubled, anxious little face altogether, and, though forbidding, a face with such a charm of its own that one who saw it once must remember it ever after. Her figure was unformed and angular. She had, like her father, fine hands and feet, but, truth to say, their unwashed condition detracted as much from the one as did the huge coarse brogues and knitted stockings from the other. She wore a skirt of black wool—just what the peasants had—so coarse that it might be taken for bearskin; a hideously-made tunic of cheap black material; no collar, no cuffs, no brooch, or attempt at girlish decoration of any kind. Such was the attire of Lord Darraghmore's daughter.

For at least twenty minutes she crouched in her window-seat, one arm resting on the deep window-sash and her cheek lying on it. The old man got up off the sofa, and, pushing the wolf-dog aside with a petulant gesture, began to walk slowly up and down the room. He had a tall figure, though the white head was sadly sunk between the shoulders, and the slovenliness of his dress, added to his slouching, broken gait, contributed almost equally to degrade his stature. The frieze great-coat, fastened round his neck by a looped thong, slipped and fell as he brushed against the table. He looked at it in a helpless, wondering way for a second, then pushed it with his foot beneath the table and resumed his tramp. The wolf-dog, whom not one of his master's gestures escaped, spied it, slunk across to where it lay, and, walking round once or twice after his tail in dog fashion, lay down comfortably. The occupant of the window viewed both incidents unmoved and approving.

The flooring of the room was oak, but crusted with the dirt of ages. There was a high oak wainscoting all round; in this sundry nails had been driven, from which hung various articles of clothing. Among them a battered black hat with a veil of new crape hanging loosely from it. In a corner was a stack of guns, fishing-rods, and spears of different sorts; powder-horns, shot-cases, and belts littered a small table in a corner. Newspapers, torn and dirty, were strewn here and there. The big deal-table in the middle of the room and the smaller one in the corner, with my lord's sofa, was all the plenishing to be seen. A wooden bench was scarcely visible in a recess, which evidently held the family wardrobe. Huge fishing-boots, tarpaulin coats and leggings, sticks, and straps, and head-gear were piled together. A little three-legged stool, set near the hearth—there was no grate, and the peat burned on the floor—seemed to indicate the place of the lady of the house.

"It's seven—past," Lord Darraghmore said at last, pausing in his walk to look at a huge old gold watch which he carried in his pocket.

The girl left her seat with an abrupt movement and crossed to the back room, swinging the door roughly behind her as she did so.

"Cawth!" she cried, after a glance round. "Cawth!"

"Well, what's it ye're needin' noo?" snapped a cross voice from another door.

An old woman, carrying a kettle of water which she had been down to the street pump to fill, made her appearance. She was dressed much like the girl, save that she wore a decent white cap on her head, and a kerchief of thick gray wool was folded across her shoulders and chest. Her face was a curious study. Wrinkled and tinted like a last year's russet apple, it presented a mixture of cunning and malignity. Keen gray-blue eyes looked from under bushy brows, and from her almost toothless mouth issued a grating north-of-Ireland brogue. She advanced to the fire and pulling towards her the chain which hung down the chimney, fastened the heavy iron kettle over the blazing stack of peats, grumbling all the while.

"Yon Connaught deevils, splatterin' and pushin' for a drap watter. See to ma coats a' wat wi' them. Loupin', roupin', Connaught thieves!"

"Go down and tell them so," was Miss Ferrard's comment after a deliberate survey of her domestic's apparel. "Cook some fish; the boats are in this half-hour."

"They're no come, though. Ye can just bide, an' I'll mak' the one job o' the cookin'."

Miss Ferrard's eyes flashed and her level brows met in a frown. She walked past her rebellious menial, who had just seated herself on a low stool by the fire, and seized a gridiron which hung on the wall close by; with the other hand she detached the kettle from its hook, then she planted the gridiron on the glowing fire and cast a glance round in search of the fish.

The beldame, furious, rose from her creepy stool and interposed a forbidding hand. Just at that moment a tramp was heard on the stairs. The old woman darted to place the fish on the fire, and the girl marched back in calm indifference to the other room.

The door was opened violently and three lads entered. One, who seemed, indeed, to have reached manhood, carried a number of lines, which he flung without more ado into the nearest corner; the other two carried between them a large open creel filled with fish—herring, skate, and different kinds of flat fish. The three might have been aged respectively from twenty to seventeen, broad-shouldered, athletic-looking fellows, dark of eye and skin, and with resolute, sullen faces, slovenly of dress and dour of manner like their sister.

Not one word of greeting did the fishers vouchsafe. The creel was swung down close by the wall, and kicking their wet boots off with some difficulty, they set to grope under tables and in recesses for dry foot-covering. These found after some delay, the two younger ones seated themselves at opposite corners of the hearth. The eldest, first kicking away an old lurcher dog who was snuffing hungrily around the creel of fish, went into the other room.

The old man paused in his walk and turned his dull eye on the new-comer.

"Ha, Clan, what luck have you had?"

"Ugh!" growled the son, "not much; no good fish." Then he seated himself on a chair by the fire and held out his hands, reddened by exposure and the sea-water, over the cheerful blaze.

Clanrickarde, Charles, and Isidor—for so were named the three sons of Lord Darraghmore by his second marriage with an Englishwoman, a dissenting tradesman's daughter, whose beauty (it was from her the family inherited their swarthy good looks) had attracted him in one of his rambles in England—had just at present a heavy task devolving upon them, neither more nor less than the imperative duty of providing the necessaries of life for their father and sister as well as themselves. Not, indeed, that it was anything unusual, for, since ever one of them had been able to set a trap, load a gun, or handle rod or spear, their services had been in requisition at odd times to supply the family larder.

It was not that Lord Darraghmore was penniless. His estates were gone it is true, but there remained something out of the burning. A sister of his who had enjoyed during her life a rent-charge of four hundred a year had died some time after they had left Darraghmore, and on the death of her husband five or six years after this income returned to the Ferrards. It was paid quarterly in instalments of a hundred pounds, sometimes more, sometimes less, being subject to the fluctuations to which all Irish incomes arising out of property of the description, namely, petty farms, are liable to. Four hundred a year might represent to some people a means of tolerably decent independence; to the Ferrards it just afforded a few weeks' riotous living, to be followed by a period of borrowing, account-running wherever they could get credit, and even actual want. They migrated from town to town according as their habits became known, and, indeed, according to the degree of temperature to which the young men raised the social thermometer. Everywhere they ran headlong into debt; every quarter-day a few of the most pressing demands were settled, and when it came to the last, abandoning such of their worldly goods as they could not conveniently carry away with them, the brood, parent birds and all, dispersed, usually in the night-time and singly, to assemble again at some given point.

The children had grown up anyhow; they were never rebuked, though often ill-treated. They were all perfectly ignorant; the national schools were of course out of the question for them, pride forbade that idea. They learned somehow to read—a questionable advantage, to judge by the style of literature they affected—and to scrawl their names when called upon to do so. The old man was perfectly apathetic; so long as he had a pipeful of tobacco in his tattered leather pouch, on which was stamped the crest and motto of the Ferrards (a falcon with bloody beak, and the legend *Rapax*), almost effaced, he cared for nothing. He sent every quarter-day a pound to London to pay his quarterly subscription to the London *Times; Bell's Life* came every week for Clanrickarde. Nobody ever looked at the *Times* save the old lord; but even Helena, or, as she was familiarly called, Hel, took an interest in the racy style of the sporting oracle. For the rest their reading consisted mainly of odd numbers of Beadle's American Library, the wild backwoods adventures, hair-breadth escapes therein related being eminently to their taste, and the less innocent histories of those British worthies, Jack Sheppard, Blueskin, Charley Wag, and the like. Now and again, when the whim took them and they chanced to have respectable clothes, which, to tell the truth, was very seldom, Helena and her youngest and favorite brother Isidor would attend church—Lord Darraghmore never went. Clan and Char were always out.

As to society, they had none. Not one of the respectable families of the various places they visited ever called upon them; a stranger was never allowed into their rooms on any pretext, and the wolf-dog and the other canine inmates of Cawth's apartment sufficiently protected their masters from intrusion. Lady Darraghmore had been as "queer," to use the common qualification of the family, as the rest of them, if not more so. Strange stories were current in Galway as to her death and the manner of it. However, she was now a week buried, and outsiders, as well as her husband and children, had grown used to the loss. Cawth McGonigle, the nurse of the children, did all that was necessary for their comfort now as heretofore. They missed her but little; it was not in the Ferrard nature to show grief or feeling. Clan took the old broken arm-chair that her ladyship used to sit in opposite to his lordship's sofa; Hel had her own creepy stool by the lug of the chimney as of old, where she sat by the hour staring with her wide-open violet eyes into the red glow of the peats, or reading by their fitful light some wild story of Western adventure, fancying herself a squaw in a wigwam by Lake Huron, or roaming the prairies with Deerslayer or the pioneers. Had she been a Catholic, some good-hearted priest would have made interest for the desolate, neglected little girl, and have shipped her across the seas to some quiet Belgian convent, where she would have been tamed and trained into piety and industry, where one day she might have taken the veil and passed a quiet dream-like life away from the toil and strife of the wild nomads amongst whom her lines had fallen. Had she been a Catholic, things would have been different; the common people would have treated the family with more respect, they would have sympathized with them as "belonging to themselves;" their misfortunes would have been ascribed to "the troubles," to their rulers, to the English, just as they laid their own wretched conditions to the charge of the aliens and heretics who lorded it over them. But the Ferrards were Protestants, stem and branch, consequently their poverty and degradation brought them only contumely. They were treated by the Catholics as the poor whites were treated in the slave states of America in former times. Despised by the negroes, and almost disowned by their more fortunate fellow-citizens, they received none of the adulation and respect accorded so lavishly to the estated heretic who drives his carriage and pair. As poor Protestants, shiftless and dirty as the Catholics themselves, they were held as creatures with whom even the devil had broken his compact. They were an anomaly, an anachronism, and unaccountable.

The young people were by no means unconscious of

this, and doubtless it was some misgivings on the subject that had prompted the flight of the senior brood. Already Clan had given some dark hints of his feelings. While his mother lived she would not hear of any change, but the young man was now growing tired of the everlasting fishing and hunting, and with his sprouting beard had come ideas of a wider range of living, of a state of existence where there was bigger game than rabbits and trout, varied in season by an occasional buck or salmon filched from demesne or river.

Cawth, the nurse, sharp-eyed and observant, watched all these signs and waited, knowing that the time was not far off when Clan would some early morning put on his stoutest boots, pat the old wolf-dog on the head, and go, as his brothers, the "lord" that was to be, and Brand and Louis had done before him, never to return. Then it would be Char's turn, unless fate by some ugly thrust, such as had cut short the life of Walter, the second son, should interfere. Isidor and Helena would seek their fortunes together, and by that time the old lord and Cawth need not care.

Such were the Ferrards of Darraghmore.

After a short delay Cawth came in bearing a huge trencher of grilled fish. She laid this on a corner table for a moment, then pulled a tattered and dirty cloth out of a drawer; this spread on the table, black-handled knives and forks were distributed round; the salt made its appearance in a saucer out of a cupboard in the wall, a large coarse pan-loaf was cut into pieces, and a platter of potatoes roasted in the ashes was carried in by the youngest boy. Cawth retired to prepare a second relay of fish, and the family began their supper.

"What's to drink?" growled Clan, looking up inquiringly.

"It's all gone," replied his father with a sigh.

Clan muttered something, then rose and strode into the kitchen. Going over to the creel of fish, he selected a couple of the largest and dispatched Cawth with these to the public-house at the corner to change them in his name for as much porter or spirits as the publican's daughter would give. Cawth was enjoined particularly to negotiate with the daughter of the house alone.

After a lapse of some ten minutes or so she returned with a can of porter, which she placed on the table without comment and returned to her fish.

Lord Darraghmore looked up with rather a pleased expression in his face.

"Ha, Clan! got money, eh?"

Clan, a swarthy-faced, silent young giant, vouchsafed no answer. He filled the blown-glass tumbler beside the old man's plate, then took a deep draught out of the can.

Char stretched out his hand to take his turn, but the amiable Clanrickarde struck it aside.

"Yes, I will," stormed the younger; "I caught the fish as well as you. Let go, I say, Clan."

Clan, whose appetite was not yet sufficiently appeased to admit of his being in humor to fight, growled a permission, which Char received with a short laugh of derision as he raised the can to his lips. When he had done he placed it in the centre of the board. Helena laid down the knife with which she was conveying fish to her mouth and gave the vessel a push towards her youngest brother.

"There, Isidor!"

"Give that over here this moment, you pup," began Clan again, stretching out an intercepting hand.

"Not I," said Isidor, seizing the cause of contention in both his brawny hands.

A struggle ensued, in which Helena took an active part, the end of which was that the porter-can was upset and its contents spilled as it rolled over, save a small quantity which Cawth, who having made her appearance on the scene with a second dish of herrings, was in the nick of time to catch, and which she appropriated without protest.

Lord Darraghmore, by whom this scene had been allowed to pass in stolid apathy, had soon finished. He rose from the table and collecting some portions of fish on his plate gave it down to the old wolf-dog. As he stooped his eye caught his frieze great-coat beneath the table. He pulled it out, shook and threw it round his shoulders again.

"Boys, nobody went to the post to-day yet," said he, as he laid himself on the sofa.

"Send Cawth or Hel; I'm going to bed. The boats go out at four to-morrow morning," answered Clan.

"I won't go," snapped Hel, who was standing on a chair, poking pieces of potato through the bars of a cage to a pet thrush.

"Isidor, go on you," said Char.

Isidor, a strikingly handsome young gypsy of seventeen, slight and fragile looking as his sister, got up and went into the back room to take his cap. It was not long before he returned, evidently excited and hurried.

"A letter!" he announced, holding up to the view of all a large square envelope bordered with black.

A letter was an event of rare occurrence in the Ferrard household—that is, a real letter. Bills they had in plenty, but they were easily recognizable, and were usually thrown into the fire at once.

Hel got down off her chair and advanced to the fireplace; Char leaned over the back of the sofa, and even Clan, who was deep in Blueskin's most thrilling achievement, looked up with an unwonted expression of interest and curiosity, which was heightened when they saw that the letter contained a check. Having glanced at this, Lord Darraghmore put it in his pocket and leisurely commenced the epistle. Written in a female hand in the old Italian style, pointed and clear, it did not take him long to get to the end.

"Your aunts want you, Hel, to go and live with them in Bath. They say you have no one to take care of you, and they have sent money to get you clothes and pay your expenses."

Lord Darraghmore said this in a weary tone, letting the letter slip down on the floor as he spoke.

"How much?" broke in Clan, eagerly.

"Thirty pounds," replied the old man, negligently, taking the check out of his pocket as he spoke and jerking it on the table.

"Bah!" said Clan, scornfully. "Anyhow, I needn't go fishing to-morrow."

"Better send word to Jim Blake, then," interposed Char, "else you'll have Mauriade after you next time you go down the Claddagh."

"Cawth!" called the old man as loudly as his weak voice permitted. "Here, Cawth!"

No answer came from the inner room. Cawth was at her dinner and evidently refused to be disturbed. Aware of her peculiarities, he waited patiently till such time as the old lady chose to make her appearance. At last, wiping her mouth with the corner of her apron, she projected her head in the door.

"Well, what are ye callin' for now? Can a body no eat a bit in Kirstian peace but ye must be a-rivin' and shoutin' thegether gin a body was a dog?"

"Here," interrupted her master, pointing to the check. "Go and get me a bottle of good port wine, and fill that," jerking his almost empty pouch to her.

Cawth's gray eyes lit up as she took the check, on the back of which Clan had scrawled his father's name. She looked at it and nodded.

"Will I pay Kelly the grocer when I get the wine? There's seven pund owin'," she croaked; "and the baker's three, an'—"

"Get some steaks, and we'll have a supper," suggested Char; "fish is nothing for dinner."

"Will I pay, I say?" repeated Cawth, looking from one to the other. "Gin Burke knows we have thretty punds he'll be down for his bill, sure's ma life; an' he'll tell the rest o't also."

The matter required deliberation. At this hour, past eight o'clock, the banks were long closed, consequently the check must be cashed at some shop; the news of the Ferrards having money would spread, and their creditors would be down on them at once, a consummation by no means to be desired.

When the offer contained in the letter of the Honorable Miss Ferrard was made known to Cawth, she looked dubiously over it, and beckoning Clan, held a whispered consultation with him. Helena meantime sat staring into the fire bewildered. Her fate, it was plain, rested with herself; Lord Darraghmore was incapable of even thinking seriously over the project—Hel might go or stay, whichever she pleased. Her absence could not make much difference to him; she formed but a slight part of a life spent lying by the fireside with Wasky, the old dog. The newspapers would come regularly; there would be wine and tobacco, and the boys would provide what was necessary, and in a week a quarter's rent would be due. Perry, the attorney at Darraghmore, saw to it pretty regularly; Hel might go or stay as she liked.

She felt this herself, poor child, and perhaps she thought she would like the excitement and novelty of a change. She had been pent up now for a whole fortnight in the house; the boys had had to go fishing, and there was no shooting, and Cawth had refused to allow her out by herself. She felt moped and spiritless for want of employment. She had read all the books, too, and wished the first of October was come that they might buy a new store at the book-stalls. She had a pet rabbit and a thrush, and a retriever puppy in the kitchen was nominally hers too. However, she was not allowed to handle it as she might the rabbit, for Clan, who had bought it for ten shillings, held that it was not good for a young dog to be mauled, and had strictly enjoined on her when he made her a present of the little warm heap of black wool that her attentions were to be confined to feeding the creature at proper times. If she ventured to take it in her lap, Cawth, who had a certain respect as well as affection for Clan, was sure to tell him, and then Hel's ears or hair were well pulled for her disobedience. Her chief pleasure was a long woodland ramble with Isidor. Daybreak often saw the two afield, Isidor's pockets filled with snares and traps, in the making of which he was an adept, Hel trudging along, her battered old hat tied down securely, her mane of black hair plaited in a tight tail, so as to keep it out of her eyes, her jacket of black wool-stuff cut and sewn by Cawth McGonigle's clumsy fingers, worn much as her father wore his frieze great-coat, the sleeves hanging loose on her back, and the collar tied at the neck with a bit of string in lack of the defaulting button. They avoided the high-roads, preferring usually the shelter of ditch or copse for their avocations. No demesne wall was too high for the pair to scale; Isidor knew every nest, from the woodquests in the highest branches of the wood to the ground-building partridge and rail, and every hare's form within a radius of twenty miles. Sometimes their operations were carried on at a still greater distance from home; a friendly carter would give them a lift. Then night-lines were set in the trout rivers, snares in the rabbit-haunted furze, steel traps in cunningly selected places; Hel and Isidor separated to keep watch in different directions, and after night-fall—never before—the poachers would return weary and foot-sore with the spoils, and with appetites keen from the long fast.

Sometimes it was by the sea-side their steps were turned on these occasions. The dogs accompanied them, and Isidor took care to carry his permit with him. If the wild ducks were too shy to get a shot at, there were always mussels and oysters at low tide, and whelks for bait if the elder brothers were going out with Jim Blake's boat. Jim Blake was a Claddagh man, who took them with him on condition of receiving all the fish they caught save a certain portion to be agreed on, which portion consisted generally of all the unmarketable refuse of the take.

Cawth and Clanrickarde had finished their consultation.

"Wull I pay, I say?" repeated the old woman, impatiently; "if Hel wunna gae, I suppose I may as weel. These Connaught thieves wull lave muckle siller wi' us. What meks ye bide here noo I canna tell. Gin I'd ma way I'd no see ane hour of Galway."

The three young men started slightly and looked at

each other with a sudden glance, and then to the occupant of the sofa; Cawth, with a cunning oblique glance, marking the while the effect of her words.

"I'll go back to Darraghmore," said the old man, dreamily.

"Darraghmore!" repeated Clan, staring at him in astonishment. "To the house, do you say?"

"We'll get lodgings in Darraghstown," said his father, speaking quietly, a sudden light sparkling in his eyes. "The house is a ruin. Yes, I'll go back, Cawth."

"Ay," assented Cawth, "I'll like that gey weel aneugh. —Weel, Hel," she added, turning her sharp eyes on the girl, "are ye minded to go to yer lady aunts, or no?"

Hel had heard not one word of what had just been said; she had been staring vacantly into the fire, picturing Bath and her life there. Would she have a coach, and ride dressed in velvets and fur like the sheriff's lady the day Isidor and she had seen her? She had been in England before, long ago. The family had migrated to Liverpool, but the life there had been little to their taste, so they had turned back again. She had forgotten it all long ago.

She looked up quickly, startled back into consciousness of the scene around her by Cawth's question.

"Yes," she said, abruptly; "I'll go to them."

"Guid," chuckled Cawth; "ye can keep that, then, my lord, an' I'll manish for what ye want."

She returned him the check as she spoke and went out; not a word was said by the party. Clan resumed his book; Char was splicing a broken joint of his fishing-rod; Isidor drew his seat in front of the fire and remained staring now into the red mass of peats, and again with a strange bewildered pucker of his brows at his sister; the old man broke open the cover of his paper and, having drawn the candlestick near to him, was speedily absorbed in its contents.

However Cawth had contrived its acquisition, she brought back with her a bottle of port wine. Lord Darraghmore looked up with something of eagerness in his face as she re-entered the room.

"Dinna be feared," she muttered, "I haena shaken it."

She proceeded then to uncork the bottle, his eyes following every movement jealously. She found a decanter, the stopper of which had been replaced by an ordinary cork, decanted the wine carefully and poured him out a half-tumbler, then she placed the decanter on the chimney-piece where he could keep his eyes on it, and went into her own sanctum.

After a while the door was gently opened, and she called to Helena softly.

The girl rose and went into the kitchen. Cawth was going to have tea; her little black tea-pot sat in a nest of warm turf ashes on the hearth, and she desired, in token of unwonted good humor, to share it with her young mistress. The family, as a rule, rarely enjoyed that luxury. At such times as they had money, beer, spirits, and wine were freely consumed, and when these supplies were stopped tea also was unattainable. Helena liked tea, so she seated herself a little less abruptly than was her wont on a kish or wicker basket, which, turned bottom up, did duty for a seat at one side of the fire. She took the cup and saucer and the thick slice of bread and butter from her nurse's hand, and ate and drank in silence.

One tallow candle stuck in a bottle illumined the apartment. The dogs lay in corners as near the fire as they could prudently compass, having an eye to the ever-ready toes of Cawth's brogues. Over near the window Helena could see her white rabbit sitting on its hind legs and staring with round pink eyes through the bars of its box. She remembered suddenly that it had not been fed since breakfast, and laying aside the tea, jumped up to look for a cold potato.

"Cawth, have you any cabbage-leaves?" she asked, noticing that the little hungry thing snuffed dubiously at the proffered edible.

"An' iv I had," was the gracious reply, "I dinna fetch kail and pay for it oot o' my ain hard earnings to feed yon fashious brutes. Kail, indeed! Hech! there'll be a clane sweep of them a' dirackly."

"Will there?" Helena repeated absently, seating herself again on the kish and stretching out her boots on the warm stone.

"Ye'll be needin' new boots, Hel, I'm thinkin'," began Cawth, surveying the coarse brogues that disfigured Helena's feet, "for yer trip to Bath, an' some bits o' claes. I'll have a job I'se warren ye, riggin' ye oot, an' the flittin too."

"When are we going?" asked Helena, indifferently enough, for she scarcely expected an answer to her question.

Cawth was not addicted to explanations or idle talk. Once a migration was definitely arranged, and, as we see, the family needed but the slightest impetus to set it in motion; Cawth settled all the rest. They had no furniture. The tables, of the commonest deal, were bought or hired; the chairs were the same, and, if needed, Clan or Char could knock a chair into shape out of a board or two in a few minutes; a kettle, two large pots, a gridiron, and a pan formed Cawth's *batterie de cuisine;* a cabin, in short, was as well munitioned as the one living-room and kitchen of the Ferrards. A settle-bed in the corner of the kitchen was Helena's, Cawth had a mattress near the fire, Lord Darraghmore had a bedroom up-stairs, which he shared with two of his sons, and Clan lay on the sofa with the wolf-dog.

"Not till ye're gone," answered Cawth, after a long pause. "To-morrow, first thing, we'll buy ye what's needful, an' I maun tak' ye to Cork. Ma sister's livin' in Cork; she'll happen gie's night roomin' till I ken aboot the packet to Bristol. Bristol to Bath's no a lang way."

"Cawth," asked Helena, fixing her great eyes questioningly on the old woman's face, "did you ever see my aunts?"

"Ay, at Darraghmore, when I was a lass like ye. There was Miss Elizabeth, a tall, braw dame, very proud; and Alice, she was gey handsome; then there was Helena —ye're named for her—she's deid."

"Well, I know that," said Hel, impatiently; "but what sort were they, Cawth?"

"Augh! can I mind sae lang? The people at the old place had tales o' them after they went back to London. They couldna stan' the gait o' Darraghmore at a'. Ye see, they were aye in England, and had English wyes wi' them."

Of English "wyes" Helena Ferrard had little conception, but the saying fell with some sort of foreboding on her ears. She put down the tea-cup and folded her hands in her lap, and pondered what might be the differences between the ways of Bath and theirs. She had some notion of a different style of living gathered chiefly from her books, and she pictured to herself surroundings of velvet—which it may be doubted if she would recognize on seeing—silk, lace, and mirrors; the last a questionable boon, considering the figure of herself with which any she had encountered presented her—scowling, overhanging brows, tangled hair, and a yellow skin. Helena was painfully conscious of her own deficiencies as contrasted with the elegant ladies of her penny-awful romances. She turned almost angrily from their trailing robes and furbelows to the chaste simplicity of the Indian heroines of the backwoods.

She felt far more akin with them, and almost emulated their accomplishments. Char and Isidor's praises of her tying flies, devising new knots for snares, and trapping birds sounded sweeter than ever in her ears. She longed and begged to be allowed to use Isidor's gun, but he, prompted by an idea that he owed it to himself, as a man, to preserve at least one branch intact from her intrusion, refused steadfastly. Helena submitted, but it was with a lively sense of injury. Neither would the lads allow her to accompany them in the boats of the Claddagh, and as they had done nothing else but fish for the last fortnight, the expenses of Lady Darraghmore's interment having caused the funds to disappear sooner than was usual, Helena had had a dull time of it. She had read and reread until she was tired of all her books, and now, out of pure weariness of spirit, longed for a change.

Cawth was the first to break the silence. She finished

her third cup of tea, replaced the black tea-pot in its corner with the cups and saucers, and then resumed her place at the fire.

"I kent weel aneugh there was a flittin' to be!"

Helena, who guessed from the voice what was coming, shuddered involuntarily. Cawth noted the shudder, and continued in a deliberate tone with a pleased sense of power and importance.

"I dreamed last night of a hole in ma shoe: it's a seer sign—just as seer's the knock on the door at midnight comes to the Ferrards before a deeth."

Helena clenched her teeth tight in a perfect spasm of endurance.

"Ye mind, I heerd it afore she died, I tellt ye, Hel."

Heedless of the nod which Helena speedily accorded, in the vain hope of stemming the flood of unwelcome reminiscence, Cawth pursued:

"I kent it weel, indeed. It was just twelve o'clock, and I wasna able to sleep for the win'. 'Deed, Hel, I'm no seer it was the win' skrieked that night. I am not seer—no, no; I've heard them skrieks afore. An' it was just struck when I heard the knock—wan clear loud knock—it rung through ma heid. Well, I thocht it might be Clan back from the fishing—ye min' he was out with Blake a' day—an' I up and doon the stair—he's an ill lad to keep waitin' is Clan; and I opened the dure, and somèthin' struck sae cold and harsh a' through me; there was nae one in a' the street—not one. I waited, and leuked, and waited—no a soul could I see. It was the same, but ye're too young to min' it, when yer aunt Helena, Mrs. Lamont that was, died; ay, an' Walter—poor Walter, that was a bonny lad."

"Cawth," said Helena, trying vainly to speak with a steady voice, "how was it Walter was killed?"

"Killed by a man named Thornhill; it was an accident, out duck-shooting in the bog. Some say Thornhill's sister—there was something in't aboot her. Augh! it's ower long ago noo. But I mind well the knocks came to the big door of Darraghmore for Walter; ay, an' he heard them an' went down an' opened the door himself—think of that, noo."

"Cawth, did he—did he see anything?"

"I canna tell," answered Cawth in a mysterious tone. "He wouldna answer if he did or no; but just ae week after that he was carried in a' wat, and wi' the red stuff o the bog on his claes an' his bonny dark face; I washed it all off mysel'. He was the finest man of a' the Ferrards, an' a gey bad ane was Walt."

"Ye'll go to Darraghmore then, soon?"

"I'll see ye off first—afore a' the siller's gone. That will na be long gin the lads gets their will wi't. Get to bed wi' ye, Hel; there's a gude day's work before ye the morn."

Just then the door opened and Isidor lounged in. He came over and stood on the hearth and fidgeted about in a purposeless way for a minute or two. At last he spoke:

"Will ye take the rabbit with ye?" addressing Helena.

"No," she replied, looking over at it wistfully, and then up at him.

"I'll feed it for ye," said he, after a sort of awkward pause.

"All right," assented Hel, thankfully. She puzzled for a minute, and then said quickly: "Isi, if you want any snares or things fixed, you know, I'll do them in the morning. You can leave the gut and line in the old desk before you go out."

Isi looked at her and nodded. He stood by the fire, shifting from one foot to the other uneasily, his hands buried deep in his pockets, and his dark eyebrows nearly meeting in a pucker over his nose. Then he went slowly back to the other room; he could not have said anything more had his life depended on it, nor Helena either, yet her eyes followed his retreating figure with something almost of pain in their look, until the door closed upon it.

CHAPTER III.

THE next day was spent packing up the family property. The boys all disappeared early; Clan took charge of the fishing gear and the guns, all of which he managed to bestow on board a steamer bound southwards. He could land at some convenient port and get across country to Darraghmore by train or other conveyance. As to wardrobe, they were not likely to be impeded in their flight by any considerations for its safety. Not one of them possessed a second suit of clothes. The only difference observable in Lord Darraghmore's out-of-door costume was that he put his arms through the sleeves of the great-coat which in the house he wore cloak-wise, fastened round his neck; an old red silk handkerchief twisted about his throat, and a black hat, dirty and crushed, completed his attire.

Cawth took charge of the money. She gave Clan two pounds for his expenses, Char and Isidor one each, his lordship five; the rest she knotted in a handkerchief and concealed in her dress. She bought Helena a pair of boots, the cheapest she could find; a black cloth coat, a ready-made black skirt and under jacket were soon found, common and ugly, but still decent. Then she got a crape collar and cuffs, and a pair of black cloth gloves, clumsy and enormously too large. A few toilet requisites of the cheapest and commonest kind, such as a servant might provide for herself, were next procured, and then Helena was pronounced to be ready for her journey.

"Ye must hev' a new hat too, Hel; that winna do at all," said she, looking critically at the battered, shapeless thing, beneath the shadow of which Helena's great eyes stared with brilliancy. "Come away down here—here's a milliner's shop."

In the window of a shop in one of the smaller streets—Eyre Square and its fashionable milliners Cawth studiously avoided—they saw hanging a collection of such bonnets as delight the eyes of the farmers' girls and those servants who are daring enough to defy custom and criticism by casting off the decent cap or hood, which in some remote districts of the country still survives, a lingering remnant of class costume. Helena cast a doubtful eye on the hideous finery as they entered.

"Cawth! it must be black, you know," she whispered.

The shopman produced his stock of black hats, some half-dozen little hard round felt saucers and conical jars.

Hel looked at them in bewilderment.

"Quite the fashion—the last thing from London—if you'd try one on, miss."

Hel removed her black head-piece and took the largest of the black cones in her hand, surveying it doubtfully all the time. She put it on her head. At least six inches too small in circumference, the hard, unyielding thing slipped of rebelliously.

"Try this one, miss. This is worn in the new style, on the back of the head—allow me, miss."

The shopman had taken one of the saucers, and tried to fix it on the back of Helena's head, with somewhat better success. Not that it fitted, but there happened fortunately to be a sort of excrescence of hair where her thick plait commenced on which the little hat could and did hang.

"Now, miss!" said he, quite triumphant.

Hel looked all round.

"Why it feels just like nothing at all. I won't wear that thing, I might as well have no hat on at all."

"It's the fashion, miss, I assure you; there's nothing else worn. You won't get anything different, indeed."

"Ye must take it, I'm thinkin', Hel," said Cawth, who was tolerably indifferent so long as Hel had a hat of any denomination or appearance, whether she liked it or it became her. She rose as if to close the affair.

Hel flashed a look of scorn and anger at both, jerked the little black saucer from her head to the counter, on which it bumped as if it were of wood too, and picking up her own hat, flung out of the shop. Cawth followed, storming.

"Up that way in Eyre Square I saw large, comfortable-looking hats hanging in a window; let's go there," said the young lady in a determined tone, setting out rapidly in the direction she indicated.

Vainly did Cawth insist and try to stop her. Helena's mouth was set in a way that was not to be mistaken.

"I'll have a hat that will keep the light out of my eyes like that, or I'll have none. Do you hear me now?"

There was no help for it; Cawth unwillingly followed the imperious damsel. They crossed the square and found themselves before the door of the fashionable milliner of Galway.

"There now," said Helena, triumphantly pointing to a black Rubens hat in the show-case. "Did not I say it? I'll have that hat."

Cawth snorted with rage, and pronounced the hat to be a "muckle pot-lid." But Helena turned a deaf ear, and they went up-stairs and found themselves in a show-room filled with the ordinary belongings of such places; a couple of handsomely dressed ladies monopolized the attention of the milliner and her assistants. Boxes of gay-colored flowers lay strewn about, feathers of all shades and descriptions; a whole case of ornaments composed of little tropical birds was on a chair near Helena. A great, full-length mirror was at one end of the room; she could see herself reflected in it from head to foot. Dresses were displayed on stands, the magnificence of which fell upon her like a new revelation. Presently her eye caught a humming-bird impaled on the spike of a brown and streaked tiger-lily; she uttered an inarticulate cry of admiration and plucked Cawth's sleeve.

The people in the shop, who had not observed their entry, turned round. Cawth looked like a peasant woman, only that her white cap was covered by a bonnet of rusty velvet and antiquated shape that had been Lady Darraghmore's. Helena's coarse frieze skirt and coat seemed to indicate the same class, but her hat and the long crape veil were also a contradiction. A girl stepped forward in obedience to a sign from her mistress.

"What d'you wawnt," she asked, speaking affectedly, and not without some trace of contempt in her tone.

Helena replied laconically, "That hat," nodding towards the window as she spoke.

The tone was not that of a common person, whatever the dress might be, so the girl civilly desired them to wait a moment, and returned to her task. Cawth frowned at Helena and stepped well forward to the group.

"Ye'll have the goodness," she began in a high-pitched, peremptory tone, "to attend to the Honorable Miss Ferrard at once—we hae no time to lose wi' ye."

The strange voice (the vulgar tones contrasting oddly with the almost peremptoriness of the command) fell like a bomb among the group. The ladies, unwilling to be rude, turned—one so as to face the great mirror, the other so that she could glance obliquely through the stands of finery;. they looked questioningly at each other. The milliner, however, who knew everybody and everything, after the manner of her kind, whispered something round the rim of a velvet hat she was displaying at the moment, at which her customers smiled broadly. She desired her assistant to attend to the odd looking couple, however, so Cawth's pride was gratified for the nonce.

Presently the ladies swept out, a rich odor of seal-skin and the best *eau de Cologne* saluting Hel's nostrils as they passed. They bestowed a pitying, half-contemptuous glance on her, which she repaid with a frown that made her brows look like one continuous line.

"A large hat," she said, irritably pushing aside a composition of crape and feather flowers presented to her view. "I won't have feathers or flowers, I want nothing but just a hat."

She spoke in a loud, authoritative voice. What business had these women to be staring at her and Cawth? They were going to be paid. Yes, she would see that unaccustomed ceremony gone through before she left the shop. Cawth, who indeed at that moment was revolving in the depths of her practiced brain a scheme to get the hat out of the shop without the preliminary, and to her view unnecessary, formality of paying the bill, might say or swear as she liked.

"Felt or straw, miss?" said the attendant, respectfully.

"Show some," said Hel, shortly; she was puzzled, but resolved not to commit herself.

"Perhaps the young lady would like a Rubens, or a Vandyke, or may be the new garden shape, or the Elvire?" and another assistant, an older and sharper dame, looked over the lid of the box she was busy at.

The young lady who did not want for presence of mind—perhaps it was that obtuseness which betimes answers equally well—stared at her stonily. Cawth, with a grunt of impatience, retired to a chair by the door to mature her scheme.

"The Vandyke, miss," said the shop-girl, showing her a hat turned up at one side with a handsome curling plume.

Helena, without vouchsafing a glance at it, fixed her eyes on the bearer with an ominous frown.

"You heard me, I think," said she, slowly and distinctly; "a large hat without feathers or flowers."

"Untrimmed hats," said the mistress, sharply. "Be quick, now, Miss Kelly; here's Mrs. Blood coming across the square, and the Miss Persses."

In a moment a number of large felt hats were placed before Helena. She selected a high-crowned cavalier hat with a broad brim fastened up at one side, which fitted down comfortably on her head. Then unpinning her crape veil, she tried to fasten it on the new purchase.

"Allow me, miss," said the attendant; and taking the

veil from her customer's clumsy fingers, she fastened it in a becoming wreath round the hat, and then put it on her head. "Very becoming to you, miss," said she, "very. Like to look at it?" and she handed a toilet mirror.

But Helena turned her back brusquely.

"Cawth," she cried, imperiously, "come here. Pay for this; do you hear? You have the money with you."

Cawth ground her teeth. There was no help for it, however, so she produced the fragment of an old apron which held her money, and untying with fingers that trembled with rage the complicated knots that fastened up her store, counted out the twelve shillings demanded by the milliner, then followed Helena, who had stalked out of the room majestically.

"Ma word!" she exploded, once in the street, "but ye're the gran' leddy, Miss Ferrard! Twal shillin' for a bit bare hat, an' 'Cawth, pay for this; div ye hear?'" and she gave a ludicrous imitation of her young mistress's tones of command; then, catching sight of Hel's impassive countenance, with a sudden lapse from mimicry to venom, "Just wait till I see Clan the night; he'll rug yer ears, ye cutty. Gae way doon the street an' in straight t' hoose; pit turf o' the fire, an' wait till I come."

Thus speaking, she gave Helena a push as they reached the corner of their own street, and they parted company. Cawth plunged down a filthy lane under an archway so low that only one person at a time could stand erect beneath it, to find a dealer in second-hand furniture from whom she had bought the plenishing of their rooms, and with whom she was now to drive a nefarious bargain, to the despoliation of the family's creditors.

Cawth, having exacted the uttermost penny, arranged that he was to come late at night with a cart and remove the tables, chairs, and beds; a candle was to be lighted and left burning by the last person—usually herself—to quit the house, and the key might be left in the door. The night mail—the last train to quit Galway—would take them all off that night. Cawth had indeed intended at first to take Hel to Cork and ship her by the Bristol packet before undertaking the troubles and perils of "flitting." But reflection had convinced her that the old lord was now too feeble, mentally and physically, to be left with safety, so she changed her programme, and decided that her master and Hel and herself were to travel together as far as they could south. As for the boys, Clan had gone before day-break; the dogs, with Char, had found shelter in Jim Blake's hut on the Claddagh, to follow at their leisure, and Isidor was to accompany them to Mallow, and thence go on with his father to Darraghstown to the hotel where Clan had already ordered rooms.

They had not seen Isidor since breakfast, and Cawth vowed vengeance on him for not being in readiness to assist in the disposition of her boxes and bundles. She also felt anxious lest he, not being aware of her sudden plans, should fail to appear in time. She hired a cart to take the luggage on to Oranmore, a station beyond Galway, where they were to meet the midnight train. The goods dispatched, Cawth prepared dinner, and having eaten it, the family lay down for a few hours' rest. At eleven o'clock Cawth rose, woke his lordship and Helena, and sent them up to the station. Helena was cautioned to wear her veil close over her face, and to avoid the crowd. They took third-class tickets, of course, and as at that late hour few were at the station save travelers and persons on business, they hoped to escape unobserved.

At the last moment, when Cawth was lighting the candle which was to serve the double purpose of blinding such neighbors as might entertain suspicions of the unwonted stir and movements, and also as a signal to the broker who was to come in and carry off the furniture, in bounced Isidor with a string of fish. His noisy outburst was checked by Cawth, and speedily comprehending her, he flung the string of fish on the floor and made off to the station. Here he found Hel and his father, both shivering in a far corner of the third-class waiting-room. About one minute before the bell rang Cawth made her appearance, the hood of her huge blue cloak pulled over her head. They took their places, and after a few minutes' delay the mail-train started. At Oranmore the boxes were ready. Cawth jumped out and saw to their safe bestowal. After that until they reached Athenry Junction, where they had to wait for a train to take them across King's County to Portarlington, not a word was exchanged between the travelers. They reached Mallow, where they were to part company, about midday the next day, after a journey through a bleak region of stubble fields and bog. The Cork train was soon ready, and Cawth, selecting Helena's bundle and black bag from a miscellaneous heap under their seats, got down. Hel stood up and prepared to get out. Lord Darraghmore was lying at full length on the opposite seat. His nose was all that was to be seen in the space between his hat and the red silk muffler which hid the lower portion of his face. She did not know whether he was asleep or not, so touched his hand timidly.

He opened his eyes with a start.

"Where are we? Mallow? Oh yes, Mallow Junction. I must get up and look out. And, damn me, I say, where's the flask, Cawth?" he called, peevishly.

"Come on, Hel, I say; will ye lose the train?" snapped Cawth without on the platform. There was plenty of time, but she was cold and tired, and this was her way of showing her discontent.

"Good-bye, papa," said Hel, awkwardly. "You know I'm going to Bath—to my aunts"—she repeated, seeing a puzzled look in his eyes.

"Oh yes; good-bye, then, Hel. Be a good little girl, eh? And," he added, with a glimpse of his old grand manner, for Lord Darraghmore had been a gentleman once, "my love to my sisters."

Helena got out and made her way with difficulty, for she was tired and stiff, after Cawth across the platform. Isidor, who had plunged out head-foremost instantly the train had stopped, made his appearance at the door of the Cork train. He leaned one hand on it after they had taken their places, and seemed trying to say something.

"Hel," said he at last, with a suffused look in his great

eyes, "the rabbit's under the seat. Jim Blake carried it up to Oranmore with the things."

"Gin I'd known he'd sic lumber in his cairt," interrupted Cawth, "I'd ha' flung it in the street, or gien it to Rusty to ait."

Hel never noticed this interpolation, and only looked her thanks darkly from beneath her cavalier hat.

A premonitory whistle from the engine warned them the time was come to part. But Isidor did not take his dirty hand off the door yet.

"Isi," whispered Helena, leaning forward so that her chin touched the ledge of the window, "I did all the gut into snares, and there's slip-knots in the cashroom cord, too, in the old desk; it's in Cawth's big box."

The train was in motion now. Isidor stepped along beside it, his eyes fixed wistfully on her.

"Good-bye," said he, thickly; "in the big desk. I'll feed him for ye."

Then he dug his hands into his pockets and walked back to his father, wondering to himself how many snares there were, and of what sizes Hel had made them, and when would it be Cawth's convenience that he should get at the desk which was in her big box? He stood by the door, watching with somewhat dim eyes and with a deeper indentation than usual over his nose, the Cork train as it steamed onwards till the last vestige of smoke had disappeared behind the hills.

Lord Darraghmore roused him presently from his reverie by giving him his flask, with directions to have it filled with the best brandy to be had at the refreshment counter, expressing at the same time a hope that Clan had not neglected to bespeak a good dinner at the Darraghmore Arms while he was about ordering rooms. Then he lifted his feet on the wooden bench, wrapped himself as warmly as possible and settled into a doze. Isidor opened the window at the other end of their compartment, and, crossing his arms on the top of the door, rested his head on them and stared out at the wilderness of bog and moor that stretched away westwards to the mountains.

CHAPTER IV.

> "Thy dark eyes opened not,
> Nor first revealed themselves to English air;
> For there is nothing here,
> Which, from the outward to the inward brought,
> Moulded thy baby thought."

HELENA and her attendant reached Cork late in the afternoon; both were tired, and Cawth gave full vent to her weariness and bad temper in a series of scoldings and revilings.

"The Ferrards were a pack of fules; shiftless, bootless crew; t' workhouse was t' proper place for 'em all, beggars and scant-o'-grace lot. An' Cawth would see them there yet. As for Hel, black nowt, her fine aunts wad soon rid the hoose ov her. Hech—she'd live to see it."

Here she was taken by a fit of asthmatic coughing, brought on by the jolting of the old covered car she had hired—for when in cash she had all her compatriots' aversion to walking—to take them to Cawth's sister's house, situated in a back street near the butter-market.

Helena heard nothing, or was as if she heard nothing; she and Cawth sat on one side of the "jingle," her parcels occupied the opposite seat. Helena was next the door, and was busy watching the crowds of Patrick Street and the gay, well-lit shops they passed by. She had eaten scarce anything since the previous night, and felt rather giddy and weak; she was anxious, too, in spite of herself, and dreaded the unknown future that lay across the sea.

She pondered Cawth's words. "Miss Elizabeth, a braw dame and prood," and those mysterious "English ways." How she wondered what they could be.

At last, after some searching and inquiry, they drew up at a house, the lower part of which was occupied by a little shop. Cawth got down first, bidding Helena remain until she came out again. After a quarter of an hour's delay she presented herself, accompanied by an old woman, somewhat stouter, but in other respects the counterpart of herself. She courtesied to Helena, and, collecting her scanty luggage, bid her walk in.

They passed through the little shop, reeking horribly of salt fish, stale vegetables, and tobacco, and passed into a queer little sitting-room behind it. Cawth put down the bundles in a corner, and telling Helena to wait for her, went out. There was a turf fire in the grate, and the girl was glad to sit down and warm herself, for the evening was chilly. So she pulled an old rickety arm-chair close to the grate and seated herself.

There was nothing to be seen from the little window; it was choked with plants, straggling, unhealthy-looking geraniums with pale, waxy leaves; over the chimney-piece hung a picture of Emmet as he stood addressing his judge, his arms folded, and, but for the attitude, not unlike the common representative of Napoleon. Jennies and Jessamies in gaudy crockery-ware decked the chimney-piece, and a dirty white cat sat on a straw stool before the hearth. The place was dirty and frowzy, and the air intolerably bad; but it was warm, and Helena, as we may imagine, was not disposed to be too critical. She took off her hat and laid it on the table; then, leaning her tired and aching head on the rail of her chair, in that uneasy attitude fell asleep.

She was roused after an hour or so by Cawth, who came in bringing some provisions in a basket. She fetched a kettle full of water from the street pump and cooked steaks for supper, in which meal they were joined by the old woman of the shop.

Helena drank her tea eagerly. She was too weary to

take part in the conversation, though she heard it all drowsily.

"An' so they're back to Darraghstown? dear me," said the old woman, "an' yon lass is to go to England the morn. Did ye speer the time o' the boat, Cawth?"

She spoke like Cawth, with the real northern accent. Thirty years of absence had in no way dulled its edge, grating and sharp as the day they had quitted their native village.

"Ay!" replied Cawth; "an' I'm away now to find Jim O'Brien; he's going over wi' pegs, an' he can look to her too. She's no just that steady that I can lat her gae alane."

And Cawth's malignant gray eyes looked over to see how this shot told. Hel had heard nothing, she was fast falling asleep again. The warmth and closeness of the little room, added to fatigue, acted upon her almost like a sleeping-draught. Her head was sinking on her breast, and her long eyelashes almost touched her cheek. She looked beautiful, notwithstanding that she was weary and travel-stained; a faint red flush colored her cheeks, and the neglected, tangled hair had fallen back, leaving her fine brows uncovered in their marble beauty.

"She's some like the others, I wat," said Cawth's sister, setting down her saucer and looking across to where the girl sat; "none so good-lookin' as Elizabeth. She's ower tawny for that."

"Tawny," repeated Cawth; "an' a rale Ferrard, black and dour; gin ye raised her she'd think little o' stickin' ye wi' a knife—my word for it she would."

The other grinned approvingly.

"Is Clanrickarde, what ca' ye the biggest ane, wi' the auld lord yet?"

"Ay," replied Cawth, "he sune winna be though;" and she nodded mysteriously. "He be after Claude to Austria, I'm thinkin', an' jest as guid; we haena enough for oorselves, let alane keepin' yon great fool. He's better off; ma word, I dinna ken the minute we'd hae the police doon on us, thievin' an' poachin' an' robbin' fra ane end o' the week to the other. He was in wi' a gang that hed a still in Galway, an' when it was taen by the polis' Clan had ta run like a deer and hide for three days. I haena peace o' my life."

"Be here!" ejaculated the listener, piously.

From Clan to Char, from Char to Isidor, Hel and Lord Darraghmore, Cawth dealt impartial justice all round. The very schemes she herself had hatched and suggested she now unfolded to her willing auditor, painting them in their blackest colors, reviling and ridiculing those whose bread she ate with a bitterness and venom that would have astonished Helena herself could she have heard her. Every wild prank or ill deed was dilated upon by this faithful follower, who, indeed, was but refreshing her memory ere she should commence the "pastures new" awaiting her among the Darraghmore gossips, though with them she would exercise a certain discretion. Cawth knew what to tell and what to keep. She would spread tales of Clan's vices and follies, but she would stoutly deny that the larder was supplied with hares and rabbits from the demesne; that it was her interest to hide, and she had a keen eye to her own interest. She would recount with painful exactitude the oaths of Char and Isidor, but she would omit the depredations with snares and traps that the youths committed in the coverts and preserves. Cawth had saved money. Although she had no wages, she had the disbursements of such part of the family revenue as was devoted to paying bills and the household outlay generally. And she was too wise in her generation not to take care of herself; and notwithstanding all this she loved the Ferrards, and grudged no exertion or labor in their behalf.

"She's going to the aunts—the lord's sisters, dear! They canna be young noo," said the old woman, thoughtfully.

"Ay, we're well rid o' Hel," was the nurse's reply, casting at the same time a glance of mingled affection and bitterness at her now sleeping charge. "Wad ye believe me, Meg, she canna mair than read a bit, an' she'll be sixteen in a month—a muckle guid-for-naethin' thing, an' ignorant as a kish o' brogues."

Cawth and her sister remained till the tallow candle which illumined their little den was nearly burned out. Poor Helena, whose child-like beauty formed a striking contrast to their weird, hag-like faces, still slept heavily. Then Cawth remembered that her task to inquire about the boat and the escort for her charge was yet undone. So reluctantly she had to forego discoursing on her congenial theme, and pulling her great blue cloak around her, set out for the shipping-office.

CHAPTER V.

NEXT morning at four o'clock in a cold, gray twilight, Helena and Cawth were standing on the quay by the packet-boat watching the embarkment of some hundred shrieking pigs, who were to form her traveling companions to Bristol. The last firkin of butter and the last unwilling porker had been consigned to their respective places, when a burly, frieze-coated man, with a red, wholesome-looking countenance set in a framing of yellow beard, approached them and shouted to Cawth.

"Mornin'; now, ma'am, where's your consignment? time we were getting aboard."

"Mornin', Mr. O'Brien," replied Cawth, with dignity; "ye'll mind Lord Darraghmore? this is his youngest leddy, an' I'm pittin' her in yer charge so far's Bristol."

Hel looked up into the cattle-driver's great face, half-curiously, half-timidly; the big man stepped back and raised, with an almost irresistible gesture of respect, his old felt caubeen, showing a broad, white forehead and a mass of curly hair above the red-and-tan of his face.

"Sarvice, miss; I'll be proud to be ony assistance to ye."

A bell rang on board, and the order to clear the ship of shore-folk could be heard. Cawth looked at Helena one moment; a strange grimace contorted her weather-beaten, cunning old face, and something of a softened look shone in her eyes as she looked at her last nursling child on her way alone and unfriended across the sea.

She hesitated one moment, then dipping her hand suddenly into her pocket, by an alert flank movement placed herself between the drover and her charge.

"Hel," she whispered, eagerly, "gie me yer handkerchief—quick!"

She snatched the handkerchief which the girl held out wonderingly, and knotted two gold coins in it, fastening them in a tight snarl with the aid of her teeth.

"Now, miss, by yer leave; 'tis time we was off."

"Guid-bye to ye, lassie; mind that now, and sae lang's ye hae it ye dinna want a friend."

Hel stooped and kissed her withered cheek, then turned, and keeping close behind her escort, crossed the narrow gangway and gained the slippery, dirty deck of the Bristol boat. It presented a noisy scene in the chill gray of the last morning of September. The live stock squealed hideously, big pigs, little pigs, black, white, gray, and red, all bemoaned their fate in various keys. Huge piles of butter-firkins, hogsheads of whisky, sacks and bales, lay promiscuously everywhere around. The captain was shouting his orders from the deck, and the crew seemed to be in their own way and everybody else's. The big hawsers were cast off and fell with a splash into the river; the paddles turned forward a couple of strokes, then back as many; gradually her head pointed outward, half a dozen quick strokes and there lay a great gulf of seething, foam-flecked water between them and the shore. She walked down to the end of the deck and mounted on a bale to look over the bulwark. The quay behind them was fast receding, and she could see Cawth in her black bonnet and great cloak leisurely walking away. Helena pulled her hat down tight, and stood watching the white terraces on the shores of the Lee glide by; gradually the river widened, the banks rose higher, and the lovely sylvan scenes of Passage lay abreast of them. The trees were putting on their autumn hues, and to Helena's eyes, accustomed to the wild wastes and stone walls of Galway, the masses of exquisite foliage almost realized in their brilliant and varied coloring her most cherished visions of fairy-land.

Down to the very edge of the water, whose ripples kissed their overhanging branches, grew the arbutus, mingled with alders, silver larch, and willows. Helena looked longingly at the shadowy aisles between, and thought how delightful a covert she could make in such a place with Isidor; he, bare-legged, with spear or snare, stepping noiselessly among the shiny pebbles, while she, on book intent, or more often keeping watchful guard against surprise, paced up and down the banks.

A harsh cry roused her from her dream; she looked up and saw a couple of gulls flying in their wake, near enough for her to hear the heavy, strong beat of their pinions, and see their hard, wolfish eyes. She had a piece of bread with her, and breaking it, flung it out to them. They pounced upon it and seized it almost as it reached the water, then rose mid-air again, swaying to and fro with almost the same undulating motion as if floating on the water. Every now and then their shrill cry reached her ears.

She went down to breakfast, summoned by the big drover, who placed her beside himself, and loaded her plate with food in kindly token of his good-will. Helena thanked him with a look, and ate her breakfast with the keen relish of a growing girl. Meanwhile he, feeling bound to do his best, thought he ought to make some conversation, and plied his charge with rough point-blank questions.

How far might she be going? and where? and to whom? and the like.

It was all meant with the best intention, but he was speedily compelled to give it up and attack his breakfast discomfited.

Helena had soon finished, and began to wonder how she might edge her way out of the narrow bench, in which she was hemmed on one side by her burly cavalier, and on the other by an equally burly priest, both of whom were absorbed in the business of eating.

Presently the drover leaned back and laid down the saucer from which he had been imbibing tea with a noise not unlike that of one of his own four-footed belongings in the forecastle when engaged at a troughful of buttermilk. He cast a side-look at Helena, whose dark eyes were traveling round the table in perplexity, then leaned back and past his next neighbor, till he reached the ear of a man seated farther up, to whom he whispered, audibly enough to be heard by Helena as well:

"The young lady here beside me, ye seen her come aboard, Smith? whisht, she's a lord's daughter, ay fait."

Smith, an English jobber, instantly leaned as far forward as he could to stare open-mouthed at the subject of his friend's remark. He did not enjoy the vision of nobility long. Helena had heard; she stood up, and turning round with difficulty, got her foot on the bench; a light spring landed her on the floor, and heedless of the general murmur and the stare that greeted this feat, she was out in a moment and away back to her post in the stern.

The sun had broken through the clouds by this and gilded the white houses among the trees and the distant Waterford mountains lying in purple and gray to the east. A salt smell was in the air, and the breeze became stronger as they neared the ocean. Helena shrunk herself close in her jacket, a wretched rag of thin cloth. She had neither rug nor shawl, and wondered, in case it was possible for her to go down to the cabin again, whether the bad smell or the cold was the most endurable evil. She decided on remaining where she was, and leaning against the taffrail, looked about her with wondering eyes. As they were passing Roche's Point her guardian presented himself on deck and looked all around for his charge; catching sight of her where she was perched on a heap of merchandise, he steered his way towards her somewhat unsteadily, for the big Atlantic rollers were sweeping up now, and the boat's motion was rather uncertain.

"Look out beyant, miss, an' you'll see a big steamer; that's an American."

Helena's eyes obeyed the direction of his finger, and

she could see a huge black vessel steaming towards the harbor they had quitted.

"Arn't you cold, miss?" asked the drover, replacing his little black pipe in his mouth, and scanning Helena's wan cheeks and pinched blue lips.

"N—o," she answered, untruthfully.

He disappeared and returned with a rug which, from its appearance and smell, must have done duty as a horse-cloth in its day; and unable conveniently to wrap it round her, the good-natured fellow opened it and handed it to her by the two corners. She drew it round her shoulders gratefully enough, and thanked him with a smile that lighted up her face. He sauntered off to join his friend the English drover, who was seated near the funnel.

"My heye!" this gentleman began, "so that's the 'Onorable Miss Ferrard, a lord's daughter—come now, railly, Jim."

Jim, whose black pipe was in process of being replenished, could spare no breath for further asseveration than that conveyed by a solemn nod. Presently, when the little cube of tobacco was in full blast, he began:

"That she is so, Smith—a rale article too; none o' yer new musharoon English lot, but a ginuine owld stock entirely. They've broke through, broke horse and foot."

"Broke! I rayther expect it, Jim; if hever I seen a lord's daughter a-travelin' that way! why look at 'er cloes."

"Smith," said the drover in an emphatic tone, "just you whist now, and let the lady alone; she's travelin' undher my care. You's a good judge of pigs, I dare say, but I never knewn you was a judge of ladies' cloes; an' a lady she is, whatdever. It's no business of ours, if so be she is down on her luck."

Smith admitted the truth of his friend's argument, and Helena was left alone for the rest of the journey.

The boat reached Bristol at about one o'clock at night, and the stewardess, at the instance of the drover, kept Helena on board and provided her with a bed. The next day he came down to the boat early, and having learned her destination, collected her luggage, a small wooden box and a bag, and took her to the railway station. He tried hard to be allowed to pay for her ticket, but Helena pushed his hand aside indignantly. He then begged her at least to keep his rug, but she declined this also. She took her seat in a third-class carriage, her esquire remained standing by the window. As the train moved off he raised his hand to his hat respectfully; some sudden impulse made Helena hold out hers. The big man grasped it cordially in his great brown fist.

"God save ye, miss, an' send you your own again wan day," said he, fervently, a flush of pleasure and gratitude covering his cheeks, and his gray eyes twinkling. Helena smiled drearily; the train swept on with a wild shriek, and the big drover was left behind.

CHAPTER VI.

> "You bring blithe airs where'er you tread,
> Blithe airs that blow from down and sea:
> You wake in me a Pan not dead—
> Not wholly dead!—Autonoë." A. Dobson.

IN the front drawing-room of one of the best houses in Plantagenet Terrace, Bath, sat a couple of old ladies. It was a pretty room, owing much more to its well-proportioned size and its handsome and massive fittings than to the adventitious aids of modern upholstery. The furniture was solid and old, the ruby velvet of the curtains sadly faded and worn, and the gilding of the tall looking-glasses tarnished, but nevertheless there was an air of solidity and antiquity about everything. There were fine pictures on the walls—a landscape or two that a connoisseur would have approved, and sea-pieces that made one almost smell the salt brine, and feel amid the half-decayed sweetness of the great jars of rose leaves that scented the air the rough caresses of the sea breeze. A large cabinet of black oak, in the top of which was set the centre-point of a curious wreathing of animals, flowers, and fruit, a falcon with the motto *Rapax*. Venetian glass of cobweb texture and quantities of beautiful Sèvres and Dresden filled the shelves; in the centre of all stood a bouquet of late flowers—scarlet geraniums and yellow lady-slipper glowing against the black background, and mignonette, its long stems heavy with little seed-bells, scattering its bitter-sweet perfume.

A long, low book-shelf ran along one side of the room and the old calf and morocco-bound volumes looked dingy and well worn. On the table stood a writing-case; open books lay about, the *Standard* and *Guardian*, some bright-colored needle-work, and in the centre a graceful marble statuette.

The younger of the two ladies was seated before the writing-case; she might be sixty-eight or seventy. A handsome old woman with imperious features, a short upper lip and a rich, mellow-tinted skin, to which the glowing colors of the hangings seemed an appropriate framing, and large full eyes. Her hair was not yet quite white, and she had plenty of it, but it was gathered plainly back out of sight beneath a cap of lace and velvet. Her dress was the finest, softest, black cashmere, and she wore ruffles of fine lace at her throat and wrists. The other old lady sat near the fire in a curious old leaning chair, on the back of which was embroidered in now faded silk a huge monogram F, surmounted by the crest and motto. She was a few years older than her sister, but was much more feeble physically and mentally. Her hair was snowy white, and her full dark brown eyes had a feeble, clouded look; she had been knitting something of soft, fleecy wool, but the needles lay unheeded in her lap, and the ball had rolled away across the rug.

"Clanrickarde has not named a day, then, you say?"

The lady sitting at the table took up a letter as she replied:

"No, Elizabeth, our nephew has not arranged a day or time." Then she fixed a pair of gold spectacles on her nose, and, for the second time, unfolded a very dirty half-sheet of paper, on which was scrawled, in the Honorable Clanrickarde Ferrard's unformed characters, the following epistle:

"DR. ANTS,

"This Is to let you kno that Helenna excepts yr offer with thanks, and she will leeve imedietly"—(Clan had made several attempts at "immediately," and the result was a terrible smudge)—"per Cork to bristol. My father is wel and all here at present, which I hope this finds you and my ant Elizabeth the same.

"Yrs obediently,

"CLANRICKARDE FERRARD."

Miss Ferrard read this effusion, which, be it observed, bore neither date nor address, and shook her head slowly. Then she folded it, put it back in the dirty blue envelope belonging to it, and opening the case of her writing-desk, laid it carefully aside. She rose and walked to the bay-window and looked across the top of the jardinière, then turned, after a moment or two, and seated herself opposite her sister by the fireside.

"I fear, Elizabeth," said she, after a pause of a few minutes, which she spent looking with a troubled brow into the fire, "we have not yet realized the responsibility and magnitude of the task we have undertaken. Were she a child it would be different; but she is sixteen, and at that age her habits, I fear, will be formed. And it is so difficult to eradicate rooted habits; think how she has been brought up."

"Well, my dear, it cannot be helped. Pray do not distress yourself on my account. After all, she is a child still; she is—" (Miss Elizabeth Ferrard stopped, hesitating, and turned her knitting in her long white fingers)—"she may be a child in many ways. I have no doubt that in point of instruction she is behind most children of half her age; but I fear the Ferrard temper. Her mother was a common person too."

"Yes, yes, my dear; but we must make allowance. It is not everybody, my dear Alice, that has been so signally blessed as we; removed at such an early time from contact with everything that was calculated to injure or harm us. So carefully trained, so guarded and sheltered. Indeed, my dear," continued the old lady, raising her dim eyes to her sister's face, "I have thought that we must be especially mindful of the great difference between us and this poor creature, and—and be more indulgent with her on that account. Now, Alice, is not that your idea too? Yes, I am sure it was. Poor little creature, we must not be hard on her."

Miss Alice Ferrard did not reply. Her brows arched themselves in a nervous angle, and her eyes strayed over the brilliant steel grate with its glowing fire, above which, on the beautiful carved marble mantel-piece, a Dresden clock, wreathed with the loveliest and most fragile little flowers and surmounted by an arch shepherdess and shepherd, with lips parted in a smile of eternal happiness, ticked so peaceably and calmly. A bronze Hermes, with upheld caduceus, was poised gracefully on a tiny sphere; and a charming Hebe, presenting a cup with nod and beck and wreathed smile, a stray sunbeam lighting up her dusky dimples, was his companion, divided from him always by the shepherdess and shepherd on top of their eminence; two long, slender glasses held tall fuchsias and a spike or two of flame-colored gladiolus, and bronze candelabra filled the ends of the mantel-piece. Everything was bright, well kept, and in order. Miss Alice noticed this with a sigh, and looked almost sorrowfully at a splendid tortoise-shell cat, who, curled on a soft, knitted cushion, was asleep at her sister's feet. She observed the ball of white wool lying in perilous proximity to the cat's feet, and, picking it up, laid it with a sigh in her sister's lap.

"Ralph said if she comes at all to-day, it will be about three o'clock. It is now a quarter past three." And Miss Alice went once more to the window to look out. Scarcely had she taken a survey of the street when she uttered a little cry of surprise.

"Some one is getting out at our door, Elizabeth. Can it be Helena? but I see no luggage. Oh! perhaps it has been taken in. Dear, dear!"

Ere Miss Ferrard could rise from her chair to follow her sister, the door of the drawing-room was opened, and Ralph, the solemn old butler, announced in sepulchral tones, "Miss Ferrard."

The two old ladies advanced simultaneously, with hands outstretched, to the tall, awkward girl, who stood, uncertain whether to advance or not, just where she had stopped on entering the room. The dim, mellow tinge of everything, the half-shade and the faint, delicate odors, after the sunlight and noise without, almost stunned Helena; she could hardly see, and groped rather uncertainly with her clumsy gloves for the hands extended to her by her aunts.

Miss Elizabeth kissed her on the cheeks; Miss Alice, who had intended to do so, forgot it, so astonished was she at the girl's looks.

Helena, indeed, was rather the worse for the journey; her hair, which had not been smoothed or dressed since she left Galway, had broken partly loose from its plait and hung in a tangled mane down her back; her face, always sombre, was more so than ever, and her eyes expressed all her bewilderment and uneasiness; her new hat cast an additional shadow over her countenance, for she had crushed the brim by sleeping on it in the train—and, indeed, at the present moment it was on with the wrong side to the front.

"Now, my dear, my poor little thing," began kind Miss Ferrard, "come over here to the fire."

And she took the girl's hand in hers, and led her towards the chair beside her own. Miss Alice, who was tongue-tied from pure wonder, followed them. Helena submitted quietly, and sitting down, stared in bewilderment at her new surroundings.

"How is your father? and did you leave Clanrickarde and your other brothers well?"

"They're well," replied Helena, abruptly but distinctly. "They're all gone to Darraghmore," she added.

"Darraghmore! back to Darraghmore! Impossible!" cried Miss Alice.

Helena looked up from under her hat.

"May be 'twas Darraghstown. Clan was writing to the hotel the same time he wrote to *yous*."

"*Yous!*" repeated Miss Alice to herself, with a horrified shudder. "This is dreadful—dreadful! Far worse than I ever expected!"

Helena yawned now, without even the formality of putting her hand before her mouth.

"You must be tired, dear child," said the elder lady, taking the girl's hand in hers and pulling off the thick glove that covered it. "Did you come by Bristol, and who accompanied you?"

"Cawth put me on board at Cork, and a man who had pigs coming over took care of me; he was very kind," answered Helena, simply, putting up a grimy hand to rub her forehead as she spoke.

English training and ways had not obliterated the Misses Ferrard's native sense of humor. Miss Elizabeth smiled involuntarily; but the smile was quickly followed by a sigh. Miss Alice turned aside to conceal a grim laugh.

"And who is Cawth, pray?" she asked.

Helena looked at her in wonder.

"Cawth McGonigle—she's always with us—the servant, you know."

"Would you not like to go up-stairs, and wash and dress? Pinner has a warm bath ready, and you would like to change your dress. I shall ring to have your trunks carried up."

And Miss Alice rang the bell.

Ralph received the order with stolid impassiveness, and Helena rose in obedience to her aunt's desire and followed her up the stairs. She stepped wonderingly on soft carpets, past a conservatory filled with flowers and strange creeping plants: a white statue holding a lamp was half concealed by the leaves and tendrils of a climbing clematis. They went up two flights of stairs and entered a little sitting-room, plainly fitted with shelves running round the walls. A sewing-machine was in one corner, an old harp in another, some pots of flowers were scattered about, and a neat little writing-table stood in the window.

"Pinner uses this room, Helena; but it is yours. You can read and study here. Did you begin to take lessons?"

Helena did not seem to hear her.

Then an elderly woman entered. She had a harsh face,

and turned a cold, disapproving eye on the stranger as she spoke.

"The young lady's bath is ready, ma'am. Do you wish that I should attend her?"

"Yes, Pinner," replied Miss Alice. "Come in here, Helena; this is your bedroom."

She led the way as she spoke into a second small room behind the sitting-room.

A snowy bed was in the centre of the room. Helena had never seen such a bed before. The pillows were frilled and laced, and in the centre was a splendid embroidered F. The counterpane was like snow, and the muslin curtains were lined with pink. The toilet-table was a marvel of white muslin and pink ribbons, and the mirrors seemed as if desecrated by the reflection of Helena's wild face. Pretty mats stood before the toilet and the marble wash-stand, and a handsomely-fitted dressing-case stood open on the table.

"Where are your boxes, Helena? See, this is your wardrobe. Pinner will unpack and hang up your things if you give her your keys."

Then, as Miss Ferrard turned round, she caught sight of her niece's luggage—a deal box painted green, with a big sprawling F, traced by Isidor's hand, on the lid. She gave a little gasp of horror.

Helena, perfectly unconscious to all appearance, though a demon of outraged pride was gnawing her interiorly, opened her coat, and pulling a piece of cord out of the bosom of her dress, produced her key.

"Pinner, get ready the bath," said Miss Ferrard.

Then, when the maid was gone, she opened the little box. In it was Helena's Galway petticoat of black wool, so coarse and thick that it looked like a garment of raw sheep-skin; her jacket of the same, a couple of linen under-clothes of the coarsest sort, and three pairs of knitted stockings.

Miss Ferrard dropped the lid aghast, and rose from her knees.

"Do you mean to tell me, child, that your father has

sent you out of his house dressed and equipped in this manner?"

"He knows nothing about me," replied Helena, sadly.

"Who got you ready? Who sent you, Helena?"

"Cawth; she bought me this hat, and this, and this, the day before yesterday, in Galway."

Her aunt nodded, thoughtful and puzzled.

"Well," she said, resignedly, "now let Pinner do what is necessary for you, and come down then to us again. You must want something to eat."

"My dear Elizabeth," she said, hastening over to her sister, "this is dreadful, fearful. I really don't know what I am to do."

"Eh! my dear. What—what is it, pray?"

Miss Ferrard almost rose.

"Oh, sit down, sit down. This creature has come here almost in a state of nakedness. Such clothes! She has a box not larger than your desk, filled with savage-looking things, like a peasant's clothes. She has nothing. Darraghmore—well, never mind—I told you how it would be. Is it not fortunate you did not send them fifty pounds, as you intended to do? I must fit her out from head to foot. It is perfectly dreadful, and before Pinner and Ralph, too."

"Oh, poor child, is that all? Ah, well, we can arrange that. Do order them to make her some tea, and have her dinner got ready."

In about half an hour's time, Helena, fresh from the hands of Pinner, presented herself at the drawing-room door. She looked like a new being. Her skin was soft and clear, and the natural olive paleness of her cheeks was suffused with a rose hue; her hair was drawn back tightly off her face, giving the low forehead its full height and adding to the width of her beautiful temples. Pinner had washed and disentangled the mass of black hair and plaited it in two huge, silky braids from the crown of the girl's head. Her collar had been put on properly, her clumsy dress somewhat adjusted to her figure; and almond soap had made Helena's hands something to admire and wonder at.

Pinner had found a pair of her mistress's high-heeled shoes, and these, with fine thread stockings, chanced to fit Helena exactly. She felt conscious of the change herself, and blushed a little as she walked in somewhat unsteadily, for she was unused to her foot-gear, and, moreover, felt a little giddy. She made her way over to the chair she had occupied before. Her aunt looked up suddenly as she approached her.

"Ah! my dear, you have come down. Yes, yes, you have had Pinner to help you, I hope. How pleased your aunt Alice will be!"

At that moment Miss Alice appeared to summon Helena to her lunch. She could scarcely forbear a cry of approval.

Helena read her surprise with a glance of her great eyes, and a slight frown traced itself in her forehead.

"Now, come down; the child must be starved." And she took Hel's arm and led her down-stairs.

Ralph was in readiness at the foot of the stairs, and flung open the dining-room door. Helena walked awkwardly behind her aunt, stepping every now and then on the old lady's trailing skirt. When she got in she was almost dazzled. The afternoon sun streamed in, lighting up an exquisitely-appointed table. A vase of chased silver in the centre held tea-roses, graceful fern-leaves, and feathery clusters of clematis. A silver tray with an urn marked Miss Ferrard's seat at the head of the table. A napkin and a little cover-dish stood before her seat. The butter was unrecognizable under the form of pale shells and rings floating in a crystal dish of water. The sideboard was opposite the window, and its plate-glass back reflected all the brilliancy. Round the walls hung portraits, which looked at Helena with a somewhat familiar expression, as do faces of people once known and almost, but not quite, forgotten. One picture in especial caught her eye—a youth with soft, large brown eyes that seemed to follow her about the room, resting one hand on a greyhound's head; long curls hung on his shoulders, and a froth of lace filled the open of his scarlet coat.

How like Isidor, she thought. It was like him; there were the same short curved lips and round chin, the eyes at once daring and sad. Helena did not hear her aunt's questions—would she help herself to a cutlet? should she give her sugar? Her eyes were intent on the picture.

"That is your great-great-uncle, my dear. Yes, Brandon Ferrard; he was killed at Ramillies."

Helena looked again. "It is just Isidor," said she, with a sudden flush of animation kindling in her great eyes. Ralph, the butler, looked up at a beauty of Sir Godfrey Kneller's—a pale lady, with dark hair gathered off her face into a cap, and troubled, large blue eyes wandering far away from the poppies and dog-roses in her hand—and from her back to the young stranger's face. There was a strong resemblance between them, and he uncovered the dish before Helena with something more of respect in his manner.

Helena's manners at table fully confirmed the bad impressions her appearance and dress had already given her new relations. She showed herself to be perfectly uncivilized. Her aunts were shocked and pained, but they decided to take no notice of her until the next day.

As soon as Miss Ferrard had crashed her cup into her saucer and had declined further refreshment, they rose to go up-stairs. Rough and uncouth as Helena was, she had yet some native sense of fitness; for, although sitting nearest to the door, which to her might have suggested that she was to go out first, she drew back instinctively to let her aunt pass before her. Miss Elizabeth looked meaningly at her sister and smiled.

"You see, my dear. Oh, trust me, you will soon tame her!"

Once in the drawing-room Helena stretched herself willingly in a low lounging-chair, and began to answer the questions with which her aunt Alice plied her.

What did she do? when did she rise? the occupation of the boys, and so on.

Hel, who was silent by nature and habit, answered as best she could; and in a short time the two old ladies were fairly acquainted with the habits of their kinsfolk. Lord Darraghmore appeared between one and two; if it was fine he took a short stroll in the sun with Wasky the wolf-dog. The rest of the day he lay on a sofa and read the paper or smoked. Sometimes she helped Cawth; mostly she was out fishing or hunting rabbits with Isidor. She hadn't been out for more than a fortnight now; and Hel, thinking of the weary days in the close room at Galway, sighed heavily.

"No, dear child, of course not, so soon after the funeral of your poor mamma," said her eldest aunt, approvingly.

"Yes," answered Helena, "the boys had to fish all the time; we had no money."

Then she fell asleep in her chair, overcome by fatigue and by the drowsy warmth and quiet. Aunt Alice started forward to rouse her, but Miss Elizabeth intercepted her outstretched arm.

"No, dear, let her sleep; she is tired, poor little thing. Just leave all efforts until after to-day. How pretty she is!"

The old ladies looked admiringly at the sleeping girl, the fine oval of whose face showed to perfection against the dark velvet of the chair. Her lips were parted and moved slightly as she breathed, showing the white, even teeth between. One foot was advanced carelessly, and the high, arched instep and slender ankle Helena had inherited from her southern kinsfolk were apparent now, clad in Miss Alice's pretty shoe and cobweb-like hose.

"Pretty! yes," assented Miss Alice; "but a Ferrard, with a Ferrard temper. Mark those brows, Elizabeth. See, she frowns even in her sleep."

"Don't say that, dear—now, don't; she is young, and she will change—she will improve."

"Ah, Elizabeth, if we had but caught her younger! I fear greatly she is set. And you know the Ferrard temper. What would we have been now if Lady Conyers had not taken us? and we were infants."

"Well, my dear Alice, we must only try."

Helena retired to bed early. Her toilet for the night

was soon made, her habits being certainly characterized by the most marked simplicity. She pulled the bows off her hair, and shook the long plaits until they felt comfortably loose. She felt afraid to go near the toilet-table lest she should break or spoil something, and she had already broken a Venetian glass in the drawing-room, so she flung all her clothes on her bed just as she had been used to do at home, and crept in. She had been told by her aunts that Pinner would take away her candle, so she left it burning on the chimney-piece. When that discreet personage came some twenty minutes later, she cast looks of horror at the pretty room and its occupant, who was already sleeping peacefully in the midst of the disorder around. Helena's shoes and stockings were lying where they had fallen as she divested herself of them after getting into bed. The black crape bows Pinner had made and fastened into the young lady's hair were thrown here and there on the floor, and the grimy black clothes were tumbled about the snowy counterpane. Pinner shook her head grimly; she picked up the litter, put everything in its proper place, collected the skirts and hung them in the wardrobe, folded the rest of Helena's clothes neatly on a chair beside her bed, and last of all took out the hair-brushes and combs and ranged them on the toilet-table. On the chimney-piece was a nicely-bound Bible; Pinner took this down and laid it conspicuously on the table among the brushes and combs, then she walked off, wondering if the young lady would take a hint next morning from these little arrangements.

Helena slept until eight o'clock. The maid awoke her at that hour, and pulling back the curtains, let in a flood of clear sunlight into the room.

Helena jumped up in bed, and rubbing her eyes, stared drowsily at the new-comer.

"Good-morning, miss," said Pinner, not unkindly; "I hope you are rested. I have brought you warm water. Would you like me to do your hair, or will you be able to do it yourself the way I did yesterday?"

Pinner spoke in an impressive tone, with her little, cold blue eyes fixed on Helena.

"Oh, I'll do it," she replied, a little doubtfully, but still with independence.

"Very well, miss," replied the maid. "You can ring if you want me, and breakfast will be ready at nine, prayers at ten minutes to nine."

Then she went away, and Helena, glad to be alone, sprang out of bed. She looked all round bewildered for her clothes and shoes and stockings. First the array of brushes and the Bible caught her eye, then a light broke upon her. Pinner had done all this after she went to bed. She noted the position of the symmetrically-folded clothes, of the shoes and stockings, and resolved never to incur that tacit reproach again; so, after an elaborate toilet, very unusual for her, she went down to breakfast, feeling slightly fatigued and very hungry.

She sprang into the dining-room, throwing the door open in such an impetuous way that it crashed against a chair behind it with such force that Ralph, who was arranging his sideboard, jumped round with a start. Even the Persian cat sat up on the stool and arched its back with a nervous shudder. Helena looked round. Her aunts had not yet come down, and she felt puzzled what to do. She walked over to the window and looked out. There was not much to interest her; a decorous, dull terrace, scrupulously clean and white. Comfortably-dressed people came and went; no bare feet, no red petticoats, or blue cloaks; no wild Spanish faces, with mournful, reproaching eyes, gazing from beneath the shade of their graceful hoods; not a murmur reached her ears, used to the shrill, strange tongue of the Claddagh. The passers were all dressed alike; not a speck of color varied the monotony of the view. She looked up and down as far as she could reach with her eyes. Away up the street the line was broken by a patch of green, and she sighed, thinking of her view of the harbor and bay, and her evening watch in Galway, sitting with her eyes fixed on Mauriade Blake's red petticoat away down on the quay wall. Then Isidor rose to her mind, and remembering the picture whose black eyes had followed her yesterday, she crossed hastily to where it was hanging, and mounted a chair to view it closer. Certainly it was like Isidor. There were the same daring, brave eyes, the short, imperious upper lip, and the dimple on the round chin. If Isidor were only dressed like that, thought Helena, surveying with a woman's appreciation the fine laced cravat and scarlet coat of her ancestor, Brandon Ferrard.

"Good-morning, Helena," said a grave voice behind her.

Helena leaped to the floor instantly. Her aunt Alice had come in, key-basket in hand, and with a shawl of some light fleecy wool over her shoulders.

"Good-morning, my dear," repeated the old lady, stooping forward and kissing the girl's forehead gravely. "You must manage to look at the pictures without standing on the chairs. Now, my dear, we shall have prayers. Do you see the Bibles over there, on the top of the bookcase. Hand them to me. Where is your own? Oh yes, I forget; run up to your room and bring down your new one, off the chimney-piece."

Helena ran up-stairs and speedily returned with her Bible. Miss Ferrard had come down meantime, and Pinner, Ralph, and a female servant whom Helena had not seen before, were ranged by the sideboard.

Helena was slightly out of breath, she had jumped almost half of the last flight, forgetting to shut the door; she advanced to receive her aunt Elizabeth's kiss.

"Now, my dear," said aunt Alice, "the door."

"Oh," said Helena, and stepping forward she gave the panel a vigorous push with her foot, and the door clapped with a noise that made her aunts jump.

"My *dear* child!" And Miss Alice left her place and opened the door again. "Now shut it always so. *So*," she repeated, as, having gently closed it, she passed Helena on her way back.

Then prayers began. Helena read her verse three times too quickly and miscalled several words, to the evident tribulation of the colony by the sideboard. At last it was over, the servants filed out, and they sat down to breakfast.

"Helena," began Miss Alice. "I wish to say something to you before we begin. You must be conscious yourself of your deficiencies of manner and deportment. Now, my dear, I think we had better begin at once to remedy the most glaring of them; and you will observe that in telling you this, I desire to have you resemble, as nearly as possible, your aunt Elizabeth."

Helena, who was gravely pouring tea into her saucer, heedless of the trickle running from the bottom of the cup on to the snowy cloth, listened attentively and with her great eyes fixed upon her aunt.

"Now, my dear, my dear!"—Miss Alice's tone betrayed the least shade of asperity—"no one out of a kitchen drinks tea so. Pour it all back into your cup, and never do that again."

Helena obeyed willingly but clumsily, and by the time the cloth had received a second libation, this time offered up to the *bienséances*, she was obliged to move away to a dry corner, close by Miss Alice. She proved an apt pupil, however, and before the breakfast was over had learned to hold and use her knife and fork, to sit and eat properly, and delighted Miss Elizabeth by her docility and eagerness to learn.

"After breakfast, Helena, we go out, you and I together. I must get you some dresses at once."

Helena thought of her shopping expedition with her nurse in Galway, and wondered how this fresh one would be conducted. Ralph was instructed to call a fly, and at eleven they set out. A fashionable mourning warehouse in Milsom Street was the first place visited, and Helena's measure was taken for three dresses. A morning dress of plain black, a walking suit of black silk, and an afternoon dress of cashmere. Then to the shoemaker's and various outfitters, dispatch being enjoyed on all as a *sine qua non.* Helena was unimpressed by everything she saw; she expressed neither admiration nor desire, and assented mutely to all her aunt's suggestions. She seemed to be, as indeed she was, utterly destitute of vanity; and the admiring looks which were directed at her in the street and in the shops, she, ascribing them to impertinent curiosity and criticism, repelled by a sullen frown. She was soon tired of shopping and of the crowd of strange faces; the novelty wore off speedily, and she wished herself back. Only that she did not know the way home, she would have slipped quietly away from her seat by the counter, and have left Miss Alice to decide between the rival merits of Bonnet's and Fournier's silks without any aid from her. Her head ached too; the stiff, uncomfortable braids into which, in imitation of Pinner, she had tortured her hair pained her, and the garish colors of the goods displayed wearied her eyes. She began to think of home, and wonder vaguely what the boys were doing. She puzzled what Darraghstown was like; not Galway, for it was not by the sea; nor Coleraine, nor Thurles, nor any of the places she had been in in Ireland. It was there her father had been born and brought up, no wonder he liked it. Cawth too was glad to go there; what could it be like? Then she remembered that it was idle for her to think about Darraghstown. She was never to see it, so she put the thought out of her head. Only for a minute; in spite of herself it came back.

"There was the Darragh river running through the town, so close behind some of the houses that you could fish out of window;" she remembered Cawth's talk over the fire, the last night she spent in Galway. "And there was the Rack full of salmon, and watched all night in the season by Lord Comerford's men." And Hel, sitting on a high-legged chair in a fashionable draper's shop, watching her aunt choose linens, felt with a sort of pang a strange longing for a hiding-place by another river well known to her and Isidor—a noisy, brawling trout-stream that ran red-colored from the bogs through one of their favorite haunts. Helena thought of the last July day she spent by it, lying so still and quiet in a shady corner that the water-hens swam to and fro almost within reach of her hand, and the swallows darted unconcernedly from bank to bank, taking now a fly from the very surface, and then a tiny shell from the grass at the edge, heedless of the sun-glare that drove the dun-colored trout beneath the sedges, and the cattle, fly-plagued, to the shelter of the woods and hedge-rows. She could almost hear the snapping of the creatures' beaks, and the hum of the bees in the branches above her.

She answered "yes" where she should have said "no" to Aunt Alice's remarks, and looked so abstracted and indifferent to the weighty discussion about the proper length of her skirts, that Miss Alice at last got angry and requested her sarcastically to descend from the moon, if it were only for politeness' sake.

At last they got home. The early dinner passed off without much mishap. Helena was attentive to Miss Alice's liberal hints, and ate her dinner slowly and solemnly. At last it was over too, and they returned to the drawing-room. Helena did not care to sit by the fire; she went over to a window-seat to look out.

It was a bright, clear day out of doors, late autumn as it was. The summer was not quite gone; just a fringe of her gay robes still trailed behind. The few trees to be seen from Plantagenet Terrace were still clad in their summer garb. The chestnuts alone showed signs of decay; their long leaves were bruised and rusty, and the chestnuts were splitting and falling from their spiked sheaths.

Helena looked enviously at the school-children, who were kicking away the dead leaves to discover the glossy, new-fallen fruit. A big boy flung stones at the high branches, and the whole band rushed with cries of delight when one or two fell to seize upon and dispute for them. Presently a policeman appeared and shook his head warningly; a nurse seized the big boy by the arm and dragged him away, scolding furiously, and the troop scattered in every direction.

Helena looked up and down the street vainly in search of something interesting; then, disappointed, she went to the book-cases, and took down one of the faded volumes and opened it to see the name. She could not read the gilt lettering on the back: "Gibbon's Decline and Fall."

She wondered what that could be about; there were no pictures to illumine her, and the long, unbroken pages did not look promising. She poked it back into its place, upside down; then tried the next row—"Blair's Rhetoric," Macaulay, Hume; then a whole row of white and gold Italian authors. Coleridge, Shelley, Keats, Wordsworth she found in one corner, and left them there.

At last an illustrated edition of "Gulliver's Travels" came to hand. She was attracted by the title and carried it off. Had she tried the bottom shelf she would have discovered the English dramatists, beginning with Shakespeare in the right-hand corner, and going on from Jonson in a direct line down to her brilliant countryman Sheridan. As it was she missed them, and having curled herself comfortably in the window, began her book.

Miss Ferrard was dozing meantime tranquilly in her easy-chair. Miss Alice was writing notes at her table and entering in a leather-bound book her outlay for Helena that morning.

Presently the leather-covered book was shut with a snap, and Miss Alice looked over at her niece, who, with both legs curled up tailor-wise in her chair, was buried in her book. In a moment she was beside her.

"Helena, my dear, a young lady does not sit so. Stand up."

Down came both legs with an impatient jerk. Helena was standing bolt upright, the book clasped wide open against her breast.

"Lay down your book, dear, if you please. Now, like me."

Miss Alice spread out her handsome skirt at each side and seated herself gracefully. Helena imitated her as nearly as she could, and her aunt walked off content.

She did not notice that her pupil, whose book had been laid rather out of reach, was obliged to disarrange her *pose* again to resume it, and that in reseating herself she completely forgot the lesson she had just received. She was allowed to read undisturbedly until Miss Ferrard woke up, then Aunt Alice called her over.

"Helena, dear, I think your aunt Elizabeth would like you to read out to us. Anything at all. See, here is the *Standard;* take the leading article and read loud and distinctly."

Miss Alice handed the paper to Helena, who turned it rcund and round, wondering what was meant by the leading article. Her aunt came to the rescue and pointed it out.

Helena began to read loudly enough, but utterly unintelligibly. Every word was mispronounced or wrongly accented and the punctuation totally ignored.

Miss Alice uttered a little scream before the first sentence had been got through.

"My dear child, that will do—that will do! Oh dear! how dreadful, Elizabeth! Could you have believed it possible?"

Then Helena was allowed to go back to the window and "Gulliver," while the old ladies discussed this new revelation.

Helena's mode of reading her verse that morning had not been unnoticed by Miss Alice. It was clear that the child had been neglected in every way, and the sooner such a state of affairs was remedied the better. A governess, of course, must be got for her, and at once; and Miss Alice decided to apply to the clergyman of the parish as the most likely to know of a suitable person.

In a few days a daily governess was engaged to instruct the Honorable Miss Ferrard in all the branches of a polite education—music, languages, English, drawing and needle-work.

CHAPTER VII.

"I will be gone;
Shall I stay here to do it? No, no, although
The air of paradise did fan the house
And angels officed all, I will be gone.
Come, night; end, day,
For with the dark, poor thief, I'll steal away."

All's Well that Ends Well.

"A MOST reliable person, so methodical and trustworthy, and so experienced; elderly—well—ah—er—my dear Miss Ferrard, elderly—yes, elderly—about that."

"I am glad to hear that she is experienced with girls; and, Mr. Cholmondely, I had feared that my dear sister Alice and myself were rather unsuited to manage our niece Helena. She is so young, and we are not accustomed to young people. She must find everything so strange here. But now, with Miss Babcock's experience to aid us, nothing can go wrong."

And gentle Miss Elizabeth looked at her friend and pastor with eyes positively beaming with gratitude.

He was a pale, meagre little man, of fifty or thereabouts, gentleman-like, with a great, deep voice, of which he seemed to like to hear the sound as it reverberated through the room; very "high" as to doctrine and ritual. He wore a priest's collar that reminded Helena of the Roman Catholic priests at home, only this one was thin and pale, and a gentleman; a tolerably clever man, but spoiled, as clergymen in such places as Bath are apt to be, by associating too exclusively with the softer sex.

Helena, from a far corner, surveyed him with something of contempt—"a sickly-looking, stooped thing; Clan could fight him with one hand." And she disliked his critical way of looking at her and asking her what she thought of England—was it not a change from "her own green isle?" Green isle, indeed! Helena's eyes flashed. And he said he found such a difficulty in understanding the people in Cork one summer he and Mrs. Cholmondely had been there; they spoke such a curious dialect—quite unpleasant to listen to—painful, he might say. Altogether, he was sure her aunts, though of course they would have a natural predilection for the land of their birth, would join him in saying England was much nicer, more—er—er—agreeable as a permanent residence.

Miss Alice assented, smiling. "Ireland, for her part, was a charming place to live out of." She had forgotten everything about it long ago.

Helena scarcely understood the little man whose sonorous voice seemed to be rolling and echoing among the Cupids and Dianas of the ceiling, but she divined his meaning fast enough and bent her dark brows in an ungracious scowl.

"Oh, yas," he continued, patronizingly, "by the time Miss Ferrard has been a few years among us she will have lost her antipathy to England and English ways." (Helena began to understand Cawth's puzzling sayings now.) "Why—er—how any one can live in Ireland except—er—in constant bodily fear, I can't imagine, really. I should be in perpetual terror of being shot—ha, ha!"

"You needn't," Helena exploded contemptuously; "we don't buy powder for nothing."

"Ha, ha, ha!" This time his laugh was thoroughly genuine, and he turned round in his chair to look at the speaker. "Why that is capital—capital! I never heard that before. Powder not bought for nothing! My dear young lady, I wish everybody would think so with regard to everybody else—ha, ha!—in your country! Excellent! though—ah! you Irish" (with a patronizing, soothing tone) "are so quick-witted; yes, you really are quick-witted now. But I must be going. Not any more sherry—oh dear, no, thank you. Good-bye, Miss Ferrard; I shall look for my young friend at St. Botolph's on Sunday. Good-bye."

"Well, my dear," said Miss Alice, gleefully, when the deep notes had died away on the staircase, waking strange echoes in that silent house, "it is settled. Miss Babcock will come to us at ten next Monday morning to remain until three. How good of Mr. Cholmondely to call and tell us all about it."

"Ah, yes!" returned Miss Elizabeth, "he is such a zealous creature. Helena, dearest, don't you like Mr. Cholmondely?" And without waiting for Helena's answer, for which indeed she might have waited long enough, Miss Ferrard pursued: "The Braziers have come back for the winter. How early the place is filling, is it not, Alice? I did remark this morning that there were a number of people in the boarding-house at the opposite corner. Did you not see them? We must call upon the Braziers directly, and the Welds, and Lady St. Johns—how nice."

"Yes. We shall have quite a gay winter, shall we not? and as soon as Helena has done something, made some progress with Miss Babcock, we must see about having the third Brazier girl—yes, Guinevere Brazier is just her age—down to take tea with her; she must have a companion of her own age. Helena! do not hold your book so."

"Dear, yes," said Miss Elizabeth, laying down her knitting with an air of astonishment that the idea had not occurred to her before "Of course, Alice, we must remember that, we must remember that."

Then the two old ladies sat down to digest the news their pastor had brought, and Helena was forgotten for the nonce. She felt in no humor for "Gulliver" now, and she began to speculate as to Miss Babcock, whose threatened apparition furnished ample food for her imagination. She ransacked her memory in vain for an example of a governess. Cooper and Mayne Reid had overlooked that character in their *dramatis personæ*, so her erudition was no help to her, and she had to fall back upon her meagre experience. There had been a governess with some family living on the Salthill Road in Galway. She recollected a shabby, quiet-looking person who was always telling the young Bloods not to walk in the dirty places, and always running after them along the road. She remembered the children abusing her and calling her names, threatening to tell their mamma if she refused to do something they wanted. A governess could not be such a terrible personage after all, Helena reflected. She remained in her place quietly for about an hour. The ample velvet curtain had fallen forward so as to hide her from the room, but she could see her aunts still seated talking cheerfully together by the fire. The dusk was falling and she could not read, neither was there anything to be seen in the street. It was quiet, and dull, and warm within. The cat lay in a ball on his cushion, and the firelight shone on Miss Elizabeth's snowy hair as she knitted and talked in her low, rich voice. The Venetian goblets shimmered on the oak cabinet, the crimson and yellow of the flowers, not withered yet, glowed fitfully among the china monsters and gods on the shelves; and on the mantel-piece the cut crystals of the candlesticks sparkled like diamonds.

Helena lounged at her ease with her arm over the back of the chair, staring fitfully at the fire. She felt weary and she did not know why; she tried to listen to the conversation, but the names were all strange and uninteresting, and she fell into a dream about Isidor and herself. They were out in a boat, near Arran, at anchor, and fishing. She could feel the strong salt breeze from the Atlantic lift the hair off her temples under her old hat, and the waves rocked the boat, and now and again a fleck of spray was blown on her cheek. The Clare mountains lay bathed in purple and gold to the south, and the horizon was flecked by the brown sails of the fishers. Rusty, the lurcher, sat in the stern, looking uncomfortable, yet confident, after the manner of dogs in unwonted positions.

Again, they were in the woods, the autumn leaves rustling under foot and flying off in sudden skifts across the dry, reedy grass. She and Rusty had chased them and kept up with the best of them many a time. The blackberries hung in ripe clusters down to the very edge of the grass, and the cones were tumbling from the high branches of the pines. There was a sharp taste in the air, and in sheltered corners an autumn smell came from the mould and the heaps of damp leaves. She would lie watching the rabbits for hours, while Isidor went to look for hares farther off, or stroll cautiously down to the weir to see if his night-lines held a fish.

Helena mused and dreamed, and in spite of herself a sort of fretting desire came over her to be back to the old scenes again. She drew a deep breath of longing for the fresh sea breezes and the heather she had reveled in all the past summer, but she inhaled only the faint, warm rose scent that came from the china jars beneath the console. Then she sighed half impatiently, then stood up suddenly off her chair as if to shake from her such vexing memories. Aunt Elizabeth turned round at the stir.

"Helena, dear child, come up here to the fire. Why are you moping down there? come now, and sit near me, my pet."

The girl obeyed languidly, and submitted to have her cheek stroked by Miss Elizabeth's soft jeweled fingers. She was not of a caressing or affectionate nature, her bringing up had been singularly devoid of all softening or lovable influences, and though a physiognomist might trace in her full lips and the ardent deep eyes capabilities of future passion, fiery and wild when once raised, she was as unresponsive and unsympathetic as some strong wild bird, which may crouch under your hand, but has its gleaming eyes fixed on the sky and its pinions straining for flight all the time.

Three days, inclusive of Sunday, had to be got over somehow before the exciting advent of Miss Babcock on Monday, and how Helena suffered in the interval no pen could describe. The heavy, steamy atmosphere of Bath was in itself depressing to one accustomed to the fresh Atlantic breezes. The orderly, methodical household, with its clock-work routine and unvarying monotony, galled the young barbarian's wild, untamed spirit, and she fretted and chafed like some caged animal. To look out of window presented little variety—rows of prim, methodical houses, whose very walls expressed the comfort, cleanliness and prim orderliness which form the glory of Bath; they had all the same bright knockers and bell-handles and snowy door-steps, cleaned at much expense of labor and Bath-stone. How useless, objectless it all appeared to Helena, brought up in the fatalistic, self-indulgent *abandon* of the Galway tribes.

She was taken out to her afternoon promenade in Milsom Street, where she and her aunt Alice walked beside Miss Ferrard's pretty Bath-chair and threaded their way leisurely among a throng of people—invalids and cripples, oddly contrasting with fresh, golden-haired girls, to look at whom made poor Helena feel wilder and more wretched than before.

Then came Sunday. The chimes from the Abbey Church made Hel inclined to throw back her head and howl as the dog in the next-door garden did. At last it ceased, and then the oppressive stillness of a Bath Sunday held its sway until morning service began to ring, and the rattle of the Bath-chairs, carrying the invalids to church, filled the whole place. Hel joined in the procession and walked demurely beside her elder aunt's chair. On they went amid the deafening clamor of the bells, and into the Abbey church-yard. The fresh look and glare of light rather repelled than charmed her, and after tumbling over the hassocks she at last seated herself disconsolately in the farthest-off corner of her aunt's roomy pew. She found some occupation in staring at the yellowing marble monuments—one in especial, where a disconsolate Sarah Green wept over an urn, her marble visage concealed by a remarkably dirty handkerchief. Hel soon exhausted the interest of this wondrous production, and pleasant memories of Sundays in the smoky, dirty room in Galway commenced to crowd upon her with a most exasperating clearness, playing beggar-my-neighbor or *écarté* for pence with Isi until the church-time was over and they could escape to the Claddagh or the fields, for even in Galway they respected public opinion sufficiently to stay indoors during service. Not all the preacher's oratory sufficed to exorcise the spirit of restlessness and *ennui* that now possessed her, and it was with an earnest vow never to enter its portals again that Helena descended the steps of the Abbey Church when the weary service was over.

Monday morning came at last and brought Miss Babcock punctually at the time appointed. She was a middle-aged Englishwoman, very plain of face, angular, and stilted of manner as became a person always on the watch for the deficiencies of others, and to whom a lapse into naturalness or ease might have been perilous. If governesses are obliged to watch their young charges, they have always the consciousness that they are themselves under a strict and malicious surveillance, and liable at any moment to be "hoist with their own petard." Ralph showed her up to the drawing-room and went into the dining-room to announce the arrival; the breakfast was scarcely over. Miss Alice took Helena, now dressed in a suitable morning dress, with neat cuffs and snowy collar and tie, above which her wild, poetic face looked doubly strange, up to introduce her to her new Mentor. Miss Alice shook hands a little condescendingly with Miss Babcock.

"This is our niece—our brother's daughter, Miss Ferrard—your pupil, Miss Babcock," she said with a glance at Helena, who stared at her, never dreaming of returning the formal and correct salutation with which the governess acknowledged her presentation.

"We shall be good friends I hope, Miss Ferrard," she said, a little fussily, for she was duly impressed by the young lady's social status. "My dear pupils, Lady Saltster's daughters, with whom I spent five happy years, were so attached to me when I left they presented me, the darling girls, with a handsome locket; all their names—do you see, Miss Ferrard?—are engraved inside." She had opened a queer old locket, half glass, and was exhibiting it as she spoke. "'Alicia, Maud, and Elinor.' They are all married now—so well married," continued Miss Babcock, as if that fact also, like the presentation of the locket, redounded to her credit.

"You will find Helena backward for her age," began Miss Alice, a little nervously. "You see—er—living always in the country, and poor Lady Darraghmore had such wretched health—dreadful—er—quite so. And in the country, in Ireland especially—"

"Oh, I quite understand, Miss Ferrard—quite! I assure you, Miss Saltster—now Mrs. Comberbatch—will be Lady Comberbatch—at sixteen could hardly write her name. You have no idea of how quickly she got on; an eldest daughter and her father's favorite. Sir John never rode to hounds without Miss Saltster until I came to them. Oh yes, I quite understand all that."

Miss Alice gave tokens now that she considered the interview had lasted long enough. And Miss Babcock rose:

"We may proceed to our task I suppose, Miss Ferrard. I have taken the liberty"—she produced a black reticule of considerable dimensions as she spoke—"of bringing some school-books, supposing that my pupil had very likely omitted to bring her own from home with her. If you have already procured them, of course I can return them to the book-sellers."

Miss Babcock fixed anxious eyes on her employer's face as she finished.

"Oh, quite right, Miss Babcock; I am glad you have been so thoughtful; it will save time so nicely. Now, if you will allow me, I will take you up to the school-room. Come, Helena."

Miss Babcock grasped her black bag, which, indeed, seemed very heavy, with a re-assured expression of countenance, and followed Miss Ferrard.

In accordance with that useful and high-minded practice which has crept into general use in British commerce of touting, or commission, Miss Babcock, like other teachers, was allowed a handsome percentage, twenty-five per cent., on all books she bought or caused to be bought at the book-sellers' she favored, so of course she was anxious to secure the munitioning of Miss Ferrard's school-room. She had noted the absence of a piano in the drawing-room; and all the way up-stairs her mind was exclusively occupied by the hope that the school-room might also be destitute of that modern instrument of torture.

They entered the little sitting-room which had been set apart for Helena's use. And Miss Babcock cast admiring glances round, glances which became positively rapturous when she discovered that her wildest hopes were realized—that there was no school-room piano.

"A charming room, Miss Ferrard, so airy, so isolated; the room of all the house that I would have selected. It quite reminds me of the dear old school-room at Lady Saltster's—oh, quite! but the aspect is different—the park, you know; and the school-room was on the ground-floor, jessamine and roses growing round the windows. A bower—a perfect bower—our school-room was."

"Well, now, Miss Babcock," said Miss Ferrard, her low-pitched but distinct tones falling musically on Helena's ears after the governess's shrill, hard voice, "I shall leave you and Helena to become acquainted with each other. I think we know what is to be done."

"Pardon me," said Miss Babcock, "did I not understand you to say that Miss Ferrard was to learn music?"

"Certainly!"

"I did not observe a piano. Perhaps you meant the harp?" She looked interrogatively towards the instrument which, swathed in its green-baize cover, stood in the corner.

"Oh, I quite forgot all about it! I must speak to my sister; it was quite an oversight. Of course a piano must be hired—at all events until we see about purchasing one."

"It is a very important matter, in purchasing or hiring a piano, to procure one suited to the touch and to the requirements of the pupil. I hope you will be good enough to allow me to select the instrument for Miss Ferrard, subject, of course, to your approval. Pedal and Truss have just got a capital assortment of pianos from London, for hire as well as sale. I have dealt there exclusively for my pupils and myself, and they are most satisfactory."

Miss Babcock had quite recently selected a two hundred guinea grand piano for a rich county family, who had confided the choice of the instrument to her; and the commission—forty guineas—had been paid down by the eminent firm of Pedal and Truss with the most satisfactory promptitude.

"Certainly, Miss Babcock; it is very kind of you to take the trouble. I shall consult my sister and let you know at two o'clock."

Then Miss Alice went away, shutting the door after her, and Helena and her governess were left together. Miss Babcock took off and shook her mangy seal-skin—the cast off, no doubt, of some Lady Saltster—and hung it, together with her bonnet, on a nail behind the door. Then she poked up the fire (the morning was sharp), placed the most comfortable chair at that side of the table next to it, and, taking her black bag in her lap, sat down.

"Now, my dear, come and sit down there—yes, with your back to the light, and see if you are acquainted with any of these books."

She opened her bag and took out a varied collection. Prominent among them "Mangnall's Questions," in a stiff, shiny cover; a French grammar, selected not so much for its undoubted excellence as for the handsome percentage allowed on its high price; a "Murray's Grammar," a spelling-book, a Brewer's "Guide to Science," a volume of Pinnock, a book of French dialogues and vocabulary, a French dictionary, a large book of elegant extracts, a copy-book, slate, and exercise-book. Helena watched the disgorging process with much the same wonder that a child watches the operations of the conjuror's magic bottle.

"Now, my dear," said Miss Babcock, surveying the pile in triumph—as well she might; her share of the spoil was to amount to about fifteen shillings—"let me hear you read, this—say;" and opening at random the volume of elegant extracts, she laid before Helena, who had never seen poetry in her life, and had no conception of even the meaning of the word, Shelley's "Cloud."

Helena began, but ere the second line was read, Miss Babcock stopped her with an exclamation of mingled impatience and surprise, and, taking the book from her hands, found a prose extract. Miss Helena read in such a manner as showed that she at least understood its sense, although her pronunciation and accent made her listener stare.

"I think we had better begin with spelling and dictation," she said. "Now, Miss Ferrard, you will learn that column. See, those marks indicate the syllabling of the word and its pronunciation. Take them one by one, and when you think you know it tell me, and I will hear you by rote." Then she drew an antimacassar in bright wools out of her wonderful bag, and, leaning back in her chair, commenced to net away, while Helena, with bent brows, pored over the spelling-book.

Long experience had taught Miss Babcock the easiest way, for herself, of teaching. So she set Helena tasks that took her an hour at a time to con, while she sat at her ease and wrote letters, knitted or sewed. Not that she was by any means disposed to neglect her charge; she only wanted to get through her task as comfortably as possible.

Helena presently handed her the book and spelled the column down creditably enough. She had read a good deal and could remember the words that she had seen before. The pronunciation, however, was sadly astray. At last Miss Babcock was compelled to resort to the expedient of reading over the words with her pupil, making her pronounce each one after herself. A couple of columns of the multiplication-table and a page of "Brewer's Science" were got through by two o'clock. Even the mental exertion undergone to produce this small sum of achievement had sorely taxed Helena; her face was lead-colored, and the drooping eyelids, languid voice and attitude showed how severe had been the strain.

Miss Babcock's self-asserting voice rang with painful dissonance through her ears. The print seemed to dance before her eyes, and the hot, close air of the room weighed upon her chest with oppressiveness.

At last the clock struck, Miss Babcock folded up the antimacassar quickly, donned her old seal-skin and bonnet, and, leaving the pile of books on the table, walked off, consumed with desire to hear Miss Ferrard's decision about the piano.

Helena followed her down slowly. The cooler air of the staircase was delightful to her, and she stretched her arms high over her head and yawned to her heart's content. How weary and sick she felt! If every day was to be like this! She shuddered with repulsion at the idea. Could it be possible? and she sat down on the stairs and buried her hot face in her hands. A step and rustle disturbed her. It was Pinner coming out of Miss Ferrard's room. Helena slipped down the stairs like a flash, across a vestibule room, and out on a balcony leading to a pretty green-house, the especial care of her aunt Alice. The ground-glass door shut behind her; she sat down on the end of a shelf. The soft, fresh perfume of the lemon verbenas and heliotropes trained to the walls was refreshing to her, and the cool green of the luxuriant ferns, the shade of the vines and creepers overhead were pleasant to her eyes, weary with gazing at the hard, monotonous columns of her book. One sash was drawn down, and she could see between the vine-stems across the gardens of Plantagenet Terrace. At the end ran a row of stables; over their roofs more houses; everywhere high walls covered with ivy and creepers; stiff, well-kept gardens with flower-beds cut out in the turf; vases filled with nasturtiums, tossed and withered-looking now, trim box-hedges and glass-houses—a bounded view certainly.

The sparrows flew to the ledge of the green-house and chirped and looked in confidently. Miss Elizabeth fed them every morning, and they were tame and saucy. A cat which lay basking on the parapet looked eagerly at them, and chattered her teeth so viciously that they all took wing and lighted in a poplar tree that grew out of the yard beneath, and whose dried leaves rustled harshly. Helena wondered if they would come back, and, heedless of the pots of balsams she was crushing, leaned forward to the open sash to look out.

Just then the door opened and Ralph's gray head looked in.

"Miss Helena, Pinner is looking everywhere for you. The dinner-bell is just going to ring."

Helena uttered an exclamation of impatience and drew back brusquely. Down went the balsam-pot with a crash on the inlaid floor.

Ralph, who was holding the door open for her, uttered a "H'm, h'm, Miss Helena."

She knelt down and began to replace the clay with her hands.

"Pray don't, miss; I'll put it to rights," expostulated the butler.

But Helena, on reparation intent, scraped up the clay, replaced the pot, and then, wiping her hands on her pretty black frock, passed unheedingly out on the stairs. There she fell into the hands of Pinner, who put on an ominous face and ushered her up-stairs.

"What hever 'ave you been doing, miss?" asked the maid, startled out of her usual correctness of language. "Wot 'ands you 'ave. And, my! Miss Helena, your lovely new frock! A young lady of your age ought to know better, indeed."

Helena let her storm away. All her irritation and ill-humor had returned, and she longed to vent it in some way. Perhaps Pinner caught sight in the mirror before which Helena was seated of the gathering storm, for she ceased her tart observations and commenced to brush and plait the long hair that hung down over the wrapper. She must have twitched it roughly, for Helena, after a few grimaces, suddenly jumped up and catching the plait pulled it away from her hands.

"I will do it; go away, you old fool!" she cried, turning away from the mirror, and snapping as she spoke the comb from the astonished maid's hands. Her eyes flashed angrily, and her white teeth gleamed. Pinner delayed not a moment. She rushed off and presently re-appeared with Miss Alice, who read Helena a strong lecture on the impropriety of her conduct and her ingratitude to Pinner, who had never been told to dress her hair at all, but had volunteered of her own good-will to assist her.

"I am shocked, perfectly shocked," Miss Alice said by way of valediction as she was leaving the room, "to think that a niece of mine could act so. Helena, you shall not come down to dinner. You must apologize to Pinner, and you shall remain here until you do."

A scornful, short laugh greeted this declaration, and Helena flung herself into a chair, her lips curved with contempt.

"If she comes near me again I'll fling her out of the window."

This defiance reached Miss Ferrard as she shut and locked the door after her.

Dinner was sent up on a tray to the delinquent, who refused to touch a scrap, and lay still undressed in the little easy-chair beside her bed. She felt chilled, for the window was open, and she had not exchanged her white wrapper for her afternoon dress. But she never heeded; she lay still in a stupor of exasperation and rage. Pinner to speak so, and to pull her hair! She was an old fool; for that matter Aunt Alice was another, and next time she came she would tell her so. Then she turned round with a jerk of impatience and looked out. The sun was still shining brightly, and above the lace and bows of her pretty toilet-table she could see the clear blue sky. The twit-twit of the sparrows came in at the open window, and to it was joined presently the cry of a goat in the garden next door. Presently Helena began to cry; she was wearied out and she was so lonely. If she had only her rabbit or Rusty, or even the thrush, to console her; but it was stupid work, locked up in that room so full of fine things that she felt afraid to move. How different from home! She longed for Cawth's crabbed face, with her old cap and her woolen shawl. Her cross voice never sounded strange and awful as Aunt Alice's did, with her dress of lace and silk and her gold chain and rings. And she cried away until with pure weariness she fell asleep.

Later in the afternoon she was awakened by her aunt Alice, who with stern countenance was standing over her.

"Helena, I should never have expected such conduct from you. Are you ashamed of yourself?"

Helena sat up; her white wrapper had fallen back, her long hair, unconfined by plait or ribbon, was loose on her shoulders and had clustered over her brows; from beneath, her eyes looked out tear-stained and dimmed, but sullen and determined.

"No," she answered, shortly.

"You ought to be ashamed of yourself to say so. Have you made up your mind to ask pardon for your offense?"

"Of her? the servant?" demanded Helena, scornfully.

Miss Alice looked at the rebel and shook her head.

"Just what I expected," she said to herself; then, aloud and sternly, "You shall ask Pinner's forgiveness, and you shall not stir out of this room until you do so. If not from your heart, at least in obedience to me."

Helena only turned her head aside with a scowl.

"You ought to remember that you owe respect to yourself, to your rank and position. Ah, your aunt Elizabeth will acknowledge now that I was right, and that she was wrong when she persisted, in spite of my warnings, in bringing such a trouble upon us."

Helena moved uneasily in her chair at the mention of her elder aunt, the genial kindness and sweetness of whose disposition had impressed even her wild nature; but she was too proud to give any sign, and Miss Alice left her as hopeless and hardened to all appearance as before.

After an hour spent by Helena in a chill torpor, the door opened and Miss Elizabeth came in. She carried a tray in her hand, which she sat down, and taking a shawl she advanced silently and wrapped it round Helena's shoulders. She submitted without speaking, only looking questioningly and suspiciously at the old lady. Then Miss Elizabeth sat down beside her and said in her usual tone, only a little lower:

"Tell me now, Helena, what is all this? I should like to hear it from yourself."

Helena did not reply, but she turned and looked into her aunt's eyes with an expression at once wistful and bewildered.

"You had done something in the green-house first?" suggested Miss Ferrard, gently. She saw that the culprit did not know where to begin.

"Yes," replied Helena, "broke a pot, soiled my fingers and dress."

"Well, dear, and Pinner was scolding, was that it?"

"Yes, and jerked my hair, and then I—" Here an eloquent hiatus supplied the rest far better than words.

"Well, now; and do you not agree with me that it would have been better for you to have spoken quietly to Pinner? Are you sorry?"

"No, Aunt Elizabeth," Helena answered, in a tone that left little doubt of her sincerity. "I ought not to have dirtied my frock; but she ought not to have pulled my hair. I am sorry for breaking the pot," she added with an air of concession.

Miss Elizabeth sighed.

"You will say, Helena, at least, that you are sorry for troubling your aunt Alice and me. Say that, dear, and come down-stairs. We shall not mind about Pinner."

"Oh yes!" assented Helena, readily enough. "I am sorry to trouble you."

"Very well, dear;" and Miss Ferrard lifted up the tangled mass of hair and kissed the fine brow beneath. "Now you will drink this cup of warm soup that I have brought you, and then dress and come down."

Helena obeyed. The reaction had set in after her fit of excitement and anger, and she felt chilled and exhausted. It seemed as if an entire week had passed since the morning; her temples throbbed painfully, and her aunts' voices sounded far off and strange, as in a dream. She remained all the evening lying in a chair by the fire, her long fingers held up between her face and the blaze. Miss Elizabeth tried to get her to speak, but abandoned the attempt after a while, and contented herself with looking at her from time to time with an expression of anxious concern.

Miss Alice shook her head ominously. She could understand the burst of Ferrard temper well enough, and make allowances for it; but this secondary attack of sullenness as she called it—nervous prostration, having its origin in physical and mental causes, it really was—baffled all her astuteness.

Helena retired early and spent the night tossing feverishly. At breakfast she was pale, inanimate, with livid streaks round her heavy eyes, and ate little or nothing. She complained of nothing; indeed, she did not know what to complain of.

When ten o'clock and Miss Babcock arrived together, she went up-stairs resignedly. Her preceptress was in excellent humor, and announced to Helena that her new piano would be home that afternoon, and that she hoped she would be pleased with it. Miss Babcock was evidently in high good-humor; and with reason, for she had concluded a very advantageous bargain with her old friends, Pedal and Truss.

Helena had not looked at one of the lessons marked for her the previous day, and, after a short lecture from Miss Babcock, who was in too good a humor to be seriously cross, to which she paid not the slightest attention, lessons commenced.

At about twelve o'clock the governess determined to go down and ask permission from the Misses Ferrard to take Helena out for a walk. Her experienced eye told her that the girl needed air and exercise. They consented at once, and in a few minutes Helena and Miss Babcock were walking out in the direction of the country. They had a fine, gray day; no sun shone, but the atmosphere was clear and dry, and the broad, white highroad was inviting looking.

Helena, little by little, began to feel the invigorating effects of the fresh air, soft and enervating as it was. They took a quiet road and soon left the crescents and terraces of the town behind. When they had walked a good distance up a hilly slope they turned and Helena could see Bath lying below; the long sweep of houses creeping up the surrounding hills gave it the look of an amphitheatre, and the rich, beautiful champaign of Somersetshire stretched itself all round her. Then, after a look, they continued their way.

"Well, my dear," said Miss Babcock, "how is your headache now? Has the air driven it quite away?"

"I don't know," replied Helena, who did not indeed know if the word "headache" qualified the state of *malaise* she was in.

"I suppose you are thinking of home. Poor child! You'll soon get over that. Don't step down in the road to let these people pass; take the wall side of the path; never forget what is due to yourself. You stepped off the path to give way to quite common people just now. They knew me and I was quite vexed. Turn out your left foot a little more, dear; you hold yourself otherwise extremely well."

Helena, indeed, was as straight and lithe as a young sapling, and many were the admiring looks cast upon her by the passers-by. Miss Babcock noted them with delight, and with no small wonder at the reception they met from the young lady.

"You must miss your brothers, I am sure; and his lordship your papa will feel quite lonely without you."

No answer.

"Darra—what—Darrastown? is that the name of the family seat?"

"Darraghmore was the name," replied Helena. "Darraghstown is the village."

"Oh, Darraghmore—more!" repeated the governess. "To be sure; the Misses Ferrard's brother is Lord Darraghmore. I always fancied all Irish names of people's places ended in 'town.' And tell me, dear, is Darraghmore a fine place—now something like that?"

They stopped before a handsome gate entrance leading into a magnificent demesne. As far as the eye could reach all round extended a park, wood and water charmingly intermingled, and the changing hues of the leaves making the elms, oaks and lighter trees look like a gigantic bouquet. Dark green, pale yellow, red, and brown glowed and lighted up the dim landscape. The swans could be seen gliding in the river, but so far away that they seemed no bigger than ducks.

Helena cast longing eyes over to the woods. One-half the great iron gates stood open, and she could see right across the wide expanse of grass. The cawing of the rooks came distinctly to her ears, and now and again the sharp crack of the guns broke the stillness of the October air.

There was a shooting-party in the wood, and the rooks seemed sadly perturbed; the black cloud flew up and down with angry cawings into the air, and settled back again in their tree-tops only to dash out again in a moment with angry expostulations.

Helena's eyes lighted up strangely, and her cheeks were suffused with a bright, fitful color.

"Look, look, Miss Babcock! a hare! Do you see her?"

"No, I do not," replied the governess, indifferently.

"Do you see the fairy ring—not the near one—the large one? She's sitting right behind it."

And Helena, speaking in a low, excited tone, pointed with outstretched black finger in the direction of one of those circular tufts of grass longer and greener than the rest, which in her native country are called by the peasants "fairy rings."

"Don't *point*, my *dear* child," exclaimed Miss Babcock in a tone of mild but earnest reproof; "no lady *ever* points to anything." She gently pulled down the outstretched arm as she spoke. "Let us go on a little farther and we shall turn back then; we have been out three-quarters of an hour."

Helena obeyed with a mournful glance in the direction

of the hare, whose expressive brown ears were just visible in the long grass, and they walked on in silence. How she longed to have Isidor and Rusty within reach. What a glorious chase they would have! Not that Rusty was much good, but if he failed Isidor had always a sharp three-cornered stone in his pocket, and his aim was unerring.

She maintained a dogged silence notwithstanding Miss Babcock's social efforts. Helena now despised her utterly and distrusted her as well. She could talk of nothing that she cared to hear—the old fidgety thing. They turned after a few minutes and retraced their steps. When they passed the entrance gate again Miss Babcock turned coldly to her pupil, who made a move as if to stop, and said:

"Pray, Miss Ferrard, do not delay. I cannot imagine what interest a young lady can have in such things. In a boy it is quite pardonable and allowable, but it is not *proper* or becoming for a young lady."

Helena darted a fiery look at her and took no notice of the speech. She walked on fast as if trying to curb her irritation. Not that she was in a hurry to get back to her school-room, for never had she felt the confinement and dullness so insupportable. The glimpse she had so unexpectedly had of the old life, were it only through the bars of an iron gate, had set her brain reeling. The wide expanse of demesne, the woods, and the familiar sounds of the birds had stirred her pulses strangely. The blood coursed through her veins rapidly and dyed her pale cheeks and lips a brilliant carmine. She pressed her fingers tight together in a perfect ecstasy of longing, and there began a sort of dull, dumb gnawing in her heart. The governess watched her face in mute bewilderment; the alternations of paleness and color puzzled her, and the excited, quick step with which the girl swung along the road. At last she spoke:

"Miss Ferrard, may I beg of you to walk a little slower? we are getting quite into the town, and people will be astonished."

Helena slacked her pace suddenly. The cold, measured voice struck upon her with a shock, scattering all her dreams and memories with a blow. She almost shivered. The old dull look came back to her face, and she walked along until they reached her aunts' house in mournful depression.

Pinner opened the door and glanced freezingly at Helena. Helena caught the look and passed on without seeming to notice it. But as she went up the stairs she felt in her pocket for the old rag of handkerchief in which Cawth's two sovereigns were knotted, and, squeezing them hard in her grasp, vowed to herself she would run off—back home—away from the stupidity, the orderliness, the oppressiveness and luxury of her new state.

Then she took off her things and resumed the interrupted studies with Miss Babcock. But if in the morning she had been incapable from heaviness and languor, she was now equally so from excessive nervousness and preoccupation. The multiplication-table stared at her blankly. She was trying to remember the streets that led from Plantagenet Terrace to the railway station, and also what were the days of the week that Jimmy O'Brien crossed with his pigs and beeves from Cork, and what chance she had of meeting him in Bristol. She must get back, she felt stifling here, and English "ways," of which she thought she had now fully realized the bitterness, seemed impossible to her; a frightful, impatient feeling took possession of her. She thought of the view across the park; the woods in all their autumn glory; the sharp report of the guns, dear to her ears; the hare sitting on its hind legs. Oh! if Rusty had only been with her, what a glorious chase they would have had! She would have leaped over every fairy ring, and run until she and the dog dropped breathless on the grass. She almost jumped out of her chair with excitement at the mere thought.

"My dear, are you nearly ready?" asked Miss Babcock, who was sitting, calm and precise, knitting away in her chair.

Helena looked at her scornfully, but her glance fell harmlessly on Miss Babcock's chignon—a candid edifice of jute and blacky-brown silk pinned on the back of her head. However, she put the imaginary coursing-match out of her brain, with the firm resolution that it should not be long until she enjoyed the reality once more; and determining to leave the hatching of her scheme of escape until the evening, she applied herself to the multiplication-table and speedily mastered its contents.

Dinner over, she betook herself to the window-seat. Aunt Alice offered her a little piece of plain sewing, but Helena's stitches were pronounced to be like dog's teeth, and she was told that Miss Babcock must give her lessons in plain and fancy sewing. Helena detested sewing, and smiled sardonically as she seated herself in her window, thinking how soon she meant to be rid of Miss Babcock and the varied scheme of torture implied by English "ways" together.

Presently visitors were announced, and Helena escaped to the dining-room in such hot haste that she left her book behind her. Having inspected the family portraits again, made some overtures to the cat that caused it to fly out of the room in rage and terror, and stared out of window till she was tired, she cast around for a book. A large-sized volume came to hand first. She opened it: a history of Somersetshire. She turned it over, looking at the views of the various show-places with which it was enriched, and found a map of the city of Bath amongst the illustrations. She had often seen railway maps with the boys at home; they sometimes guided their cross-country expeditions by them. She wondered could she find out Plantagenet Terrace among all the cross lines. It was not long before she found the name. Then it suddenly flashed on her that she might discover the railway station and the route to it. She remembered she passed the Abbey Church and up a cross-street, and turned into the terrace from it. She ran her finger down along the lines. At last she caught the black stripe that indicated the railway. She read the words Great Western and followed it along to the square marked terminus. She was not long tracing the route from the terminus to Plantagenet Terrace; it was not far, and she learned off by heart the names of the streets. Then, after another tracing with her finger to make assurance doubly sure, she shut up the map and book and replaced it. She felt Cawth's two sovereigns in her pocket and walked up and down the room in an ecstasy of delight.

All she needed to do was to find out when the boats sailed, and at what hours the trains for Bristol started. If she could get off by one early in the morning, so much the better; she would not be missed then so soon as during the day. The morning or evening train was her only chance. And now all her energies were concentrated on finding out somehow the hours of starting. Ralph knew, of course, but she dared not question him. He was in the room just now preparing the table for tea. She watched his solemn, deliberate movements; spreading the cloth and placing the tray, urn, and various dishes in their exact places, moving about without the slightest noise, almost as softly as the cat, which had returned to its cushion and was coiled up, one green eye—that next Helena—open, watching everything with grave interest. The drawing-room bell rang now and Ralph went to let the visitors out. Helena, impatient, ran out too, just in time to knock against an elderly lady in an immense fur cloak who was passing through the hall; she never said a word to excuse herself, but jumped back and stood against the wall to let the other pass, staring at her in a shy, wild way. The old lady looked at her in astonishment for a second, then a smile, half admiration for the pretty, startled face, half amusement, succeeded to the surprised look, and she went out and down the steps to her carriage which was waiting. Helena, displeased, ran up-stairs two and three steps at a time.

In the drawing-room, not yet lighted for the evening, her aunts were seated in their accustomed places, talking so busily that they did not hear her entry. She crossed straight to the window, and took up her position behind the curtain to muse on her scheme. The voices from the other side of the room reached her fitfully.

"Mr. Cholmondely—the marriage at seven in the morning, new style. In a traveling-dress, too—and then they leave by the—what train did she say they are to leave by, Alice?"

"The eight o'clock train. They will have to be up very early to get the whole affair over by that time."

Helena felt interested at the mention of what was uppermost in her own mind, and she pulled back her curtain to hear distinctly.

"Silver-gray poplin and blue velvet, orange-blossoms and a veil over her bonnet. I do wonder rather at Gwendoline. I had fancied she was the sort of girl to like a fine wedding. Lady Beauchamp doesn't seem too satisfied over the settlements. Charlie is not getting by any means as much money as they fancied."

"N—no," answered Miss Alice, absently. "I wonder where Helena is?"

"I'm here," said her niece, presenting herself suddenly.

"Oh, dear child! you ran off, and Lady Beauchamp had heard of you and asked if it was you she had seen walking with Miss Babcock this morning. She asked so much about you."

"I saw her in the hall as I came up," replied Helena, shortly.

"We must speak to Miss Babcock to teach Helena how to come in and out of a room. She always turns her back and slams the door; and when she has learned that, she must come down whenever we have visitors who ask for her."

Miss Alice looked approvingly at her niece, for Lady Beauchamp had spoken in high terms of her beauty.

"Shan't you like that, Helena dear?" asked Miss Elizabeth.

Helena replied with a shrug and a pout.

The piano arrived that evening, and was carried up to the school-room. Helena, when going to bed, walked in and surveyed it indifferently. It was a little cottage piano, woody and dull of tone, and needing all the weight of hand and wrist to force a sound out of the stiff keys. Miss Babcock had lost no time in executing her lucrative commission. She presented herself next morning with a musical-primer and exercise-book, the most expensive she could think of, as well as an atlas, and a large work on Physical Geography. She had forgotten these, she said, presenting them to Helena with her most agreeable smile.

Helena took the atlas and opening the map of England, asked her preceptress to show her Bath. Miss Babcock's knitting-needle was promptly laid on the spot.

"And out here, this is the sea?"

"Yes," said Miss Babcock; "and that pale-colored slip there is the coast of Ireland."

"Where is Bristol? I came from Bristol," asked Helena in tones of unwonted interest.

"There is Bristol; and see, there is the line marking the railway track; do you see it goes all along? And look now, in this direction lies London. You see it?"

"Yes; but Bristol, how long does it take to go there? I forget how long I was in the train."

"Not more than half an hour or so, I fancy. It is not many miles off."

"Have you ever been in Bristol?"

"Yes, several times. I went down last month to spend a day there."

"Did you? You went and came back the same day?"

"Yes; went down by an early train. Now come, my dear, begin to read."

"What train did you go by?" Helena asked, boldly, as she opened the reading-book.

"My dear child, I forget, but you can ask your aunts for their railway guide, and it was by the earliest train I could find. Now don't delay any more, if you please."

One more question Helena must ask, if she died for it.

"Miss Babcock, what is a railway guide? Is it a book?"

"My dear, what a silly idea! Of course it is a book, published by the railway companies for the convenience of travelers."

Then the lessons were droned over as usual. Helena was now indifferent and preoccupied, and Miss Babcock several times was on the point of getting angry. The multiplication was abandoned as hopeless before one o'clock. Helena had a fit of fidgets on her, and Miss Babcock, by way of diversion, proposed to give her some lessons in deportment. Then Helena was taught to come into and leave the room without turning her back to Miss Babcock or slamming the door. She was easily taught, for she was naturally graceful and supple of motion. Two o'clock came at last and the governess took her leave, carrying with her the amount of her book-seller's bill, of which she pocketed a full fourth. She had not earned the money, she knew that very well; indeed, in her own opinion, it was a slightly peculiar dispensation that she should pocket it; but it certainly was no wrong to her employers; they lost nothing by it, for if Miss Ferrard had bought the books herself she would have paid precisely the same sum. The book-sellers were the sufferers, if, indeed, they did suffer, for they sold a great many more books under that system than they would have if there were no intermediary. Miss Ferrard would have bought Helena a book at a time just as she wanted them, whereas Miss Babcock generously supplied her with a round dozen. Considering the stimulus indirectly imparted to trade by the commission system, it is hardly wonderful that book-sellers flourish, or that, when teachers stoop to such dubious practices, their honorable profession should have fallen into disrepute.

Helena was in an abstracted fit all day. Several times at dinner she relapsed into her old habit of eating with her knife, and she did not bear her aunt's corrections as well as usual. She looked constantly at the picture above the book-case opposite her. The sun fell aslant on it there; the frame glowed like a circle of gold, and the carmine of the coat, somewhat dimmed by time, lighted up and set off the fine white hand, and the neck and the blonde curls that clustered round it. The eyes laughed down to hers; she pictured to herself Isidor's when, in a few days now, she would be relating to him her achievement.

After dinner she spent searching, without success, through the book-cases for the mysterious railway guide. She could think of no other place to find it, and was almost in despair.

It was impossible for her to ask any one the question, and she vainly beat her brains for some device whereby to ascertain the desired information. She sat still, biting her thumb in perplexity, and staring blankly at the bit of sky to be seen up the Terrace—a dull October sky of Indian-ink-colored clouds, with strange, weird rifts, through which shone a faint, changing green.

"Helena!" called Aunt Elizabeth, in perplexed tones, from the hearth—"Helena! In the drawer of the sofa-table, dear, look if there is a needle; one of mine has gone, and I do not know where."

Helena got up and opened the drawer. In it were stowed the odds and ends that collect in some drawing-rooms—ends of wax candles, packs of cards, counters, knitting-needles, rolls of twine, and a quantity of little books. One of these was lying face uppermost, and on its blue cloth wrapper Helena read "Guide to Bath and its Environs." She quickly took it out of the drawer, and having given her aunt the needle, returned to her seat and diligently set to work to master its contents.

She turned over the map and the plates, skipped through the letter-press until she came to a page entitled "Hackney Carriages." That, too, she glanced carelessly over; and the very next page presented her with the desired railway guide—"Bath to London; mail trains, parliamentary, weekly, and Sunday." She ran her finger down the column. "Bristol!" At last! She drew a long breath when she read "Bath to Bristol." Train at eight ten. Could it mean ten minutes to eight or after eight? She was not sure; but she would take care to be at the station early—long before eight; and the fare, only a few shillings.

She put back the little book in the drawer, delighted

beyond measure, and began—so excited was she that she could not sit still—to pace up and down the room.

To-morrow! To-morrow would be Friday. Cawth hated anything to be done on a Friday; it was so unlucky. She said Walter was killed on a Friday. And for a moment a dark fear took possession of Helena's heart; a strange sensation in her throat, such as she felt once before when Isidor, trying to get an otter that he had shot, fell into a deep, dark weir-pool. But then, if she waited longer? Saturday there would be no boat, then Sunday would have to be passed here. No; she would go to-morrow morning. She would be up at the first break of day and slip down to the greenhouse or to the vestibule, watch her opportunity from behind the curtain, and get out when the coast was clear. The milk-woman came very early, long before she was up on ordinary mornings, and the hall-door was always opened then. If she could slip down directly the cook went away with her bowls, she would reach the station in time.

Once at Bristol she could take the Cork, or for that matter the Waterford, boat. As to her aunts, of course they would be in a terrible fright about her. Ought she to leave them a note, just to say she was gone; that she was obliged for all their goodness, but she couldn't stay?

She stopped her walk and leaned her back against the oak cabinet with her arms folded, thinking what she should do. That it was her duty to stay never entered her head. She was stifling in the close warmth of this well-ordered English house. It seemed to her as if voices were calling to her from the woods and the sea to return to them. A great open space swept by the breeze invited her, and she drew a deep, broken sigh of longing desire.

Never did the scent of the roses, of the camphor-wood and Russia-leather-bound books seem so oppressive as to-night. Her head ached, and the weight of her crown of plaits seemed intolerable. She went out of the room and ran up-stairs, hoping to find it cooler there. The fire was out in the school-room as she passed through it, and she opened the window wide in her own room.

There was light enough yet, and she sat down in the chair beside her bed to arrange what she had to do. She meant to put on her old clothes—those that she came in. Where were they, though? She recollected her aunt putting the little green box into the wardrobe, and in a moment she was over and opened it wide. No box was there. The drawers and shelves were all taken up with her new outfit. She could not find her old boots or the coarse stockings anywhere. She must wear the things she had on—the pretty new dress Aunt Alice had bought for her, the fine high-heeled shoes, and embroidered coat.

She returned to her chair, and sitting down, sighed heavily. She was disappointed in being obliged to wear the new clothes; for somehow she did not look upon them as her own now, and she had resolved to go exactly as she had come. A fit of gloomy depression seized on her, and folding her hands together she sat in a sort of dull torpor for a long time—it must have been more than an hour.

The moon rose and filled her little room with a flood of pale light; the white curtains of the bed and the pretty draperies of the toilet-table looked ghostly and strange.

Helena felt half afraid now of her enterprise. What if there should be a storm—if she should be drowned, and it should never be known what had become of her? Isidor would be sorry, and—and who else? Aunt Elizabeth? yes, she would be sorry; she was so gentle and nice. And for a moment or two the little savage was softened.

What if she stayed after all? She glanced round the room at the pretty things which had all been placed there for her. In time she would become used to them, perhaps like them. And then a vision of the many hungry days she had spent watching, without food perhaps, from sunrise until the hunters would return late at night, came back to her memory. Often they came empty-handed, and she had gone to bed supperless. And how kind Aunt Elizabeth was! Even the pet canary knew her and sang his loudest when she came near his cage. What if she did stay? How would it be?

Then she heard herself called to tea and ran down quickly. She was so full of her new idea that she forgot to shut the parlor door after her. Aunt Alice's voice soon recalled her to her senses.

"Helena, the door is open again. What a draught you are letting in on Aunt Elizabeth. Now go at once and shut it, please."

Helena jumped up, a dark frown wrinkling her brows, and shut the door with a vigorous clap, shutting out at the same time—alas!—all her better thoughts, her good angel's whispers.

"I never could!" she said to herself as she sat dowr again. "It's no use at all!"

Then she returned to her plans for the following morn ing, brooding over and elaborating them with sullen determination. Her aunt Elizabeth was not feeling very well, so she did not speak to Helena or call her over to sit by her all the evening. Miss Alice's time was too much occupied in attending to her sister to notice what the girl was doing. So she spent the rest of the time until she went to bed lounging in the window, watching the few passers go by in the lamp-light, and picturing herself by that time next evening on the deck of the steamer, watching the green and white of the waves, and looking back at the long white furrow that stretched in their wake.

She woke next morning at six and sprang out of bed. It was still dark. She looked out of window up eastwards over the gardens, and saw the faint red and green of the sunrise just breaking through the clouds. She dressed quickly and noiselessly, and then sat down on the edge of her bed to listen for the hall clock to strike seven, at which time she meant to steal down to the vestibule on the first landing. She could hear the chirp of the sparrows in the ivy of the garden wall, and now and again the rumble of a cart through the streets reached her ears. It seemed a long time to wait, and she was frightened lest she should have made a miscalculation, and that it was later after all.

At last, however, the dull boom of the great hall clock struck her glad ears. She counted the strokes, holding her breath as she did so. Seven! Seven! Then she got up and looked round.

She had on her Galway hat, which her aunts had allowed her to retain for every-day wear, her new coat, and her morning dress; in her pocket was Cawth's ill-starred parting gift, still tied in its rag.

She opened the bedroom door gently and peeped out. Not a stir could she hear. Then she opened the door wide enough to pass through, shut it again after her, and with cautious, gliding steps, carrying her boots in her hand, reached the vestibule. To ensconce herself behind the curtains and pull them close again was the work of a minute. And now for twenty minutes, which seemed to her as many hours, she remained concealed, scarcely breathing and dreading the beating of her heart should betray her.

At last the hall-door bell rang. She heard the cook shuffling up the kitchen stairs and along the tesselated pavement of the hall. The chains and bolts were unfastened one by one, the ponderous key turned in the lock; then the door was gently shut, the cook shuffled back to the lower regions, and Helena knew that all she had to do was to lift the little latch-handle and the open street would lie before her. She was just pulling the curtain back to slip out of her hiding-place when her quick ears caught the trail of a skirt on the upper stairs. She drew back instantly and not a moment too soon, for Pinner, who was hurrying down-stairs to look after hot water for her ladies, would otherwise have caught her infallibly. She passed on unsuspectingly, however, and Helena, having waited to hear her get to the bottom of the kitchen stairs, darted down like a flash. She passed on tiptoe—

for she had contrived to pull on her elastic boots—through the hall, opened the door without a creak betraying her, closed it after her, and set off across the street as fast as she could. She kept on straight to the left, then turned, as the map and her memory both suggested, into a hilly street leading downwards, passed the great old Abbey Church, and she was at the terminus. It was twenty minutes to eight when she entered the station. The ticket-office was not yet open, and she had to wait a full quarter of an hour. It was a raw, gray morning, the first of the coming frosts was in the air, and she was glad to warm herself at the waiting-room fire. She unknotted her handkerchief and took out one sovereign, which she held tightly in her hand, trembling so that she could hardly clench it. At last she was able to buy her ticket, and then flew up-stairs to the platform, nervously looking all round, to take her seat in the farthest corner of the third-class carriage. She thought the bell would never ring; it did at last. A crowd of people poured in, most of them Irish reapers going home after the harvest, rough, wild creatures, with their gleaming sickles hanging round their great bare necks. Helena was not afraid of them; what she dreaded most was to see Ralph's gray face poked in the window in search of her, and hear his solemn voice demand Miss Ferrard.

At last eight struck by the great clock on the platform and with a wild, deafening whistle, which fell on Helena's expectant ears sweeter than the finest music in the world, the train moved out of the station. Helena looked out triumphantly; she could hear the church bells sound now, and she smiled to think that Pinner, with can of hot water in hand, was at that moment entering her bedroom to awake her. What at all would they say?

Her traveling companions now began to smoke and eat. Helena was almost stifled; her hunger vanished under the sensation of nausea produced by the frightful odor around her, and by the time the train reached Bristol she felt miserably ill. A walk up and down the platform in the cool fresh air somewhat restored her, and she drank a cup of tea at the railway refreshment-stall. One thing alarmed her seriously, everybody stared at her so. The girl in the refreshment-room watched every motion and fetched in other women to stare too. As soon as she had done she set off to look for the Cork boat. She discovered, to her horror, that the Cork boat would not leave until the afternoon tide at four o'clock, but there was a Waterford boat just about to start. She guessed that would do as well; she could easily get from Waterford home to Darraghmore. At any rate, there would be another train from Bath at twelve o'clock, and it was more than likely she would be followed, so she made her way to the dock where the Waterford steamer, having discharged her load of pigs, cabbages, and poultry, was taking in return machines and dry goods. She got on board and paid her passage, then went on deck to watch from a sheltered situation the noisy operation of stowing the cargo.

She was the only cabin passenger; her companions of the train were stowing themselves aft, or, having driven a bargain with the captain to be allowed to work their way across, and placed their sickles and the red handkerchiefs which contained their personal effects in a place of safety, were engaging in the hard work of loading the crane and turning the machine which worked it. The steam was escaping noisily. The captain, leaning over the taffrail, was bawling hoarse oaths and orders to the crew and to the shore-men. Some of the reapers lounged over the side, and chattered and laughed together. Newspaper boys and fruit-sellers offered their wares vainly. A horrible smell of grease, bilge-water, and dinner came up in a hot steam from every aperture. Helena, crouched behind the mainmast, seated on one of those high, uncomfortable camp-stools, the carpet seat of which was wet and sooty, felt miserable and sick. Still she was not sorry, and she counted the chimes of St. Mary Redcliffe's with an anxious heart. She dreaded lest twelve o'clock should arrive and the Bath train with it; Ralph, or, worse still, perhaps Mr. Cholmondely, would be sure to come by it, and she would be easily traced. She watched the heap of merchandise, the endless sacks and boxes and huge bales, diminish by degrees; fresh cart-loads ceased at last to arrive. The steam from the escape-pipe grew thicker, and great puffs of black smoke were vomited from the funnel. The hold was full, and a row of wooden cases was piled on the deck. At last, after strenuous shoutings from the captain, the last package was dropped on board. A big bell was rung. The reapers, with their heads tied up in bright handkerchiefs, leaped on board, the gangways were pulled ashore, the hawser cast off, and the steamer, grunting and snorting, steamed slowly through the dock-gates and dropped down the Avon gently. The trees that clothe its banks looked lovely in the clear, bright sunlight, and the rushing, foaming stream, mud-colored from the rains, that swept angrily along, rising in a great wave behind them, was flecked here and there with a beam that lighted it up into almost gold color, and made the rest look black by contrast.

There was no fear of Ralph now, or Mr. Cholmondely, thought Helena with a smile of triumph on her pale lips, and she got up and walked up and down the deck. It was sheltered and pleasant so long as the steamer was in the river, but presently they neared the mouth, swept out and past the band of clay-colored water that extended some distance into the channel, and Helena felt the cold sea-breeze she had so often longed for kiss her cheeks.

They passed the little islands that here and there dot Bristol Channel, glowing now like emeralds in the midday sun. The sea-gulls, with their wild, faint scream, sailed overhead, and a whole swarm of them, like silver dots, marked where a shoal of fish had risen. A great ship passed them close, all her snowy canvas filled, dipping and gliding noiselessly, so calm, so graceful, in contrast to the fussy, noisy packets. Tug-boats, green and red, like hideous big parrots, darted to and fro. The yachts—those swallows of the sea—were all gone into winter quarters. Grimy colliers steamed slowly southwards; the channel was alive with ships for a little while. Presently they got beyond the track of the coasters. The water was bluer, the waves larger, and the pleasant breeze be came a stiff blast that soon drove Helena down-stairs. She went to bed feeling cold and sick; the stewardess offered her dinner, but she could take none of it. At last she fell asleep, worn out, and until they reached the quay at Waterford next day she never stirred.

CHAPTER VIII.

"J'approche d'une petite ville, et je suis déjà sur une hauteur d'où je la découvre . . . . Je me récrie, et je dis: Quel plaisir de vivre sous un si beau ciel et dans ce séjour si délicieux! Je descends dans la ville, où je n'ai pas couché deux nuits que je ressemble à ceux qui l'habitent; j'en veux sortir." LA BRUYERE.

SIX months had passed since Mr. Satterthwaite's visit to Darraghmore. He had bought the estate of Rosslyne when it came to the hammer a few months after his departure from Ireland, but business of various kinds had delayed his arrival and final establishment in his new residence. He had for a considerable time meditated seriously taking up the profession of farming, as he had tired of traveling and desired a steady occupation, and to the dismay of his friends had determined to make his first experiment in Ireland. He had been for a long time casting about for a suitable investment for the spare thousands he intended to devote to this purpose, and Rosslyne, whose beautiful situation won his heart as soon as he beheld it, thus became his property.

So it happened that a squally April day saw Mr. Satterthwaite on the hurricane deck of the Holyhead steamer *en route* for the South via Dublin. The day was cold at sea although the wind blew from a mild point, and the soft Irish rain that came driving down at intervals from the Wicklow mountains felt almost warm. Every now and again the sun broke through the clouds and chased away the pale mist that hung between the peaks of the

Sugar-loaves and Bray Head, gilding the rich pasture-lands that skirted the shore, and lighted up the spray and foam that the paddle-wheels tossed up until it looked like a shower of diamonds. They swept past the Kish light-ship, rocked like a cradle by the ground-swell, left the cliffs of Howth to the right with its light-house, up to which the surge was licking with long white tongues, and to the left Dalkey Island and its old gray tower; and then in a few minutes rounded the battery wall and into Kingstown Harbor.

Just as the black nose of the steamer was pointed straight to her berth along-side the Carlisle Pier, a sudden squall came tearing down between the Three Rock and Killiney, and curling the tops of the waves inside the walls, swept right in Mr. Satterthwaite's face, wetting his eyes with the spray so that one might fancy he was crying, and half blinding him. A sailor was standing near and laughed.

"That was a squall for you, sir. I wonder will it reach the fishing-boats there off the Mugglins. I've seen a yacht capsized in the bay by a less one."

Then the sunlight shone out with redoubled strength from behind the little black cloud that had caused the mischief, and leaping from rock to rock along the coast, lit up the whole bay as with a smile. The long white terraces of Kingstown shone out as if newly washed and clean, and the wet black hull of the great man-of-war ship glistened above the dull, dirty green of the harbor water. Mr. Satterthwaite turned to have another look at Howth, but the packet had reached her birth, where the express train was drawn up in readiness; then began that scene of confusion and disorder so familiar to travelers. The steam from the boiler began to escape with a noise that was absolutely deafening, and to this was added the screeching of the railway engine, intensified by the echo in the roof of the hideous and utterly useless black shed erected under pretext of shelter on the pier. The porters pushed and shoved and fought with each other, to the admiration of a crowd of hangers-on who were in every one's way.

At last, abandoning some of his effects in the hope that

their being fully addressed to his hotel might insure their safety, Mr. Satterthwaite in despair took his seat in the express. The last lady had been helped in, the last ravenous porter had been satisfied, or at least silenced, the engine had taken on its load of newspapers, etc., and away went the express to deposit its freight on the platform in Westland Row, when the same pell-mell of confusion again awaited the weary travelers.

By dint of strenuous exertion Mr. Satterthwaite got a couple of porters to burden themselves with the most important of his packages, and he reached at last a side-door where cabs were drawn up in waiting. One cabman was disputing with a solitary old lady, who wanted to drive a bargain with him. A brother cabman, driving off in glory with a pile of luggage and three unprotected females, cracked his whip at him as he passed and shouted excitedly, "Arrah, Mooney, man! leave her to God, and run down there to the gintleman wid the trunks."

Mr. Mooney, thus adjured, seized his horse's head and dragged his vehicle to where the gentleman with the trunks was standing; but Satterthwaite, laughing as he was, ordered him back to his fare and mounted an outside-car, telling the porters he would send a man from the hotel to claim his property, and so with difficulty got away from the Babel. It was fine and sunshiny, and they splashed along through the lakes of mud, which form the wonder and delight of the visitor to Dublin, at a rapid rate. The hotel was soon reached, and Mr. Satterthwaite, having dispatched a messenger for his property, sat down to a good dinner, for which his long journey had given him an excellent appetite.

The next morning he left Dublin by the American mail at nine o'clock *en route* for the south. It was a gloomy, drizzling morning, and the bleak vista of bog and treeless, weed-grown fields which form the central plateau of Ireland was desolate looking and depressing in the extreme. The rich pastures and woods of Kildare, with the far-off glimpse of the Dublin mountains, were soon left behind, and the long, dun-colored reach of the Bog of Allen, of which the monotonous outline was broken only by sedge-grown pools, overhung by a tawny mist, out of which the gray herons rose with a startled cry as the train passed, stretched before the Englishman's eyes. He got out at an intermediate station to meet a friend with whom he had some business to transact and parcels from London to deliver, and in the afternoon a later train picked him up, and about seven o'clock deposited him at the district station nearest to Darraghmore. He found his baggage waiting for him on the platform, and gave the station-master orders to keep it until carts could be sent over to carry it to Rosslyne.

As he turned out of the little wooden shed which did duty for a railway station, he was hailed by a voice which fell somewhat familiarly on his ear, and a dusky figure clad in a tattered frieze coat jumped forward.

"Glad to see your honor back. Want a car, sir? Sure I'm the boy drove you to Darraghmore from Ballycormack then, last autumn."

"Are you indeed? Then you may take me back to Darraghmore now; never mind anybody else, my man, I'll settle that."

And Mr. Satterthwaite swung his valise on one side of the mail-car, and mounting on the other, wrapped his ulster round him.

The driver grinned with delight, real or affected, and whipped up his horse. Plunging and rocking, they reached the stony, hilly lane which led up to the station. As soon as the level high-road left him at liberty to disengage his attention from his steed, the jarvey turned his head round and surveyed his fare amicably.

"I hope you like Rosslyne, Mr. Satterthwaite, sir. Rale proud I am to be drivin' you home this night."

"Ha! how did you know I was Mr. Satterthwaite?"

"Augh! sure, 'tis well known the English gintleman was here last autumn bought Rosslyne; an' a purty spot it is—lovely grass land as there is in the county. You bought a rale bargain, sir. I hope I'll be drivin' 'herself' across wan of these days soon."

Cruikshank's or Leech's pencil alone could do justice to the expression of the countenance which the carman bent sidelong on his fare. The inquisitiveness, drollery, and cunning therein blended were beyond mere description. Satterthwaite shook his head gravely.

"No offense, your honor." Then with a reckless dash, "Sure we were all hopin' to see the mistress comin' in along o' you. Houses do be lonely widout the ladies whatever. Sure meself, now, afther the owld mother died, till I got married, I didn't know what'd become of me."

Mr. Satterthwaite indulged in a silent internal laugh for a moment or two, then abruptly turned the question.

"Whose land is this we are passing on the river-side?"

"'Tis Lord Comerford's, sir, all you see along there; 'tis no good."

It was almost too dark to see anything. Satterthwaite could hear the harsh, dry rustle of the reeds as the swift eddies of the stream caught and swayed them, and a faint sound came from the dark net-work of the trees above. There had been showers all day, and the hedgerows, wild and tangled as they were, gave out a sweet spring odor. The blackthorn trees were covered with snowy blossom, and pale primroses lighted up the dark recesses among the briers. Late and half dark as it was, the blackbirds were noting to one another, and their clear, bell-like voices filled the woods. Right or left Satterthwaite could discern no traces of lights or a house; not a sound, not even a dog's bark, gave token of the presence of human beings. The road was good and fairly level, and the old mail-cart bowled along smartly. After a short interval of silence he hailed the driver again.

"What is there new or strange in Darraghstown since?"

"Sorra much, yer honor," replied the driver with alacrity. "We got wan of the Miss Perrys married to a Dublin gentleman—I forget his name—anyhow, they were married afore Lent came in. An' let me see, Bill Kelly run off and let in the bank for seventy pounds of a bill; he did so, my blessin' to him. I suppose you hard the old lord was come back. Did he come before or after your honor was here?"

"What old lord do you mean?"

"Old Lord Darraghmore, to be sure, yer honor. I was tellin' you about the family when I drove you past the owld house on the other side of the town towards Ballycormack."

"Oh dear, yes; the Ferrard family—to be sure, I remember. And do you say they have come back to that old ruined house?"

"Not to the house, yer honor; they've taken Milligan's house at the corner of the Comerford Road. They came here just the first week of October. The owld lord and wan of his sons landed down to the hotel and they stayed a week or two there; then the owld nurse that's always wid them hired rooms in Milligan's; but, faith, Milligan found it better to give them up the whole house to theirselves, so he an' the wife went off out to live on their farm at Ballycormack, and the lord is to pay twenty pounds a year for the house."

"What on earth brought them back?"

"I dunno, sir; he's breakin' up fast, an' may be, as the people say, he wants to die in the owld place, or near to it."

"How many of them are there?"

"Himself, an' two boys—two divils-clips of boyoes the same—oh, bedad, yis; and the daughter, a tall, swarthy-looking thing with a pair of eyes like two burnt holes in a blanket. The big fellow wint off since they came here. I hård he went to Austria to join the army along with the step-brother. No wan knew he was goin', or a thing; he slipped off wan morning, went across the fields to the train, and a bit of a note came in a few days to 'himself' to say he was gone out to Claude—at laste, that's the account Mistress M'Gonigle, that thrawn owld wan that lives wid them, gave in the town."

"That leaves but one boy at home, then?"

"No, no, yer honor; this was the big one, Clan. He has three sons by the last wife. There's Char and Isidor there yet."

"And how old is the girl, Miss Ferrard?"

"Augh, a slip; seventeen, or less. She was sent off, I believe, to her lady aunts in England somewhere to be edgicated and brought up, bud fait she walked in one morning as cool as a cucumber. 'Twas myself druv her over. She got out of the train wan raw, cold morning, there, last October, an' she looked all round her as wild and startled just like a hare; an' at last she come up to me, an' says she, 'Do you go to Darraghmore?'—'No, miss,' says I; ''tis Darraghstown to the hotel I'm goin'.' Wid that she sat up on the car. Young Devereux, the son of the farmer that has the old place of Darraghmore now, grazin' it be the same token, was sittin' on the same side wid her. An' he went to say somethin' p'lite to her, the misfortunate gossoon. She gev him a look, he towld me, near took the sight out of his eyes, an' she gother her skirts up about her—och, pillilew! He thought he'd never get off the car, though they're the best of friends now." And the driver laughed at the recollection till his old vehicle shook. "An' when we got to the place and stopped, she lays a five-shillin'-piece on the seat of the car—an' the fare only a shillin', mind you, and for the matter of that I wasn't goin' to take it from her father's daughter at all at all—an' she up the stips of the hotel as light as a fly. Well, well! Blake, the landlord, he towld me she asked him as grand as you plase, 'Is my father, Lord Darraghmore, here yet?' so he said not, an' pointed out Milligan's house up at the corner of the Comerford Road, and said he was there, so she turned herself round an' away wid her up home."

"Is she there still?" asked Mr. Satterthwaite with a tone of real interest, and breathing a hope that he might yet get a look at this strange specimen of humanity.

"She is, av coorse, yer honor. I seen her out walkin' yesterday with them tear-coat Perrys. Augh, musha! to see them together! 'tis like this owld garron harnessed wid wan ov me Lord Comerford's fine-bred hunters. There's nothin' like blood, sir, nothin'. The walk of her, and her head set straight up! an' she niver turns to look to the right or left of her, while them Perrys' necks is like the pivot or the weather-cock, not a blue-bottle fly bud they must look after it; an' the feet o' them! bedad, they might walk on the wather like St. Pether, any day."

The car drew up now at the hotel where Mr. Satterthwaite intended to put up for some days before translating himself to his new residence at Rosslyne. He had made a cursory examination of the house the previous autumn when at Ballycormack. The roof was in fair order, but the chimneys were all choked with rubbish, the jackdaws having, with the usual perverse taste of that animal, chosen to build in the chimney-pots in preference to the fine pine trees of the wood. These and many other matters the new owner of Rosslyne revolved in his mind as he sat, after dinner, noting down in his memorandum-book the various items as they occurred to him to be considered on his visit to Rosslyne the next day. There was the garden to be made, and a charming one that southern slope—studded with graceful beeches and gnarled old hawthorns that extended beneath the drawing-room windows—would make. He remembered how prettily the pond lay at the foot of it when he had seen it last autumn. The overhanging chestnuts and alders half in shadow, half in sun; the little water-hens darting to and fro; the long-feathered heads of the bulrushes and cat's-tails dipping in the glassy pool and mingling with the fading autumn tints of the foliage reproduced in the water. Wild and neglected as the place was, it had charmed him. His friends had laughed at his project, and declared it was an impossible freak, but Satterthwaite vowed to make a little Eden of Rosslyne, and then bring them to witness his success.

Between seven and eight in the evening the landlord came into his room and disturbed his reverie by presenting him with a card.

"The gentleman is below, sir, and has called to see you."

"Mr. Perry! oh yes," said the Englishman; "show him in."

Then a burly man about fifty years of age entered. He held his hat in one hand and advanced with the other outstretched to greet the stranger.

"Mr. Satterthwaite," said he in a loud, resonant voice, "allow me to be the first to welcome you to Darraghstown. I am delighted to make your acquaintance."

Satterthwaite shook hands cordially enough with the big man, and invited him to be seated, running his eye as he did so critically over his new friend. He knew him to be the lawyer of the district, and he certainly did look an intelligent, thoroughly wide-awake customer, but the well-worn, ill-brushed suit of tweed, rough hair and unshorn chin, gave him rather the look of a working farmer than a professional man.

"How did you come to think of settling among us, Mr. Satterthwaite? An Englishman like you, and from London too, now, to come and bury yourself in this outlandish spot, hay?"

He spoke in a hearty, sincere tone, with a smile that showed a set of large, white teeth, not altogether a bad-looking fellow. The gray eyes were rather obliquely set, however, and the irregular profile was imperious enough for Jove himself.

"My friend can bully," thought the Englishman, "when he cannot wheedle, or I am mistaken."

"Well, sir," replied Satterthwaite, "last year I was staying at a shooting-box the other side of the mountains with friends, and I liked the country and the natives so well that I, being on the outlook at the time for an investment for some spare thousands, thought I'd buy a place here, so Rosslyne chanced to suit me, and I've come over to put it to rights."

"Goodish lay of land along there, now. That side of the Rack is very fine grazing land. The wood, too, you've the right of clearing, ha'n't you? The man that had it before you went in for fancy farming, ruined himself very fast; machines and patent manures; went in for tillage, in fact. A thundering mistake that."

"Do you say so? I had entertained some notion of

breaking up the low meadows at the back of the house; I flatter myself I'm rather a dab at farming. I've a fine home-farm at Langdale."

"Ah, yes—in Buckinghamshire; that's a horse of another color, Mr. Satterthwaite. I have three farms now of my own, leaseholds anyhow, in this place, and I've every inch under grass; grazing and dairy, that's what pays. Why, sir, it stands to reason: look at the cost of labor; and mind you, it's not the rate of wages I mean by that. No! it's the amount of work you get for your money; their whole plan is to scheme and idle the day away. They've an idea they make work for themselves that way—just like those trades unionists."

"Do these people belong to a trades union then?"

As he asked the question Satterthwaite rose and rang the bell.

"Not they. A laborers' union was tried here and fell to pieces directly; they have all the faults of unionists, anyhow. The rascals!" continued the attorney, "every moment they steal from you they consider a gain to themselves. Tillage, sir, is impossible in Ireland as things are now. They must get high wages, and they won't give any work in return; I defy any amount of capital or patience to withstand the cost of workmen here. An honest day's work is not to be got out of them."

"Then you don't consider that the high price of meat, or the climate, as some say, caused the wonderful change in farming here?"

"Not a bit of it; did I not try the experiment for myself there ten years ago? I'd have to be up before them in the morning, and I'd have to stand over them all day long in the fields and never take my eyes off them. Slieveen vagabonds—I never will make up what I've lost by them. I've sublet two of my farms to a Limerick butter-factor, who pays me eleven pound a head for each cow and provides his own servants and dairy-woman. In fact, I just draw an income from it and have nothing to do. People can't be got to work a farm so as to leave you any profit, and you look after your own interests."

Then the landlord entered in response to Mr. Satterthwaite's bell.

"What can I offer you, Mr. Perry? Bring me a pint of your best pale sherry."

"As usual, Blake," replied the attorney, nodding to the landlord, who vanished, speedily to return with a tray bearing the desired bottle of sherry, and a smoking kettle and decanter of whisky for the lawyer.

Mr. Perry lost no time in mixing himself a huge tumbler of reeking toddy, and pressed his host to follow his example, but he declined and kept to his sherry. The very smell of the concoction was stifling.

"Still, Mr. Perry," said Mr. Satterthwaite, returning to the subject, "there is a good deal of tillage land in Ireland; surely everybody does not find it the dead loss you do?"

"Certainly not, sir; the small farmer finds it profitable, may be, to till; that is, he can make a sort of living by it, more than I could by tilling my eight hundred acres. I'd be in the work-house in five years—less, be gad! Up to twenty or five-and-twenty acres you could do fairly with tillage."

"How so?"

"Why! because the small farmer does the work himself; the wife looks after the dairy. Ay, an' 'tis from those same small farms the best butter comes. It's not the professional butter-maker with her eighteen and twenty pounds a year that makes the best butter. The case lies in a nut-shell, Mr. Satterthwaite. They do their own work; their profits are not carried off by the hired laborers; the man has no outlay, if he has no capital itself. Of course a good deal is 'slobbered,' as we call it here, for want of labor and so forth, but in the long run the fellow scrapes a living, and sometimes a profit, out of it, more than we should do, I promise you."

"Humph! I must reconsider my project," thought Satterthwaite; then aloud: "You have a fair sprinkling of respectable people hereabouts. Any society?"

"Society—um—well—there's the bank manager and

his wife; a Miss Murphy from Dublin; and there's a great friend and crony of mine, Tom Fair—you passed his place coming up from the station. Then there are the Hollahans of Castle Darragh there above on the Ballycormack Road. A couple of daughters there with more pedigree than money, I take it. And then the other Hollahans, their cousins, a great family living in a big old place called Brophystown, as you go out towards Rosslyne; not to mention the Reallys of Bella Vista, as you come down to the bridge where the Rack and Darragh meet."

"Really—*Realè* perhaps." The Englishman repeated the name with the Italian pronunciation. "Surely that is foreign."

"Foreign, Mr. Satterthwaite—haw, haw," and the lawyer gave forth a huge laugh. "That's a good one; a butter-factor from Limerick that married a Protestant Shoneen, and turned his coat, and then his decent father's name from Reilly to Really. He is very wealthy; the wife is a queer soul. She was brought up abroad with relations of hers who held high positions in Vienna, I believe. She kept house, I know, for some general there. When he died she had to go as governess or companion, and met Really at Harrogate, or some English watering-place, and married him—just for a living, I suppose."

"Humph!" said Satterthwaite, carelessly. "Among them all you manage some society, I suppose? There are a good many young people, are there not? Try this cigar."

"Society, well—um—thanks; that has a real fine smell. Ye see, this is a queer spot—so it is. As people rise in the world they generally try to kick down the steps behind them; not only that, but to keep down the next comer. And as to society or social intercourse in Darraghstown, there's none. The bank manager, Scanlan, was all very well till he married a Dublin girl. Then when he brought her here, a few of the county families from outside called upon her. After that, of course, not one of the towns-people would she notice. So now she's left in solitary state; and the grandees, having paid their duty, left it there, I suppose; she's never seen them since. Then the Hollahans of Castle Darragh won't recognize their first cousins, the Brophystown people. Why, I don't know. And the Reallys are queer devils that nobody could keep terms with. She has a tongue like a knife, and he's a born fool. Tom Fair's wife and daughter, again, won't know the Hollahans of Brophystown, and the Castle Darragh people won't know them. Augh!" concluded the attorney, "you must ask some of my women-folk the ins and outs of it. I don't bother my head over it. Right good cigar this is, sir."

"What a microcosm of Irish society!" thought Satterthwaite to himself, with difficulty restraining a laugh. "As well as I can follow my friend, not two families of the half-dozen seem to be on speaking terms with one another. What extraordinary, blind folly! And I suppose they are thirty or forty miles from a town. The idea of willfully destroying the only possibility of making life bearable in such a backwoods settlement as it is.—Well, well!" said he, aloud, "one would imagine people would bury all their little differences, or agree to differ, just—er —for the public good. You have the elements of a tolerable society now right to hand if only properly used."

"Augh!" returned the attorney, "what sort of place is it to be spending the best of a man's life in at all? Pooh!" he continued, wrinkling up his snub nose with an expression of disgust. "A wretched hole like this! Dead-alive one is all the time in it. I've been here now, since I settled down in my father-in-law's place, thirty years, sir; and I never thought to be half that time in it. Augh, sir, London for me! There's some life and stir of business in London. We're wretched, miserable creatures here; lost and wasted entirely. The people here are barbarians—pure barbarians. If I had my will I would not spend an hour in this country. What's the use of making money in such a place? Lord, man, you live more in one week in London than in a life-time here! Ireland's so poor, so behind the rest of the world. I'm sure you noticed Dublin yourself—a wretched, one-horse place!"

"Is it any wonder," thought the Englishman, "that this country is in the state it is? and yet this fellow doesn't scruple to make his money in it. The better class Irish are as bad as the absentee landlords. Absenteeism, indeed! They are all infected with it. I have no patience with this!"

"Ah, well!" said he, aloud and as gravely as he could, though there was a tone of contempt in his voice; "I don't approve of this crowding up to town. There's quite too much of that sort of thing. I declare London is too large, too overgrown. Society is utterly overthronged for comfort. Upon my word, it isn't decent to ask your friends to your house in such numbers that there isn't actually standing-ground for them, and you know it. I am quite in favor of decentralization. Now, Mr. Perry, as a practical man, will you give me your opinion of Home Rule? I look upon Home Rule with rather favorable eyes, considering, as I do, that the deportation of talent and—er—everything best worth keeping in this country is a serious loss to it. Now give me your candid opinion."

Mr. Perry took an enormous draught of high-colored toddy, then laid himself well back in his chair, stretching his long, sturdy limbs to their full length, as he replied:

"My individual opinion, which you may take, Mr. Satterthwaite, for what it is worth, is summed up in the word 'Bosh!' But though I shouldn't care for that to be generally known, if you'd care to hear the opinions of Darraghstown as affording a fair sample of those held throughout the country in general, I'll repeat them to you. I'm pretty familiar with them."

"By all means."

Mr. Satterthwaite's attention was divided between the attorney and his talk. Perry certainly was a study in his way.

"Well, first of all, you know it has been asserted that the Home Rulers would interrupt the trade—I mean the export—of cattle, butter and whisky between this country and England; that's the only trade there is. Not a herd of cattle goes along the road to market but the lookers-on breathe prayers for the day of Home Rule to come, when all that fine food will be kept at home for their use instead of being carried off by the English. They'll say to you, 'Look at the prices of meat and butter; sure, we'd have it dirt cheap if it was not being sent out of the country.' And not only here, but in the large cities, where they are supposed to be more enlightened than the peasantry, the same mischievous notions are current. The only thing to be said in reply to this is, that the people who hold these notions are not voters."

"Ay! but you know one of the darling projects of the agitators is to extend the franchise. That's their game in earnest."

"Right you are, Mr. Satterthwaite; if they are in earnest about anything. Then the fixity-of-tenure people; they go in for Home Rule in a sort of blind way, thinking they'll get their demands settled by it. There are also a set of out-and-outers—I don't know well what to call them—who insist on a heavy absentee tax; and, indeed, go further—would confiscate the lands of all English proprietors. Faith, I think the native ones wouldn't be let off scot free, either! One or two returned Americans have infected the lot; they want a republic, a president—O'Donovan Rossa, I suppose—and a Fenian treasurer; in short, a New York Government. Haw, haw! Home Rule was the fashion here a while ago among the Protestant gentry—that is, before the Tories got in again. I remember old Fitz-Ffoulkes, the rector, before he commuted, compounded, and cut, declaring himself for it, body and soul. Augh! the Liberal spill extinguished a good deal of their patriotic fire. The whole thing is a humbug to my mind. These Irish are not fit for self-government at all."

Satterthwaite turned so as to face the lawyer and said in a cold voice:

"I fancied, Mr. Perry, that I had seen your name in a list of people attending a Home Rule meeting, the Monday—"

"Law, yes, I belong to the association, of course; every one must, you know. But that doesn't hinder me having my own opinions of it all the time."

This was uttered in a tone of cool effrontery, as if he were unconscious of the meaning of his own words.

The Englishman nodded gravely and changed the conversation. He was disgusted at the duplicity of his new acquaintance; but, unhappily, not surprised, for he had only too good reason to believe that it was nothing out of the common.

"Who is the clergyman that has taken Mr. Fitz-Ffoulke's place?"

"Oh! some man comes over by the last train on Saturday night, and goes away by the first on Monday morning. I've heard his name, but I forget it."

"You have a doctor?"

"A couple of them. Old Bruton—past his work now nearly, but if I wanted any one I'd have him before any other—and a young fellow just down from Queen's University with a license to kill; decent sort of harmless chap he is; lives up next door to me in Comerford Terrace."

"Take some more punch, Mr. Perry?"

"No more, Mr. Satterthwaite, thank you. I must be going. I wanted to mention that I'm driving across to Ballycormack to-morrow; if you're going near Rosslyne, I'll be happy to give you a seat. And, Mr. Satterthwaite, will you give us the pleasure of your company to dinner when we return? My wife and daughters will be very glad to see you, in a plain, neighborly way."

Satterthwaite drew a quick, short breath as he replied. He had his doubts as to the desirability of making the acquaintance of the Perry family, who, to judge from the specimen now before him, must be far below his own rank and position. Of course, as a single man, he was, in a way, unfettered and free to choose any or every class of associates. Besides, accepting an invitation to dinner in this way did not bind him to the people; it might be a mere business overture on the part of Perry. At any rate, the Carringtons and Newtons of Crosshills were away, and he might just as well go as not. Then, too, he was curious to get a glimpse of the interior of the Perry household; it would be a new experience. So, prompted by a purely exploring instinct, he replied, cordially:

"I shall be very happy indeed—very. At what time do you start for Ballycormack?"

"Will eleven be too early for you—no? Good-night, then."

"Good-night," replied Satterthwaite.

And so ended his first day at Darraghstown.

CHAPTER IX.

"Il y'a une chose qu'on n'a point vue sous le ciel, et que selon toutes les apparences on ne verra jamais: c'est une petite ville qui n'est choisée en aucuns partis; où les familles sont unis, et où les cousins se voient avec confiance . . . . où la querelle des rangs ne se reveille pas à tous moments, ou le doyen vit bien avec ses chanoines, où les chanoines ne dédaignent pas les chapelains, et où ceux-ci souffrent les chantress." LA BRUYERE.

THE next morning at about eleven o'clock Satterthwaite was lounging in the window, waiting for Perry and killing time with a London paper two days old, when at last the sound of a vehicle without made him look up. There was Lawyer Perry pulling up his gig before the door. A tolerably well-bred horse was in the shafts, as Satterthwaite, who took a good long look at the turn-out while waiting the lawyer's message, acknowledged to himself. However, the animal was ill-groomed and dirty, the mud of a week at least was crusted on the wheels and splash-board, and the harness-plates were nearly green.

"Good-morning, Mr Perry," said he, descending the steps; "a charming day."

"Ay; you do well to bring an umbrella, though—it will rain, I've no doubt. Come along, Mr. Satterthwaite, I'm a quarter late."

Satterthwaite jumped in and took his place on the dirty cushion beside Perry, who, holding up his horse tightly, turned into the main street at a racing pace.

"Curse those pigs!" he exclaimed, suddenly, cutting with his whip at a long-backed pig that dashed almost under the horse's feet. "One of these days I'll break my neck among them. You'd think the street was made for them."

"Have they no pig-sties in these parts?" asked Satterthwaite, looking at the row of wretched cabins along the side of the road.

"Pig-sties!" repeated Perry with a scornful laugh. "If they'd a pig-sty they'd go live in it, and let lodgings in the house. Look at those cabins there, stoop your head and look in the doors; did ever you see fitter pig-sties than those!"

"I never saw more *unfit* housing for human beings. Why, you should have any amount of fever in this town."

"So there is," he replied. "Ask Cartan; they die mainly of fever hereabouts. And look at all the sore eyes; every second man or woman has bad eyes, whatever's the reason of it."

"Bad air and food, of course. That's your chapel, Mr. Perry; I was in it last time I was here."

"Ay, fine building, isn't it? Cost eleven thousand pounds."

"Eleven thousand! eleven thousand!" repeated Satterthwaite, as if he doubted his own ears; "surely you don't mean it; where is there anything to show for it?"

"Faith, I don't know; but then I'm no judge. I know there's that much paid already, and there's more to come yet."

"For that building! oh! it's fabulous!" said Satterthwaite, astonished; and he turned round and looked in amazement at the unimposing block of gray limestone.

"Father Quaide, the parish priest, wouldn't like to hear you say so, I can tell you. He has spent ten years between begging and borrowing—God forgive me, I was going to say stealing—to get the money together. You see the way they do it is to fix upon a plan, and then the architect runs up the building and the bill. What do priests know of business?"

"Is the whole proceeding left in the priest's hands then? Do you not have a committee appointed to inquire into the expenses, and approve plans, and that sort of thing?"

"Phew?" whistled Perry, contemptuously. "His reverence does it all. I'd like to see the man who would interfere with him. We pay down our money and look pleasant over it, and ask no questions. Sure it's the best after all. He worked hard to build that church there, if ever man did; and spent his own money on it, if he spent ours too. He sent a man to America to beg for him, and told him for every pound he brought for him he might keep one for himself."

"I don't think the American subscribers would approve that, would they?"

"What matter? the fellow was able to stock a fine farm when he came home. There's only one thing I dislike in it, and that is the altar. Why couldn't Quaide get an altar made in Dublin? 'twould be a sight handsomer than that Italian stone one he has there. The priests, I declare, think nothing's right unless it comes from foreign parts. Those statues now, those grand painted ones. What do you think of them, Mr. Satterthwaite? He brought them all from Munich."

The lawyer turned a doubtful eye on his companion as he asked the question. Satterthwaite, who had a vivid recollection of the gaudy red and blue-clad giants, could scarcely refrain from laughing—not at them indeed, but at the idea of an educated man like Perry having a doubt on the question. Tempting as it was, he restrained himself and answered, demurely:

"H'm! I knew they came from Munich; yes, the style is unmistakably German. What in the world has Christian art come to—what frightful revolution has taken place," thought he to himself, "that such hideous mockeries should be sanctioned!"

"They're all the fashion," continued Perry; "at least, so I'm told. Anyway, I see every priest buying them for the chapels. Faith, they're too like big dolls for my taste."

"Well!" said Satterthwaite, sharply, and with a tone of contempt in his voice, "why did you not have a committee of the leading towns-folk to lay out this money—your own money, and for your own church?"

"Bah! that's never done, and down here, who would be on the committee? men that know nothing and care nothing about what ought to be. The church cost eleven thousand or twelve thousand, and there it is; every one knows it, and it does well enough. Chuck, chuck! woa there, will ye?"

The horse showed some restiveness at having to pass a cart or two on the road, and his attention was concentrated on him for a moment or two. His great strong hand soon brought the animal to a sense of its duty, and they spun along at a fine pace.

"That's a neat-built animal, Mr. Perry; young too."

"Well, yes; rising five, right good serviceable horse now," he added, turning his sharp gray eyes upon him, "for anybody wanting a good hack to ride or drive. I got him over a year ago; my eldest daughter takes a turn of him too, betimes. He's a sweet-tempered beast enough, just in want of exercise, that's all; and then—"

Mr. Perry turned a greedy, scrutinizing eye on the gentleman beside him, who, reading his meaning as clearly as print, made haste to answer him in an off-hand tone:

"I must get my horses over as soon as this place is fit. I really forget what the stabling is like; I've a hunter or two that I ought to have got rid of before leaving England."

Perry took this in with a contraction of his bushy eyebrows and a smile at the same time, as if he, though disappointed, could recognize an equal in the game; he answered cheerfully:

"Bad time to be selling hunters, unless they're not worth keeping over for the next season. Devereux, a neighbor of mine, raises some fine horses on his farm at Tobergeen. He has all the ground on the river side of your place. It was the property originally of Lord Darraghmore."

"Lord Darraghmore—ah, yes. Mr. Perry, can you tell me anything of that strange brood? They're living beside you now."

"So they are; wish they were farther, too. A litter of foxes would be as pleasant neighbors to my poultry-yard.

I hear of a couple of ducks missing this morning; the servant says no fox took them. I wager 'twas that Char Ferrard."

"Is it possible? are they in the habit of that sort of thing?"

"Habit! I believe you! They have about four hundred a year, I collect it for them, but it all goes like smoke. Clan Ferrard bought a couple of dogs—he gave twenty guineas for them—last November; took them off with him when he found it convenient to clear out. That gypsy of a girl is much like them, too; she now and again favors my folks with her company, but they can make nothing of her. Augh, they're a wretched pack, wretched! Most these real old families are the same here, run out of everything, utter vagabonds. I could point out half a dozen no better than Darraghmore, if they were only as poor."

"Dear me! I thought that sort of thing was extinct here, since the famine and the Encumbered Estates Act, anyhow."

"Some of them managed to weather that storm, and 'twould have been just as well they hadn't. Look, down there beside you is Darraghmore."

The gig was now at the very spot where Satterthwaite and his friend the driver had halted that September day the previous year, and it was with a smile of recognition that he obeyed his companion's behest. Down below them apparently, although it, too, was on the top of a slope, lay the great old house. The fine stretch of demesne before it leading down the edge of the river was dotted with cattle, and the remains of the old plantations, where araucarias and laurels were struggling for life among brambles and furze, yet were plainly visible. The Darragh, swollen by the rain, tore impetuously past; wreaths of pure white foam glistened in the sun and encircled the little water-falls among the rocks as with a collar of gemstrewn lace, and the noise and brawl of it reached their ears on the top of the hill. The willows dipped long branches into the water, and through the dark net-work of the woods the faint green of the promised leaves was stealing.

"We take a turn here now towards Ballycormack, and then a by-road takes you to Rosslyne. It's a pretty spot that, but there's a good deal of waste land. That pond now at the foot of the slope to the side of the house, you know, that ought to be drained."

"Drain the pond! why, that's the prettiest thing in it. Wait till I get water-lilies stuck in it, and have the slope laid out in a pleasure-ground. I wouldn't drain that pond for half the purchase-money. It will be the centre of my garden."

Perry looked at the speaker with an expression of amused disgust.

"We don't go in for that sort of thing here," said he; "and that slope would grow vegetables very handy and convenient to the house."

"Right under my drawing-room window!" cried Satterthwaite, as if doubting his ears.

Perry's under lip only curled the more, and his aggressive snub nose took an upward cast. Just then they turned a sharp corner, and the by-road leading to Rosslyne entrance gate was before them.

"It looks fairly dry, Mr. Satterthwaite, and I must ask you to excuse my leaving you up to the door. I have an appointment at twelve, and it will take me seven or eight minutes to climb that hill; in fact, I'm due this minute. If I come back for you in an hour and a half from this, will you drive across to Kershaw's, five miles out to the left there on the Dublin Road?"

"I will, thank you; I shall do very well now," replied Satterthwaite, getting down carefully off his perch. "I'll look out for you about two, then."

The attorney drove off, and he turned up the narrow road, keeping in the middle of it—footway there was none—to avoid the low-hanging brambles and hawthorns which hung down so thickly as almost to bar the passage. A quarter of an hour's walking through what might not have been out of place as an entrance avenue to the castle of the Sleeping Beauty in the Wood, brought him to a swing gate opening on a pretty but weed-choked carriage-drive. Following this, up hill every step, he found himself facing Rosslyne, a three-storied building of limestone—luckily not plastered over, as was the custom among the benighted natives—with windows somewhat in the Elizabethan style, perched on the very brow of a hill, woods to the right and left, and before and behind a fine clear open. It looked inviting enough just now, lonely as it was; the mildness and sweetness of the air, the music of the birds—it must be alive with woodquests, their cooing seemed to form the bass to the melody of the thrushes and blackbirds—lent it delightful charms in the eyes of its new owner. He stood for a few minutes enjoying the prospect, then turned to follow the winding of the carriage-drive, which, indeed, the trees alone indicated, for it was carpeted in grass as thick and close set as that of the turf beside it, and had pursued his way for a few yards only when a sudden commotion roused him. A hare dashed across the lawn, hotly followed by a great brown dog. Puss doubled and turned, and finally both disappeared among the undergrowth at his side. Satterthwaite, anxious to see the sport, rushed quickly after the dog, but found his passage barred by an impenetrable thicket, so he ran back again to the open and looked about, listening eagerly from the other side. It seemed to him that he could hear the crashing of the dead twigs as if feet were rapidly passing, and then a tall figure in a dark dress flitted by an opening among the stems.

He crossed the lawn hastily and entered the wood. Not a sign or sound was there to be heard; then he pushed his way with difficulty down to the chestnuts by the pond. There was a ruined summer-house near it, and he opened it and looked in. No, it was empty and the spiders' webs were undisturbed.

"No use going farther," thought he; "these poachers know the place better than I do, and I must get my work over before Perry comes. Some of the Ballycormack people, no doubt. I'll teach them a lesson;"

and Mr. Satterthwaite, in his vexation, heedlessly walked ankle-deep into the green sludge formed by the overflow of the pond. He picked his steps out and crossed to ascend the hill again to the house, but a sudden sound—a laugh actually, behind—caused him to jump round quickly. He was barely in time to see a female figure disappear in the thicket.

"Well," thought he, "what a fool I was not to have looked behind that summer-house as well as into it! Who on earth can that be?" Then he laughed at his own discomfiture and walked away into the house. He reached the library in time to see the same dog recross the lawn with the hare in his mouth.

"This is by no means a joke," thought the lord of the manor, scratching his chin thoughtfully. Then he went to work examining and measuring, and found the time pass quickly enough. Perry's gig drew up at the door before he had half finished.

"Well, how are you getting on? It's in very fair order, is it not?" said he, looking round.

"Fair order!" repeated Satterthwaite; "it's in a shocking condition, I think. But I saw some poachers at work here." Then he detailed his adventure on the lawn.

Perry looked thoughtful for a moment.

"What sort of dog? A big old brown brute, eh?"

"Exactly; he stopped the hare pretty thoroughly."

Perry laughed out.

"Be gad! that's the Ferrards! You have had a visit from the tribe, I wager. You saw no one?"

"I did, though. When I turned off after searching the summer-house I heard a laugh, and I got sight of a tall female figure in black darting off through the trees."

"Well, that was Hel, no doubt of it. She hunts in couples with Isidor, the youngest brother. By Jove! there, last October they played the deuce among Comerford's pheasants. They never could be caught, but they got off the birds without ever using a gun or trap. Boiled barley, Paddy Sheehan told me, with a hog's bristle in every grain, just choked off the pheasant quietly, and then they bagged them; and the salmon the same. Char, I'm told, stands to his neck night after night in the Rack, and see how he's never caught."

"Do they sell them? What the deuce does it mean? I can tell you I'll allow none of these tricks in this place."

"Sell them!" repeated Perry, "laws no, eat them. They never think of selling them, though indeed I think the shop-keepers where they deal come in for some of the spoils. They never sell them. But you see this whole district was once their own, and the people all know that and have a sort of feeling for them in consequence."

"Oh, that's the way, is it?" said Satterthwaite, dryly. He was stooping on the floor busy with a foot-rule, though, indeed, Perry's words interested him so infinitely more than his measurements that he had to make them all over again.

"Are you taking the measure for a carpet?" asked the attorney.

"Yes, and new wainscoting. I shall want more than that, too. I'd better send to Dublin for a man to come down to make an estimate. I want painters and fitters of all sorts."

"Dublin! oh, don't do that; you can't go past Dan Cassidy that way. He'll do it all up for you, or you'll be very unpopular if you go to Dublin for anything. I daren't buy an ounce of tea out of Darraghstown."

Satterthwaite stared at him as he folded up his foot-rule.

"The cases are slightly different, Mr. Perry," said he as stiffly as he could. He was intensely amused at his new friend's presumption. He half suspected him of touting, and the attempt with regard to the horse in the morning had made him a little suspicious.

"True for you," returned Perry, who was by no means obtuse. "Of course I'm bound to deal with the people I get my living off; it's not so with you. All the same, you'd better keep on neighborly terms with them, I can tell you."

Satterthwaite bit his lip.

"My servants will give them their custom, I dare say, but I doubt I'll consent to poison myself with the vile drugs they call tea and wine for the sake of their goodwill. Let us go and have a look at the stabling."

They went out into a large yard at the side, sadly in need of new paving, into a four-stalled stable. The fittings were in tolerable order.

"There's a good poultry-house, nice closed yard, too, for your fowls," said Perry, pointing to a well-fitted-up outhouse.

"Ay; it will be time to stock that presently."

"Hah! for the Ferrards' accommodation!" grinned the lawyer.

"Wait till I catch the Ferrards—Miss Hel, as you call her. I'll put her in the stocks—pound! What instrument of punishment have you here?"

Satterthwaite was not in earnest, but he was irritated by Perry, whose manner had assumed a dictatorial freedom rather offensive. He turned his back to him, and opening a small door in the yard wall, walked into what was once a garden, a large open slope, bordered on one side by a row of beautiful beech trees, and at the west and south by high, red brick walls. The fruit-trees, which had once been trained to this, had grown out of all shape and in many cases had fallen forward and away from their fastenings. Privet hedges, which had perhaps not known pruning-shears for ten or more years, had grown together, so that the alleys were impassable; the centre of the garden had been ploughed up and cropped with potatoes the year before, and in a sunny corner lay the ruins of a green-house.

"What a desert!" said the new owner, looking round; "I wonder if there were grass-walks here? I think I'll have them laid down, if not. Whoever chose this site knew what he was about."

"I've heard Bruton say this was a monks' garden once —ages ago, you know; before Cromwell, I suppose; and there used to be a ruin down in that field below, but the stones were carted off out of the way. Bruton can tell you, I dare say. There's a fine well there under that tree."

Satterthwaite walked over to a thicket of privet and box. He could see the opening of a well, surrounded by a little flagged rim which was moss-grown and damp looking, but he could not get near enough to look in. A sun-dial, on the face of which a tuft of grass had taken root and was flourishing, stood there.

"That old rubbish can go, I suppose," said Perry, nodding contemptuously at the old thing.

"I'll see about that," said its owner, distantly, who indeed by this time had formed a poor opinion of his friend's æsthetic judgment. "The walls look solid enough. I'll ripen peaches easily there."

Perry sneered.

"Peaches! I'd think a deal more of cabbages."

"We can have cabbages too, Mr. Perry, but not on the walls."

Then they drove away. When they reached the town, Satterthwaite got out at the hotel to write and forward his orders to the Dublin tradesmen, and in about an hour presented himself at the hall-door of the Perrys' house.

A dirty servant-girl showed him into a room on the right-hand side of a narrow entry. It was dark, but she returned presently with a large lamp which she set on the centre-table, and then Mr. Satterthwaite had means to indulge his curiosity. The room was not large and was lighted by three windows, two in front and one at the back; these were curtained by dingy, faded green damask hangings. There were no muslin or lace hangings, and the white blinds were dirty. The carpet was green with bouquets of enormous roses and lilies, and the chair covers were the same; a chiffonier with plate-glass back, which reflected the vase of wax pears and fuchsias which stood before it; a cottage piano, piled with torn and dirty music; no ornaments, no knickknacks, pictures, or books. On the table lay some once gaudily-bound volumes; "'Books of Beauty,' I suppose," said he to himself, and a thick green and gold volume of Moore's "Melodies" served as a stand for the lamp. Satterthwaite, whose quick eyes took in everything, opened one of the "Books of Beauty," as he at first fancied them; it proved to be a "Life of the Blessed Virgin," uncut, though grimy.

"This looks promising," said he to himself, and walking to the fire-place he placed his back against the chimney-piece, where under a broken glass shade an old gilt French clock enjoyed a sinecure. "What a room! I can hardly fancy there are women in this house; however, I suppose these antimacassars and bead-cushions represent them. Not a flower—even a primrose—faugh!"

Then the door opened and the Perry family trooped in. Mrs. Perry, a faded, untidy-looking woman, with a weak face and a querulous voice, introduced her four daughters to the stranger. They were healthy, bright-complexioned girls, hideously dressed, and with fringes of ash-colored hair. The eldest, a tall, awkward girl, with a shy, self-conscious manner, sat down near Satterthwaite, who, as soon as he had replied to her mother's commonplaces about the weather and his journey from London, good-naturedly began to talk to her.

"What a beautiful country this is, Miss Perry; I admire the scenery greatly."

"Oh, do you? I wonder at that now! we hate the country so."

Miss Perry spoke with a very strong brogue, drawling and unpleasant to the ear. He turned to the other sisters, who with wide-open, pale-colored eyes were staring at him.

"Is that so—you hate the country?"

"Oh yes," they all answered together; "we had rather—"

But the door opened at this second to admit their father, and Satterthwaite observed the sudden change that took place in the manner and bearing of the girls and their mother. She seemed, indeed, to shrink before his eye, and the younger girls looked demure. Miss Perry alone seemed unaffected.

"Why isn't dinner ready?" he asked in a bullying voice.

"We are waiting for Doctor Cartan. He promised to be here at six," Mrs. Perry said, deprecatingly.

"Go and tell them to send in dinner! Go!" he repeated, addressing the group of younger girls.

"Go, Lizzie," whispered the tallest of the three to the second.

"I won't. Do it, Eily. Eily!" As she spoke she pushed the youngest, a rather pretty girl of fourteen.

Miss Eily turned round a rebellious countenance, but meeting the fiery glare which Perry turned full on the trio, she decamped instanter.

"Cartan may be in Ballycormack; who on earth would wait dinner for him? That's the worst of being a doctor," he went on, addressing Satterthwaite; "you never have a moment you can call your own, especially a dispensary doctor. Bah! if he got anything of a decent salary even."

Then dinner was announced, and they adjourned to a back-room on the other side of the hall. The dining-room was a much smaller apartment, and was, if possible, more ugly and squalid than that which they left. The dinner-table and its equipage left much to be desired in point of cleanliness and comfort; elegance or refinement Satterthwaite did not expect. The dinner consisted ol meat almost exclusively. A large boiled leg of mutton was the *pièce de résistance*, and a dish of beefsteaks was at the foot of the table; two dishes of potatoes were the only accompaniment.

Mrs. Perry apologized to her guest for the simplicity of the fare, which was not even well cooked.

Satterthwaite was hungry and contrived to eat the dinner; he thought to himself that he had never seen such a table in his life. The spoons and forks, of massive silver, were dirty, and black thumb-marks decorated the plates.

"I wonder what the Ferrards have for dinner to-day," said Perry with a laugh, in which his wife and daughters joined. "My ducks, I'll vow."

"Indeed, I don't know that. I'm not at all fond of believing everything Mat says." Mrs. Perry said this in a tone of feeble protest.

"Humph," grunted her lord. "I dare say there are plenty of thieves beside them—but all the same, I don't know anybody would dare take anything of mine but that Char."

"Well, Hel wouldn't, and Isidor never does anything she dislikes." Miss Perry said this.

"I dare say," said Perry with a scornful laugh.

Then the ladies left the room. A servant carried in a tray with whisky and hot water. Perry brewed a tumbler of strong punch, but no entreaties or inducement would make his guest follow his example.

"I never drank punch in my life—never!" he protested. "If you will let me have cold water I will take some grog. I prefer it to the sherry? Yes."

Satterthwaite did indeed think it less dangerous than the brown, fiery compound he had been forced to drink at dinner. He was a judge of wine, and moreover a very moderate drinker. He was astonished at the quantity of punch Perry drank without its taking effect on him. They talked chiefly of farming for about an hour, then, his host showing unequivocal signs of drowsiness, Satterthwaite rose, and after some demur rather faintly pressed by Perry, went into the other room.

Mrs. Perry was nodding in an easy-chair. The eldest girl was playing, but ceased at his appearance and turned round on the music-stool.

"I wish I were out of this," thought Satterthwaite; "however, there is no help for it now." So he took a chair beside the lady of the house, who in her husband's absence seemed inclined to be talkative and cheerful; she no longer drooped her eyelids and stammered as if in the expectation of being set right every moment.

"I wonder, Mr. Satterthwaite, you came to live here—after London, now, too!" she exclaimed, open-eyed.

"Oh yes, you'll never stop at Rosslyne!" echoed her daughters.

"I like it immensely. I mean to live there always. I like Darraghstown too, ever so much." Satterthwaite said this with malice prepense.

"Augh!" cried Mrs. Perry, "I hate Darraghstown. I wouldn't live a day out of Doblin, if I could help it."

"You don't care for the country, then. I think the views round this place are simply charming."

"Augh!" cried they all in one melodious chorus, "I'd rather have Grafton Street than all the views in Ireland."

"Or the Pier o' Sundays."

"Or the Exhibition Promenades."

"I don't know why Mr. Perry likes it so much," said their mamma, plaintively.

"Does he, indeed?" said Satterthwaite, thinking of something the worthy gentleman had said the previous evening. "I fancied he disliked the place too."

"Augh! don't mind him now," said his wife; "if he was out ov it he'd be dyin' to get back again. Look at him there last summer, when we were up in Kingstown; he couldn't stop a week in it. He should be back home. No, indeed, Mr. Satterthwaite, Mr. Perry couldn't live out ov Darraghstown."

"It's a horrid place. There's no society at all," said the lady on the music-stool with a plaintive expression of face.

"No society?" said Satterthwaite, turning and looking at her inquisitively. "Are there not a great many families here? I thought I heard of half a dozen from Mr. Perry."

"There's the Hollahans, of Brophystown," began Mrs. Perry in a droning voice; "but ah! they're such very plain, old-fashioned people now, though my girls and theirs were at school together at the Sawker Cure Convent. I don't care for them mixing at all now. An' them Reallys are queer—very queer."

"Who are they, Mrs. Perry?" asked Mr. Satterthwaite as maliciously as before.

"They live up there in that out-of-the-way-lookin' house on the hill—Buona Vista they call it. She was reared off abroad somewhere with an uncle, a marshal or general, or something, and Really met in with her. She was a governess at Harrogate, I believe, an' he married her.

They say she thought he had money, and he thought she had. I don't know—but I never got on with her. She has an awful temper."

"You know her then, Mrs. Perry?"

"Augh, yes, in a sort of a way; but we don't get on. She has a big telescope up there in their drawing-room window, and I think she'd rather be lookin' through that than anythin' else. She can see all over the town, and knows everybody and everything."

Satterthwaite felt glad he had broached this subject. And he determined to make Madame Really's acquaintance without loss of time.

"She must be a character," thought he. "My friend seems to resent the telescope even more than the temper. I expect I shall have some amusement here yet, unpromising as it does look."

"Then there are the Castle Darragh Hollahans," said he, intent on working the mine further.

"Stuck-up lot—drive their carriage and pair, with a footman on the box. They're cousins of the Brophystown people, but don't visit them. They called on Mrs. Scanlan of the Bank, but only ask her to tea; they know no one at all. The Newtons and Carringtons won't have them, and we in the town ain't fine enough for them. Mrs. Fair and Miss Fair, we know them now, but they're a long way off, and Tom Fair is—"

Mrs. Perry broke off with a shake of her head, which conveyed to Mr. Satterthwaite the impression that Tom Fair was not a most estimable character.

"As well as I can gather, not two families of the whole place seem to be on terms," thought he. "So far for society; now let's see what remains." So, turning to the eldest girl, he said:

"How are you off for books? You have a library in the town?"

"No," replied she, "there is no library. The nuns have a few religious books and story-books, and they lend them out at a penny a week."

"Why don't you form a book-club, and get down books

from Dublin? In England people do that. How do you live without reading?"

"Oh, we don't mind," returned the young lady in a languid, careless drawl. "We borrow a book now and again. We don't care for reading."

"Do you know the *London Journal?*" said the youngest, Miss Eily, looking up pertly at him.

"Eily! if you ever bring the *London Journal* from the kitchen again I'll tell Father Quaide on you," her mamma spoke in peevish, scolding tones, "and I won't allow Julia to bring it into this house. You know he doesn't approve of light reading."

Satterthwaite stroked his mustache thoughtfully, and asked Miss Perry to play. He got up and turned over the leaves of her music for her—not a very easy task, so dilapidated and ruinous was their condition. Miss Perry's music was of the most ordinary and most unbearable class—operatic airs with frightful variations. The piano was bad and out of tune to boot; the pedal required the exertion of both her feet to work it and performed a hideous *obligato* of its own. Satterthwaite stood patiently and turned over the leaves for the performer with a gravity that was at times imperiled by the criticisms on his personal appearance which reached his ears distinctly from behind. He heard the door of the room open and shut as if some one had entered, but he did not turn to look, thinking it might be the master of the house.

At last, at long last, the fantasia closed with a score of awful crashes. The musician let her hands drop into her lap, and swung round towards the patient Mr. Satterthwaite.

"Thank you, Miss Perry; that is really a treat." He meant the finale. "You must practice immensely."

"Oh no, Mr. Satterthwaite, I assure you I never touch the piano. I don't really know when I practiced my pieces; 'pon my word I don't, now."

Miss Perry repelled the accusation, just as all young lady pianists of her calibre do, with as much warmth as if it conveyed an imputation of a discreditable nature.

"Mr. Satterthwaite," said Mrs. Perry from her easy-chair, "let me present you to the Honorable Miss Ferrard."

Satterthwaite, almost doubting his ears, turned round to find himself, to his still greater surprise, facing a tall young lady, dressed in an elegant and well-fitting robe of soft black stuff mingled with silk. She was standing on the hearth-rug, silent and gloomy-looking, and acknowledged his low bow by an inclination of her head, accompanied by a look from a pair of, what Satterthwaite thought, the most magnificent eyes he had ever seen in his life. There was something of fear in their expression, and recognition, too. In the lamp-light, and shaded by the beautiful dark lashes which now drooped over them, they looked almost black. She appeared a little uncomfortable and ill at ease for the moment, but Satterthwaite could not help noticing the difference between her simple naturalness and the clumsy affectations of the Perrys.

"Sit down, dear," said Mrs. Perry, good-naturedly.

The new-comer seated herself in the vacant arm-chair opposite, and folding her hands in her lap remained demure and silent.

Satterthwaite took up a position beside his hostess, and while conversing with her managed to reconnoitre the features and lineaments of his new acquaintance, she meantime replying indifferently and in monosyllables to the questions of the other girls who had gathered about her.

What a contrast she presents to them, thought the amused watcher. A low, broad forehead, from which the hair was brushed back smoothly; strongly-marked eyebrows and long dark eyelashes, curling and thick like fur. The eyes were violet-blue, and the nose—he had to wait until she turned her head sideways to determine its order—*retroussé* ever so little. The upper lip short to a fault, and the strong round chin almost cleft by a dimple; the skin was pale, colorless olive.

The Perrys, with their ash-colored hair, red noses and ears, and straggling loose mouths, and undecided pale eyes, looked washed-out, faded creatures beside her. Satterthwaite smiled as he thought of the carman's not inapt comparison. . The feeble attempts of Mrs. Perry to make conversation received but scanty encouragement at his hands.

"This is my poacher," thought he with an amused smile. "A Diana, indeed. She recognizes me, the young gypsy that she is. If I had caught her that time behind the summer-house! glad I did not."

"Mr. Perry must have his nap. You'll excuse him, Mr. Satterthwaite. He never wakes up till tea. Eily, darling," continued the matron, "run and see what Julia's at."

"Why didn't you come out for the walk to-day?" Satterthwaite heard the eldest girl say to Miss Ferrard. "You know you promised us, and we walked up and down ever so long waiting for you."

"Isidor wanted me," replied she in a demure, low voice, after a pause, looking down shyly as she spoke, but with a faint smile.

"Were ye ever in Louth, Mr. Satterthwaite?" Mrs. Perry went on. "I was thinkin' ye might have made the acquaintance of my first cousin, Hyacinth O'Maloney. He's sub-sheriff of the county this year."

"No," replied he, "I never was in Louth, and don't know the name."

"Ye might have met him at the Castle in Doblin," she persisted in spite of his disclaimer. "They go to the levees and draw'n'-rooms regular—all of them do. They've a lovely place, O'Maloney Castle. There's never less than fourteen horses kept up constant, and as for—"

"What did Isidor want you for to-day? Say, fishing?"

"N—no!" answered Miss Ferrard, with a conscious look at Satterthwaite, who had turned his eyes on the fire and did not look at her again till Mrs. Perry had got to the eight sets of real lace drawing-room curtains at O'Maloney Castle.

"A walk then?" pursued Miss Perry.

Satterthwaite strained his ears but could not hear the reply, and when he next stole a glance across the hearth-rug Miss Ferrard, lost in a reverie, was looking into the fire, and her companion seemed to have abandoned her efforts at conversation in utter despair.

Then they all went to tea in the dining-room. The host had awakened and was standing with his back to the fire, his wiry hair all on end. He nodded with a satirical smile to Miss Ferrard, who either did not see or disregarded the salutation, then yawned aloud.

"You don't nap after dinner, Mr. Satterthwaite, eh?" The "eh" developed itself into another yawn of most alarming extent. "Driving in the open air always makes me sleepy. I could not do without a snooze after dinner—'tis a most wholesome plan, I'm told."

"I prefer to smoke," said Satterthwaite, who had contrived to place himself opposite Miss Ferrard.

Perry took his own arm-chair at the end of the table, and glancing at Miss Ferrard and from her to Satterthwaite, winked meaningly. Satterthwaite frowned and turned away his head. The young lady, however, said nothing, and continued calmly buttering her bread.

"How's young Devereux's foot, eh, Miss Hel?" asked he then with a malicious twinkle in his eye.

"I don't know," she replied, looking up quickly, a red flush mantling on both cheeks.

"H'm—I saw you in that neighborhood to-day; so fancied you might be around inquiring for him." Then he winked again and took an enormous bite of the edible on his plate.

"What happened to young Devereux?" asked Satterthwaite, turning to Perry; "and who is he?"

"He's the son of the man that has Darraghmore now," answered Mrs. Perry, "and he hurt his foot a while ago breaking in a young horse, I believe."

"You never do have the rights of any story, Mrs. P.," snapped her amiable lord, who had disposed of the mouthful of cake. "He was leading the horse in and it stepped on his toes. Wasn't that it, Miss Helena?—you were there. By-the-bye, has he made up his mind about going to Australia, yet?"

10

"California, pa," said Miss Perry.

"Well, it's all one, isn't it? Do you know, any of ye?"

"California is not in Australia," said Miss Ferrard, speaking in a decisive tone; "it's in America."

"Is it, indeed! Thank you, miss," returned Perry, with a mock gratitude for the information, which his daughters had not dared to supply.

"We haven't heard," returned the young ladies, who had glanced to each other and tittered when their guest made her daring assertion.

"Well, if ye haven't heard it," grumbled their parent, "it's not known, for I'm blessed if an egg is laid in the barony without your having the first intelligence of it."

At this compliment they all laughed boisterously, Miss Ferrard excepted—a sneer curled her lip, and she did not raise her eyes again during the meal. After tea, Perry and Mr. Satterthwaite went into the study. The rest returned to the drawing-room.

The study was a small, untidy room with one window which looked out on the front. Cocoa-matting covered the floor; one side of the wall was occupied by bookshelves, which in their turn were occupied by a great many things besides books. A large green-covered table, strewn with books, paper, maps, and all sorts of litter, filled the whole centre of the room. Mr. Perry's saddle and top boots lay in one corner, and whips, rods, and guns graced the wall. They had seated themselves at the fire to smoke, when a knock at the door caused Perry to jump up.

"That's Cartan, now," said he. "I don't want to be bothered with him here." Then he opened the door and said to the servant as she passed:

"It's Doctor Cartan—tell him I'm busy, and show him into the drawing-room. He's a decent poor fellow," said he. "'Tis a pity he drinks so."

"A rather serious disqualification that," said Mr. Satterthwaite, gravely.

"Ah, in these country towns men have a frightful life of it. I have seen I don't know how many go to the dogs in this little hole of a place with drink. The bank-clerks get together of an evening up in the billiard-rooms of the hotel—what else have they to do? A man has a terrible life in a place like it."

"Evidently," replied Satterthwaite, absently. "Nothing to do but go to the dogs and drink," he repeated to himself. "What a state of society! I declare I don't wonder at their wanting Home Rule. If I thought it was to put any healthy life into them, I'd go in for it too. The education must be at the bottom of it.—Tell me, Mr. Perry," he continued aloud, "how are you off for schools here?"

"There's the Christian Brothers and the National School, and the nuns have a boarding-school in Ballycormack; and there's the National, too, for poor girls, I mean."

"Have you no better class schools for boys?"

"No; and that's a terrible loss. We have to send boys off to the Diocesan College; there's nothing between that and the Christian Brothers, and for that matter they'd be better taught by the brothers."

"No day-schools, then, of that class?"

"None; ah, these National Schools are a great humbug. There's a teacher above there appointed by the parish priest, and he's no good. He won't appoint any one trained in the model schools, and so the Christian Brothers easily distance them as teachers. Wherever they can manage it, the priests get the nuns to take the National Schools; and they appoint anybody they choose to the village male school. If he gets them up to the mark for the inspector, it's enough. They're humbugs."

"That, it seems to me, is the priests' fault. Why don't they get proper teachers?"

"No proper teacher would work for the pay; and the position, moreover, is too poor a one. National teachers are just priests' servants and dependents; no one recognizes them, or respects them."

"Ergo, neither do their scholars."

"I declare to you, Mr. Satterthwaite, if the people can thumb their prayer-books instead of their rosaries at Mass on Sunday, they think they know everything, and their teacher is precious little better than themselves. Believe me, under the hedge-school system, with its odd scraps of Latin and Greek, they were better off; they had a glimpse, anyhow, that there are fields of knowledge beyond those comprised in the National school-books. And they tried to reach them, aye, and some of them did. Some of our greatest men, sir, got their first taste for knowledge at the hedge-schools; now a National School would just turn them out smart, self-conceited shop-boys. It is a scandal that all higher class education should be impracticable—should be denied. I dare say in this very place, poor as it is, there are forty or fifty boys whose parents could afford to send them to the old intermediate schools now (there may be a genius or two among them), and who are forced to put up with the National School. There's nothing between it and the Diocesan College, which is inconvenient and costly, and good-for-nothing into the bargain."

"In that case why don't you get a classical master? You could easily find one. You have the remedy in your own hands."

"He'd have to be a Catholic, otherwise it would be impossible; and where would you get a Catholic classical scholar now? And along with that the priests want the Diocesan colleges supported."

"Why, that's absurd, you know; and what has the school-master's creed to do with his scholars?"

"Hah, there's the whole trouble, sir; there's mixed education. You see," continued Perry with a bitter grin, "ignorance is no sin—no hinderance to salvation, whereas a mixed education is most perilous. There, I'm quoting last Sunday's pastoral. Another point: the people here are very peculiar. They value nothing that costs them nothing. And if you made them a present of the finest educational scheme in the world, they would neither thank you nor value it. They paid something in the hedge-schools, and something more in the intermediary schools, so they respected them. I assure you it is the same all through; they don't consider the dispensary doctor fit to bleed a pig, because he costs them nothing. It's a fact."

"What is the meaning of that?"

"The hate and distrust they have of everything devised by Government for one thing, and I suppose there is at bottom something of independence of spirit for another. God bless me! I recollect poor Mrs. Fitz-Ffoulke, when she was here, getting up a coal-club and clothing fund, and collecting money to treat the poor to blankets and fires when the cold weather set in. Well, she and her committee did manage to make a lot of the old rascals comfortable; and what do you think my wife and daughters heard them say? in fact, it was the generally received belief among them, that Mrs. Fitz-Ffoulke and the others were making *some profit out of the charitable enterprise for themselves*, else they'd never have gone to all the trouble they did. Haw, haw, haw!"

"That was gratitude, by Jove!"

"Yes, and it was all done in pure charity, no souping, swaddling mixture whatever. The Fitz-Ffoulkes had none of that about them. We'd better go into the drawing-room if you have finished your cigar."

Satterthwaite was not sorry to return thither. He felt curious to see more of Miss Ferrard. She was a new experience to him, and her beautiful face and wild, troubled eyes as they met his for the first time, seemed somehow constantly before him.

They entered the drawing-room. Mrs. Perry was in her easy-chair, Miss Perry and Doctor Cartan were seated a little apart. He rose and bowed to Satterthwaite; he was a fair-haired, heavy-looking young man of perhaps six-and-twenty, with a soddened, bloated face. His manner was uncouth and rough, but he did not seem devoid of intelligence. Miss Helena and the other girls were teasing a kitten on the rug, but they left off and seated themselves decorously on their chairs. Perry dropped himself into the easy-chair and drew it nearer to the fire. The girls moved farther off, and Mrs. Perry's nervous manner returned. Miss Ferrard seemed utterly unmoved by his approach, and glanced disdainfully at him sideways. He saw the look, and eyed her for a moment as if he were about to speak, but thought better of it. Timidity evidently formed no part of her character.

"Why didn't you come to dinner, doctor?" said Perry.

"A call to Ballycormack," replied the M.D. with a sigh.

"Mrs. Doyle, eh?" laughed Perry.

Doctor Cartan nodded with a sulky look.

Satterthwaite did not care to talk to the dispensary doctor, whose appearance had impressed him unfavorably. He was thinking what to say to Miss Ferrard that would entail a longer reply than yes or no. He had not yet heard her speak, and wished to make her do so. At last, in despair, he said, looking directly at her:

"Do you play?"

The Misses Perry glanced at each other maliciously and laughed.

"No," was her curt answer, accompanied by a searching look, as if to see if he was in earnest or in jest.

"Or sing?" went on Satterthwaite, desperately. The young ladies telegraphed still more mocking glances to each other, and looked with a pitying, patronizing air at their friend.

She seemed as if she did not hear him, and rose from her seat. She crossed the room, passing by the sofa where Doctor Cartan and Miss Perry were holding a very one-sided conversation over the family album, to the chiffonier, on which lay some numbers of an illustrated weekly; these she began to turn over deliberately.

Mrs. Perry and her daughters exchanged looks expressing reprobation of such flagrant ill-manners. Satterthwaite, who was repenting his boldness, turned in his seat so as to command a view of her profile, which showed to perfection in the window corner against the glowing damask curtain.

"You won't mind her," whispered Mrs. Perry, apologetically, "Mr. Satterthwaite. She's such a temper; and then she's never had any opportunities, the poor child. Such a bringing up, ye know. Left there to run the country, and no one to do anything for her but a horrid old servant."

"What a pity, is it not?" said he in a sympathizing tone. He wanted to hear more.

"Augh, 'tis!" continued Mrs. Perry; "but those Ferrards are all so wild, ye know. She was sent over when her mamma died to aunts of hers in England, and she ran off in no time. So I heard. The old nurse told the story herself, so it must be true. She wouldn't learn a lesson or anything; and they'd got a governess into the house and everything for her. Helena nearly killed them all, and made her appearance home here without a thing but what she stood in. So Cawth said. An' her aunts packed everything, clothes and books and all, over to her. 'Twas very good of them, now; and, indeed, it's little thanks I'm afraid she gives them or anybody. Only a while ago she struck my Eily for something she said to her just for her good—she did indeed."

"Served her right!" was Mr. Perry's approving comment; "teach her to give impudence another time. Helena's a trump."

"Of course, Mr. Perry," said the lady, plaintively, "you always set every one up over your own."

"She is strikingly ha—er—good-looking girl, don't you think?" said Satterthwaite, looking at the subject of conversation; Helena was now standing upright, her tall, straight figure and finely-set head showing to advantage.

"Oh, do you think so now, Mr. Satterthwaite?" hastily replied Mrs. Perry, with a touch of truly maternal jealousy showing in her eyes and voice. "I never could fancy that dark skin; and she has such a displeasing expression. Oh, now, I'm surprised at your taste!" Then she bridled her head, and glanced at her three chicks, as if wondering how any one could prefer Miss Ferrard's dusky beauty to their blonde charms.

"Why, Mr. Satterthwaite," continued she in a loud, impressive tone, "the girl doesn't actually know how to write her name!"

"Yes she does," interrupted Mr. Perry again, and this time more tartly than before. "Yes she does, Mrs. P., and knows a blessed sight more useful accomplishments than any of your precious girls. If I wanted a dinner, I wager Miss Hel wouldn't be a bad warrant for it." And he winked at his guest and laughed long and loud.

Mrs. Perry assumed an air of long-suffering and resignation. Satterthwaite looked at his watch and rose to go.

"Ten o'clock, Mrs. Perry. I must take leave of you—no, thank you, I could not stay longer this evening. If you will allow me, I shall have the pleasure of leaving Miss Ferrard at her own door. I pass it, you know, on my way to the hotel."

Miss Ferrard looked up in bewilderment and indignation.

"Now, Miss Hel, hold up your head," laughed the master of the house, standing with his back to the fire. "Do you hear? There's money bid for you."

Miss Hel only turned on her heel and went round the table to say good-night to her hostess.

Satterthwaite saw by her looks that she meant to ignore his offer—made, indeed, in pure kindness. He fancied that, as a mark of attention and respect, the young lady would overlook the imaginary offense of his question a few minutes before. He did not know what to do now, and stood irresolute. Doctor Cartan got up yawning and said to Satterthwaite:

"I'll be down the street with you too, I'm going—"

But his proposition met with such a storm of opposition from the family that he sat obediently down again. Satterthwaite went into the hall to take his hat.

"You will allow me to see you home then?" he said to Miss Ferrard, who appeared disinclined to wait longer, and was taking no notice of him.

"Do you hear?" added Mrs. Perry in a sharp tone. "You must not walk home alone. You ought to thank Mr. Satterthwaite."

By the light of the one candle which illuminated the entry, Mr. Satterthwaite could see the young lady's eyes flash a gracious look in the direction of her hostess from under a great broad-brimmed hat which she now slouched over her face. She remained still, however, till he opened the hall-door, and then they went out together.

It was dry and mild, and the night air seemed heavenly in comparison with that of the stuffy room. Miss Ferrard threw back her hat and drew a deep breath of relief.

"Is it not a lovely night?" said he, looking up. Not a cloud veiled the myriads of stars above. There was no moon, but everything was clear and distinct, and the scent of the wall-flowers and primroses under the holly trees hung heavy in the air. Everything was soft with a drowsy sweetness; it was like stepping into a new world, the half dark, the silence, save for the rhythmic murmur of the branches rocked by a little breeze overhead.

"Yes, it is beautiful," she replied.

They walked on a few steps in silence, then suddenly through an opening between the houses came a hoarse, dull murmur.

"That must be the river we hear," said he, halting for an instant.

"It is the river," said she, with something more of animation in her tones than he had yet heard; "it runs behind the houses. It is very full after the rains. Look," she continued, pointing with outstretched hand, "you can see where it goes."

Satterthwaite followed the direction of her hand with his eyes, and could trace the broad lead-colored band that stretched itself eastward from where they stood, moving on slowly between two high banks of reeds, the rustle of which was borne to their ears on the breeze.

"Good-night," said the girl, abruptly, stepping down as she spoke through a swinging gate into a flagged walk considerably lower than the footpath. A dog jumped up from under the bushes and approached her snuffing and wagging his tail.

"Allow me to knock or ring," said Satterthwaite making a movement to follow her.

"Don't come in," said she, imperiously.

The dog, as if divining her wishes, crouched with an ominous growl. There was nothing to be done; he lifted his hat and crossed the road to gain his hotel, feeling thoroughly amused with his adventure; but before he had gone far it struck him that he had not heard the door open or shut. What could the meaning of that be? and he turned and looked back. Just as he expected; the young lady had not gone into the house. There she was, seated on the parapet of the old bridge, the black silhouette of her figure clearly defined against the sky, and her canine protector seated close beside her. Satterthwaite stood still, perplexed. He should have waited until the hall-door was opened at least; then his responsibility had ended, but he had not fulfilled his duty, and now this impropriety was the consequence. He could not go home and allow her to remain in such a dangerous place. Who could tell what drunken strollers might be about? What if she lost her balance and fell over the parapet? "Bah!" thought he; "I'm a fool! she knows what she's about." Nevertheless, he stepped off the path and down into the soft roadway, and walking quickly reached the delinquent unnoticed by her.

She was sitting sideways on the coping-stone leaning on one elbow, and with the other arm wound round her dog's neck. Before Satterthwaite got up to her he could catch above the noise of the river under the arches the sound of some queer old ballad she was crooning in a low voice to herself. The words reached him distinctly:

"Mauriade, ny Kallaght,
This good skene beside me
Had drunk the last drop
Of thy young heart's—"

Satterthwaite laid his hand on her dress before he spoke. Her back was turned to him, and as she was unconscious of his approach, he feared to give her a sudden start.

"Miss Ferrard," he began in a distant, reproving tone, "are you not afraid to sit here? I thought I left you at home."

"Well, sir!" she said, breaking off her song and looking up at him defiantly and coldly as if wanting an explanation.

Satterthwaite had expected an excuse, or at least a precipitate retreat on her part. He faltered for a moment. She changed her position to an upright one and stared at him insolently almost.

"I cannot think of leaving you here at this hour; you do not know who might see you. It is neither safe nor proper," he added, severely.

Her lips curled, but what answer she meditated he never knew, for at that moment a side-door in the mill-yard opened and a voice shouted "Hel!" Almost simultaneously an old woman appeared and made straight for his companion. She clutched the girl by the arm and dragged her off her seat and away towards the door, abusing her vigorously the while.

"Ye trapesin', night-walkin' cutty, come awa' in this minute; gin I had Clan here, but he'd rug yer heid. Naethin' wull do ye then but larkin' this hour of night; I'll—"

The loud bang of the door and the rattle of the bolts cut off the rest of the discourse. He could hear them crossing the garden and yard, the old woman's shrill tones alone reached his ears, and he could not distinguish the words. Then another door clapped and all was still. He stood quietly and listened attentively, but no further sound came from the mill-house.

He walked across the bridge and looked from the other side of the water at the bleak old building, every window of which was dark.

"She is safe, anyhow," said he, turning once more homewards; "what a wonderful collection these creatures are! Miss Hel is something quite out of the common. The house and everything seem to match each other."

Then as he crossed the road he glanced once more at the front of the house; in a top window there was a pale light as of a candle. He smiled as he saw it.

"Safe enough this time. I wonder has she had a whipping? she looks as if she wanted one."

Then he, too, went home and to bed.

The Darragh river ran close behind the houses in Comerford Terrace; so close, indeed, that in course of time it might be expected to eat away the bank next to them in such a way as to endanger their foundations. At one time, so the oldest inhabitants said, a good-sized field had separated the garden, hedges, and walls from the watercourse, but the swift current had gradually widened the elbow which the stream assumed a quarter of a mile above the Comerford bridge, and which elbow or curve just touched with its centre the end wall of the mill-house garden. This wall was not high, just high enough, indeed, to admit of a person sitting on it with ease and comfort; though very close to the bridge, it was not overlooked by the loungers who all day long leaned against the parapet, owing to the fact that the wool-store was between the bridge and the garden, and with its high limestone wall formed a thoroughly efficient screen. Immediately below the garden wall, which was in a very ruinous condition, lay a narrow bank of grass and stones, some three or four feet wide, bordered by rushes and waterweeds, and outside of it ran the river, tawny of color, swift of current and bearing along on its bosom trophies of its conquests in the rocky beds above by Darraghmore and Ballycormack, in the shape of flecks of foam in which were mixed dead leaves, broken twigs, and atoms of moss torn from the tree stems and the stones. Flocks of gray and white geese crossed and recrossed the river, never troubling themselves to swim; they launched out confidently on the water and were borne over by the current, from which at their will they disengaged themselves by a deft stroke or two. The ducks were not so venturesome and were content to disport themselves in muddy pools by the edge, leaving the deep water to their larger kindred. Right opposite the mill-garden were fields sloping to the water's edge, where the cows came down to drink, and in hot weather stood knee-deep in the splashy ooze to cool themselves and gather new energy to withstand their torturers the flies. Altogether the view from the garden of "Milligan's," as the old corner house was called, was not destitute of picturesque charm. It was pleasant enough from the moss-grown wall to watch the course of the stream from beneath the dipping branches of the trees at the fork where the Rack met its waters, down under the arches of the old bridge, winding past the cabins whose indented, irregular roofs were glowing with every tint of brown and green, gray and crimson, on until it spread out beyond the sedges that lined its banks in a wide silver expanse.

Between five and six, one mild, gray evening in April, two figures, one male, the other female, were seated on the wall, one lounging with a book, the other idly throwing bits of mortar and loose pebbles into the stream. Both were silent. The student seemed engrossed in her book, and the boy equally intent on hitting a bit of dead wood that had got tangled in a tuft of rushes. The monotonous ripple of the water hurrying by was lost sometimes in a sudden burst of cackling from the geese as they straggled homewards. A hoarse voice came occasionally from the bridge, and now and again little impatient yelps from the brown water-dog, who was aggrieved that the stones were not thrown in the water for his amusement.

"Hel!—I say, Hel!" began the boy, dropping a bit of mortar and leaning with both hands on the wall; "what sort of looking fellow is this Satterthwaite that has come to Rosslyne?"

"I don't know," replied the girl, without taking her eyes from her book.

"Don't know," repeated he, impatiently, "why, you saw him last night at Perry's. Was it the fellow who ran after us at Rosslyne yesterday morning? Wake up now and say."

Isidor, who had grown a full inch within the last six months, stretched out a long arm and laying a hand on the student's shoulder pushed her amicably.

"Dear," said she, drawing back impatiently, and keeping one finger close pressed to the line where she was reading, "how can I tell you what he is like? A big man—"

"Fat, eh?"

"No, not fat; he looks well, a big strong man and very polite."

And as Miss Hel pronounced this last part of her description, she wrinkled up her pretty nose.

"Polite," repeated Isidor, "humph! Tell us, though, was it he you came home with last night? and what was all that row with Cawth for, eh? I was in bed or I'd have come down. What was it?"

"Oh, ay, you didn't know," answered Helena. "He walked with me to the door, and when I thought he was gone I went round and sat up on the bridge to try if I'd any chance of seeing the otter, and the fool came back after me. I don't know what he was saying when Cawth ran out like a wild-cat and dragged me in."

"He's just gone out a while ago on Dowling's car, up to Ballycormack I suppose, and he doesn't look a bad sort either. I wonder what kind of fellow he is, now?"

"Pooh! what's that to us! Look, Isi, before the middle arch there's a fish leaped this instant."

"Ay," returned the boy, his eyes kindling with a sudden interest, and he turned them in the direction indicated by his sister. "I wish I'd gone out this morning. That Englishman has brought over grand rods—you ought to see them, Hel! gaffs, and nets, and everything. They say he has a permit from Lord Comerford to fish the Rack. Char says he's going to rent the shooting of the demesne, too, next season. He's enormously rich. His father was in trade in England. Old Perry heard all about him—he made piles of money. This fellow was a member of Parliament till the dissolution, and he's come over here to study this country. We'll never have any fun out on Rosslyne side again, I fear."

"No," assented Helena, dreamily, her eyes fixed on the far side of the river.

"What do you say to go up to Darraghmore in the morning? Jim Devereux is all right again, and we'll go through the old house and look at his new colt."

"Yes," replied Helena. "The Perrys wanted me to drive

over to Ballyslane, just because that Cartan is to be there. What a fool he is! I won't go."

Then they were both silent again for a time; the girl read, and the boy stared moodily at the stream running by the tuft of brambles beneath which the otter was supposed to lurk.

"Hel!" croaked the old woman's voice from a broken window in the house, "come in wi' ye to your supper. Come in!"

The pair turned round and beheld Cawth's uninviting countenance projected through a broken pane, from the draught of which she shielded the candle in her hand. It was not nearly dark yet, but the sunken ground-floor rooms of the old house were dingy and ill-lighted, and the old woman's sight was not too good. Helena looked back over the river, folding her arms indifferently, and heedless of the eloquent entreaties of the dog, who, understanding the import of the summons as well as his masters, began to fidget and snuff impatiently. Isidor of course was not going to stir until his sister did, and as long as Cawth remained at the window she chose to seem starkly impassive.

"Did ye hear!" cried the domestic at last, her tone showing clearly that her stock of patience was exhausted.

Not as much as a look did either of her hearers vouchsafe. Then she made a dash at the back-door, and they heard it slam to and the rattle of the bolts as the old dame fastened them, in the avowed intention of keeping them out. In less time by far than it takes to tell, Isidor had vaulted over the end wall and run round the house to the front. Ere Cawth had leisure to divine his movement and frustrate it, he had opened the back-door again and called Hel, who picked up her book and sauntered in lazily and triumphant.

They passed the kitchen and went into a front room, low ceilinged and dingy, where the dinner was spread. The furniture was something more civilized than in their Galway lodging. There was a sideboard, rickety enough certainly, against the wall, and an old round table stood in the centre of the room. On a hair sofa by the fire, which, though the day was close and mild, was piled high with turf sods, lay the old man, much the same in appearance as when he left Galway, save that his eyes seemed duller and more sunken, and his under lip trembled constantly. He raised himself with an effort and took his place at the table. Char rose from a corner by the window, where he was trying to read with his book held close to his eyes, and they all sat down together. The dinner consisted of a leg of mutton and fowls. Plentiful fare, as was usual with the Ferrards while their money lasted. The table was laid in somewhat more orderly fashion; wine-glasses and tumblers were placed to each, and from Helena's behavior it was easy to see that the glimpse she had had six months before of civilized life had not been completely forgotten. The old man ate little, and drank quantities of whisky and water. Char and Isidor disputed just as Clan and his second brother had done when he was at home. Char was quieter and more lazy of disposition than either of the other boys, and as Helena always took Isidor's part, the dissensions were of short duration. The dinner was soon over. Lord Darraghmore lay down by the fire with his newspaper; Char collected the fragments and whistled the dogs out to the yard, sparing Mrs. Milligan's fragments of carpet in deference to Helena's suggestion that the dogs could eat more comfortably off the stones, and moreover ran the risk of being choked by the multifarious shreds and patches that covered the floor.

Isidor was rummaging in an old escritoire in a far corner, and Helena, after a wistful look out of the window, sat down in the arm-chair opposite the sofa. Presently the old man filled his pipe and called Isidor over to light it. He obeyed, taking a red glowing crumb of peat and dropping it into the bowl, and then the room was filled in a moment by the strong reek of the tobacco. Helena got up and slipped gently out.

It was too soon to go to the kitchen; Cawth's supper could scarcely be finished yet, and until that event had taken place she would be no welcome visitor; so she went up the narrow stairs to her own room on the second story. Isi and Char had each a room to himself, for they were not pinched for space in this old rambling house. Behind the dining-room and separating it from the kitchen was a small but warm room, appropriated to the master of the house and his inseparable companion the old wolf-dog. On the other side of the narrow hall was a room originally intended for a drawing-room, but which the young people used as a receptacle for their miscellaneous properties; guns, whips, rods, and lines littered it. Furniture there was none.

Helena's room was very differently munitioned from the pretty chamber she had left at Bath. A huge old four-poster filled the centre of the room, looking, with its enormous mahogany pillars and thick, dusty curtains, like some great catafalque. It had been bought by the former occupants of the house at a sale held at some old family seat in the county. There was a legend that William of Orange had slept in it, and Mrs. Milligan on getting it home had liberally sprinkled holy water over all the four posts to rid it of the contamination left by his Protestant Majesty. A mahogany wardrobe held Helena's clothes, and on a table near the window was her dressing-case, which, with the rest of the things purchased for her by her aunts, had been sent over as soon as they discovered her whereabouts. On a shelf over the fireplace were piled her books, all of them bearing traces of use. A looking-glass, cracked and dull-colored, and an old box, formed the furniture of the room; in the projecting gable window, however, there was a seat of some kind, with a shawl disposed cushion-wise upon it. On this the girl threw herself and leaned with her elbow on the sill to look out. There was a wide view from the little queer opening of the gable window. She could see down the street to the Darraghmore Arms, past the post-office, where the mail-car was just starting for the train, surrounded, as usual, by a group of idlers; and by turning her head a little to the left, she could follow the course of the Darragh for a long distance as it wound among the flat meadows and the snipe-haunted sedges away towards the sea. It looked like a silver ribbon, so still and white, as it wandered on. The meadows had taken a pale bright green, and the lambs were out yet; she could still see their white fleeces against the dark background of the hedges. The window was open, and the busy twitter of the sparrows in the ivy and the even-song of the thrushes filled the air, as did the strong bitter smell of the young shoots of the holly trees in the front. A few faint red streaks lingered in the west; she could see them through the trees that crowned the knoll where Really's cottage was; and the black net-work of the naked boughs, with the crows hovering noisily over it, looked picturesque and weird.

Then she could see the new arrival, the all-absorbing sensation of the hour at Darraghstown—the Englishman who had bought Rosslyne—saunter out of the hotel, cigar in mouth, and come down the flagged pathway leading to Comerford Road. "Going to Perry's, no doubt," thought Miss Helena. For pure curiosity she watched his progress. He came nearer and nearer, and at last disappeared under the hedge. She could not see what way he turned from her own window, so ran into Char's room opposite and looked up the road. No, the Englishman was nowhere to be seen. Where could he have gone? She slipped down-stairs, and passing the lobby window caught a glimpse of his low soft hat and gray coat as he crossed the bridge, evidently meditating a stroll on the river road on the opposite side.

Cawth, of course, knew all about him; so Hel dived into the kitchen and found the presiding genius seated in her accustomed place by the fire, knitting in hand. The dishes were washed and put away, the dogs curled up in their respective corners. A few sods glowed on the hearth and cast a mellow, subdued light on the yellow walls and the ancient painted presses. An old clock, long past its work, stood in one corner, and opposite it was Helena's rabbit-hutch. It was not a clean, cozy kitchen; no polished pewter or copper was ranged on the walls, no trim dresser, no flowers spoke for the taste of its inhabitant. Seen in the daylight it was a grimy, ill-kept den, admirably characteristic of its owner. But now the soft, warm light of the peats lent a charm to it, and the half-darkness covered charitably the more noticeable defects.

Cawth's white cap and wrinkled countenance, her red and gray shawl, and the bright gleam of her needles, might have attracted a painter's eye. She glanced up as Helena entered, and stooping pulled out from beside her own chair a three-legged stool which she pushed across the hearth. She evidently bore no malice for the ante-prandial scene. Occurrences of the sort were no novelty in that house.

"Why didn't ye go wi' the Perrys out to Ballycormack?" asked Cawth, looking cunningly across at the girl.

"Pah! It's the dispensary day at the village, and the doctor was to come back that road."

Miss Ferrard's short lip was curled with disdain.

"They're losin' time wi' Cartan," said the old woman with a grin of derision. "His brother is talkin' to Miss Sweeny of Cork for him; ay, an' she's three thoosan' pound. What a fule he'd be to take that trapesin', lang thing of Perry's; not but she's ower good for him," added Cawth the impartial—"a drucken, stupid cratur, drinkin' all day long."

Helena made no answer. She was in one of her reveries; her elbows on her knees, with her chin resting in both hands.

"She'll be settin' her cap for Satterthwaite, the Englishman; I'll warrant ye she has cheek enough, an' her fule o' a mother too, that niver has a penny of handlin'.* Perry niver lets her hev one farthin' to spend. Satterthwaite's a rich man. Ah!—terrible rich! A' them English be's rich. Much good may it do them! Really was callin' at the hotel to see him the day, an' Hollahan's

* "Handlin'" signifies the disbursement of moneys.

fro' the Castle stopped their carriage to lave cards, an' it plaze ye. Hech! they didna come sae gleg to call on huz; gin they hed, Clan wud hev set the dogs on 'em, sich trash! Really, the awd butter-factor—I kent his stall well in t' butter-market—an' madam, quare divel that she is. Satterthwaite has sent to Dublin for painters and builders, an' I ken what not, to put Rosslyne in order; and Cassidy is in fine rages wi' him that he's na gotten the job, the auld foosterin' fule. He's to bide wi' Blake at t' hotel till Rosslyne's ready for him. A fashous partic'lar deevil he is; mun hae a bawth every mornin' o's life. He'll hae somthin' the matter wi' him, I'm thinkin'. These English are aye raisin' a steer wi' their ways, as if they were niver to die—"

Helena nodded impatiently. She was waiting for a pause in the speech to say something.

"Cawth," she broke in, suddenly, "I want to know how to knit. Give over that stocking and teach me."

"To knet!" cried Cawth with a scornful laugh. "Ma word, Hel, you're jokin', seerly. What wad ye be doin' knettin'?"

"Give it here," said Hel, impatiently; and she took the gray stocking and needles from Cawth's hands—she, indeed, was too surprised to offer any resistance.

As soon as Helena had the implements in her fingers, she found her own impotence. Cawth grinned maliciously as she watched the clumsy efforts of the tyro.

"Hech! that's it! drap the stitches an' mek a hole; an' where's yer ball? Ay, Hel, ye'll do it awm seer."

Seeing that Helena paid her mocking no attention, she changed her humor and gave her some directions, by which guided the stiff, unused fingers found their proper places, and Helena, to her own delight, was able to make two or three stitches. She knit her brows and frowned, holding the needles as though they were iron bars; but determination won the day, and she mastered the first steps in a few minutes. Cawth went on talking while watching her.

"Blake sez he has got the fishin' of the river fro' Lord

Comerford, an' he's to put men to watch it; an' there's not an otter but he'll root out. He disna' believe it's otters takes the fish at a', an' he'll hev every one caught up to the assizes an' get the full penalty o' the law. Catch up that loop, Hel."

Hel's eyes lighted up with a strange gleam, and she half rose from her sitting posture, letting the knitting drop to the floor.

"Up to the assizes, Cawth! Oh! where's Char? Does he know?"

"He's awa' up at the billiard-room, I suppose; but he's goin' oot ta fish the night. He was sharpenin' the spear there afore dinner. I hearn him tell Dirty Davy to be round in time. He winna listen to ye, Hel."

Cawth spoke with a keen relish of the ill news she was relating.

Hel made no reply; she remained sitting still, and, to all appearance, calmly; but her heart was beating fast with terror and perplexity. She did not need Cawth's asseveration to tell her that Char would heed no warnings of hers. Isidor would stay at home—he always did whatever she wished; but opposition of any kind only intensified the sullen obstinacy of the other lad. And Satterthwaite had rented the fishing, and set men to watch it! "He looked like one who would keep his word too," thought Helena, with a dreary sigh, as the image of the Englishman's florid, handsome face, with the well-cut mouth and clear blue eyes, rose to her recollection. She seemed to hear the clear, quick sound of his voice, which alone seemed to express an activity and decision that contrasted strangely with the current tone of Darraghstown society. She felt sure Char would be caught; and if they caught him, he might use his knife. In a rage, Char stopped at nothing; and then—then who could tell what might happen?

Just then a tap was heard at the kitchen-door; it opened gently and the figure of a man presented itself. He noticed Helena's presence, and, as he entered, took off his old rabbit's-skin cap respectfully and stood well back in the shadow, his keen, bright blue eyes fixed inquiringly on Cawth.

Dirty Davy was one of the hangers-on to be found in every country town of Ireland—idle, dissipated, and good-for-nothing creatures—half clad and fed, and ready for any odd job that promises the minimum of work with the maximum of excitement in any shape or form. This particular specimen had attached himself to the Ferrards immediately on their arrival; and, as their new mode of living entailed some additional labor, Cawth was glad to have the aid of a "boy" to fetch and carry for her. Clan and Char found Davy of use in their nightly expeditions, whether to the river or the demesne. He was not one whit more trustworthy than his fellow-servant in the kitchen; but the Ferrards, with characteristic recklessness, never knew or cared how much or how little he told. This much we may be sure of, that every rabbit or hare bagged by Isidor and Helena became a score at least, and every trout Char took was magnified into a salmon; while, as for pheasants, Comerford Park never held the numbers alleged by Dirty Davy to be consumed in the Ferrard mansion. Cawth and he used to spend the greater part of the day sitting over the fire together, communing of the iniquities of their masters and the like kindred topics.

Helena, who seemed disturbed and anxious now, got up from her stool by the fire after a short time and went in search of Char. Neither he nor Isidor were to be found. She went into the parlor; her father had retired to his bedroom, and the wolf-dog was stretched before the embers in the grate. She put some fresh sods on from the heap that lay ready piled in a corner, and sat down to read until the return of the boys.

"Paul Clifford" kept her entranced for an hour or two. It was nearly eleven when the two lads came in. Char had lost some bets and was more sulky than usual. He snatched the candle from beside Helena and proceeded to search the corners of the room for some of his missing gear. This found, he struggled into a pair of water-proof boots that reached to his waist. She sat patient as he, with sundry grunts, fastened the straps that held them in their position. Then he took a couple of spears and held them in the light, examining them closely to see the condition of the points. Dirty Davy was fixing a lantern, by the glare of which the fish were to be attracted to the corner where the poachers, with their sharp spears poised, were in readiness to transfix their prey.

Helena sat brooding, watching the preparations. At last, as Char turned to leave the room, she rose with a movement so sudden and abrupt, letting the book fall on the floor unheeded, that Char and his attendant both looked round in surprise.

"Do you know," she spoke in a warning tone, "that Satterthwaite has set men to watch, and if any one's caught he will have them up—yes, up to the assizes?"

"It's a lie!" growled Char, defiantly. "Davy, come on with that lantern; have you no more candle than that bit?"

"It's not a lie!" put in Isidor, who was leaning against the mantel-piece, kicking the pieces or turf about. "I heard it, too; it's watched for three miles above the bridge."

"Who cares, then?" retorted Char. "Come down the garden till I get over the wall. Davy, mind the light, and give me that box of matches."

Then, taking his spears under his arm, Char led the way through the passage and out the back-door to the strip of waste at the back; picking his way cautiously among the cabbage-stumps and refuse which strewed the ground, he soon reached the low wall. Then he gave the spear to Isidor to hold, and scrambled noiselessly over. The moon was veiled by a little flying cloud for a moment, and a chill breeze swept the river in tiny, murmuring ripples. There was no one on the bridge or on the road opposite, and the cabin windows were all dark. Not a sound was there to be heard, save the rustle of the water-flags and the swirl of the eddies round the arches of the bridge. Dirty Davy, burdened with the lantern, jumped noiselessly on the damp grass; his bare feet awoke no echoes. Char snatched his spear down from his brother's hand and turned off without further parley, taking great clumsy strides in his fishing-boots, and splashing among the weed-grown pools by the edge.

Helena had stolen down to the wall and stood leaning on it, watching the departure of the poachers with a gloomy countenance. Suddenly, as if impelled by some uncontrollable impulse, she stooped forward and called after the retreating figure:

"Char! Char!—I say."

He turned round and strode back, sullen impatience in every move of his loose limbs. Helena seemed almost afraid as she saw him coming towards her. She repented her audacity and moved back a little and hesitated.

"What?" growled he in a fierce, impatient undertone.

"Oh, Char, will you mind the keepers? Satterthwaite has—"

But Helena was not allowed to finish the sentence. Char muttered a curse on her folly, and, flinging down his spear, set to scramble up the wall, vowing vengeance on her for making a fool of and delaying him. Isi seized Helena by the arm and hurried her off to the house, into which they bolted themselves securely, and the irate Char, baffled, picked up his spear and betook himself after Dirty Davy, who, hugging the lantern under his tattered coat, was stealing along under Perry's garden walls.

They kept their way in silence by the water-side, past the balustraded wall of the parish priest's pleasure-ground. Clematis branches just beginning to bud hung down nearly to the water-edge, and the smell of the March violets filled the damp night air. Char stepped cautiously among the stones. Then they came to an open piece which had to be crossed before reaching the upper bridge, where the Rack parted company with the Darragh and swept away to the left into Comerford demesne. This was perilous ground, for any straggler or belated countryman might easily see them crossing, and their appearance at that hour would certainly be looked on with suspicion. It was a dangerous time, for the new-comer Satterthwaite had offered a reward for information.

They halted under the corner of the garden wall and held counsel for a moment. Then Davy, handing the lantern to Char, crouched by the end wall and advanced stealthily until he gained the edge of the footpath. Then he stooped forward his head and looked, cautiously and long, up and down. There was no one stirring, and the long reach of high-road looked white and ghostly. So he crept back to report matters to his master, and, taking up the lantern again, they both stole cautiously and quickly to the desired shelter of the bridge. Here there was a dam to be crossed, no easy feat in the darkness, and with the consciousness that on one side lay a steep, rocky incline, down which the overflow rushed noisily, and on the other a dark, silent pool, concerning whose depth awful legends were in circulation; this was overshadowed by a couple of ash trees, whose dry, knotted branches clanked eerily in the breeze. Char stepped on the edge of the dam and drawing a long breath, braced himself, and in a couple of well-balanced strides reached the opposite bank. His companion preferred to grope his way on the incline beneath, and scrambled from one high stone to the other with difficulty. This feat accomplished, they had crossed the river, and the way lay now along the channel of the Rack; Char went first, stumbling in the darkness over the rocks overgrown with wet moss, now and again stepping into deep holes and splashing up mud and water at every stride. At last he quitted the water-side for the shelter of a high hedge, rounded a copse of larch and firs cautiously, for he dreaded an ambush, and at last, having put two good miles between him and the village, commenced his operations. He had not yet got over his ill-humor, and blundered viciously and at great expense of shoe-leather over the stones that obstructed the path, cursing them liberally as he did so.

Dirty Davy, with that keen sense peculiar to the lower animals and to inferiors, fully appreciating his master's humor, kept at a respectful distance; he was painfully conscious by experience of the Ferrard temper, which was indeed far more munificent and prompt of blows than words, so slunk along behind his master, stooping almost double to find the path and avoid, for the sake of his bare feet, the rough bowlders that strewed the way.

Char halted first and looked round angrily for his follower.

"Curse you! you slieveen, come here with that light."

Davy stumbled up, holding out the lantern and gasping energetically. Char snatched it roughly.

"Go on now, go on up there to that bend and watch. See!" he whispered, "look into the plantation. I think I feel the smell of a pipe." Then he plunged into the water knee-deep, holding the lantern in one hand and in the other the spear poised in readiness to his shoulder.

Davy quickly scrambled up the bank and down the other side into a field. Once out of sight and sound of his master, his behavior seemed rather unaccountable. First he threw himself full length on the grass and remained thus prone for a breathing-while; then he got up and shook his head and stamped on the ground, letting off the while a voluble monologue of curses deep and earnest. Again he lay down in an easy posture, and again after a short interval rose. Having relieved his mind by these exercises, he shuffled off towards the fir plantation indicated by Char.

How he employed himself there for the space of a full hour must remain a mystery forever; but at the end of that time he groped his way back to where Char had taken up his position on the edge of a pool famed among the fishers, legal and other, of Darraghstown as a haunt of the salmon. One fine seven-pounder lay gleaming on the bank, the wound fresh bleeding in its neck showing where the spear had passed.

"Whew!" said Davy in an exulting whisper, passing his finger through the gill and lifting the prize to feel the weight. Then he cut a switch from a pollard willow near at hand, peeled it carefully and ran it through the fish's head artistically. Char, in somewhat better humor, looked on half approvingly.

He was kneeling now on the extreme edge of a flat rock, which, covered with about half a foot of water, projected over the deep pool. Leaning forward as much as he dared, he searched with keen and skilled eyes in the circle of water lighted by the torch for the infatuated victims lured by the glare from the dark recesses of the pool. Davy lay on the bank shivering, for the night was cold, and hoping that the sportsman would be contented when he had taken the second fish. Suddenly Char made a deft move back. His right hand rose to the level of his shoulder, remained poised a second, then a swift downward dart! The sharp point of the steel flashed a second; the next, a smothered cry, a loud splash! Char had overbalanced himself and fallen into Morty's Hole. The lantern rolled off with a crash and sunk too.

"Mother iv marcies!" shrieked Davy, exuberant always of emotion, flinging himself down to the rock.

But in a moment Char, a practiced swimmer, sprang on to it again, spluttering wrathfully at his heedless follower, whose ill-considered outburst might have brought the watchers upon them.

"Whisht! whisht!" suddenly cried Davy. "Oh, be gob, Char! I hear them!"

Char held out his hand, and both paused a second in breathless attention. Sure enough, they could hear regular and stealthy footsteps approach. Char grasped an overhanging branch and was across the dyke in an instant. Davy made a rush for the salmon lying behind them, and was just in time to see, as he grasped it, the head of a keeper on the other side of the bank. With a yell of real or simulated terror he dashed down the stream. Char was half a field off already. The watcher leisurely looked after his flying figure.

"Musha! then, betther you wor in your bed, Mr. Ferrard. Anyhow 'tis tin shillin's to me!" he muttered.

Then he looked about to see if the fugitives had forgotten anything. He could find nothing. The lantern was at the bottom of Morty's Hole, where it furnished food for much wonder and speculation to the denizens, finned and other, of that usually peaceful retreat. Two days after a large salmon with a spear sticking in its back floated up and was taken at the weir a half mile below.

Satterthwaite was seated at his breakfast the fifth morning after his arrival in Darraghstown when the landlord entered, walking in a shuffling, hesitating way, and with an expression of mingled doubtfulness and cunning in his face.

"Beg pardon, sir. Thady Conlon's without, wanting to speak to you."

"Thady Conlon!" repeated Satterthwaite, laying down a letter he was engaged in reading. "Conlon! who's that, eh?"

"One of Lord Comerford's men, sir. About the salmon fishery he wants to see you."

"Send him in," said he, quickly. He divined from the early appearance of this messenger and the significant expression of Blake's face that something or another had occurred.

A tall, strongly-built fellow presented himself at the door in obedience to Satterthwaite's orders, and stood awkwardly shifting from one foot to the other and looking anywhere but in the direction of his eyes.

"Well, Conlon, what is this?"

"Watchin' the fishin' last night, yer honor, an'—an'—"

"You caught some of the poachers, say, did you?"

"Seen him, anyhow, your honor; but he got off."

"Got off as a matter of course," Satterthwaite said to himself. "Well," he went on aloud, "you saw him. Could you swear to him now?"

"Augh, bedad!" and here the keeper permitted himself a broad grin. "That 'ud be aisy enough, yer honor. Sure them Ferrards."

"Oh, ho! to be sure, Ferrards. Well, there's your half-sovereign. You can go."

The keeper, whose state of *malaise* seemed to vanish as soon as he got the piece of gold into his fingers, took himself off with profuse thanks, his rubicund visage lighted up by a broad grin. His employer rose and walked up and down the room in a fever of perplexity.

"This is a defiance!" he said to himself; "a defiance—nothing less! Am I to prosecute the young rogue or not? An ungracious task certainly; and considering everything, one likely to breed ill-will. There is the example to be considered. Example, indeed! If I put him in the Bridewell, that gypsy sister of his is capable of executing a *vendetta* upon me with her own fair hands. It's a pretty mess! I must only wink at it, I suppose. The only way out of the dilemma will be to make friends of the delinquents and give them the run of the river. How am I to manage this either? Miss Ferrard did not seem particularly amicably disposed the other night. If I cannot contrive it gracefully it would be better to leave it alone. These Irish devils! what a hornets' nest I have discovered!"

He was standing now by the window looking into the street, when there suddenly passed, walking in the middle of the roadway, the tall, slender figure of Miss Ferrard herself, dressed in black, and with the same broad-leaved hat slouched over her eyes. She looked neither to the right nor left, but held on her way by the high-road that led out past the chapel. He looked after her wonderingly. "If I could meet her," thought he, "get into conversation with her, I could—"

He was about to seize his hat which lay on a side-table when the thought flashed upon him that if the idlers in the street were to see him accost the young girl in that manner—nay, more, running after her thus, their curiosity and comments would be excited—country towns are all alike. So he laid down the hat unwillingly and returning to the window, looked after her again. Far away up the road he could still see the tall, dark figure moving along with firm, elastic steps. "How she gets over the ground!" thought he; "I shouldn't mind having her for a companion on a long walk." A bend in the road now hid her from his view. "I wonder what her eyes are like in daylight!" Then he remembered some business at Perry's, and started off to catch the lawyer before he set off for the day.

It was nearly eleven o'clock and some one was in the

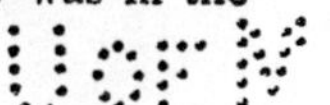

study with the attorney; so Satterthwaite, to his extreme annoyance, was forced to go into the drawing-room to wait for him. Here he found Mrs. Perry and her two eldest daughters sitting near the fire. They were all in morning costumes. Miss Perry wore an out-door coat buttoned up tight to her chin, and her fringe of hair had disappeared into a number of tiny curl-papers. They took his unexpected appearance with an absence of *gêne* which did honor to their sincerity, if it was slightly unflattering to him.

"Good-morning, Mr. Satterthwaite," said Mrs. Perry; "please excuse us, 'tis so early—we're not dressed yet. Mr. Perry's in the office with Jim Devereux—in one minute he'll be disengaged."

"I am fortunate to find him at home," said Satterthwaite. "I was afraid he would have gone to Ballycormack."

"No," replied the wife with a genuine sigh; "he'll be at home all day, so far as I know. Girls, did any of ye hear Mat ordered to get the gig?"

They replied in the negative. He was amused to see the depressed expression of their faces. Plainly the absence of Perry *père* was a desideratum with his family. In a few minutes the study and outer door banged. And then the lawyer's coarse voice was heard shouting:

"Julia—I say, Julia—damn ye!" roared he, "will ye answer me?"

Miss Eily slipped off her seat, after an instant's delay, to see whether the servant was disposed to obey her father's summons or not, and ran out.

"Who was that at the door, an' why the devil was not the name and message sent into me at once, you good-for-nothing imp?"

"He said he'd wait till you were done," whined Miss Eily. "'Tis Mr. Satterthwaite, an' he's in there."

The lawyer made no reply but banged into his office, prehaps to recover his equanimity before presenting himself before Mr. Satterthwaite. The ladies exchanged meaning looks.

"Devereux, wasn't it?" said Mrs. Perry, tremulously,

and blinking her weak eyes. "It's trespassers again I suppose."

Satterthwaite regretted sincerely that he had not had the presence of mind to insist on waiting for Perry on the pavement without. The lady of the house moved uneasily in her chair and looked uncomfortable and nervous. The girls were the same, but responded to his efforts to talk. He was sorry to have caused, however innocently, this domestic annoyance and resolved, if possible, never to enter the house again. Perry seemed a perfect Turk, though, indeed, these jelly fishes needed something of a powerful stimulus to keep them going.

Their amiable lord and sire marched in presently, high-colored and sonorous as ever; all traces of the disagreement had vanished.

"Come into the office," said he, leading the way without further ceremony.

Satterthwaite's business did not take long; when it was over he rose to go, but, as if moved by a sudden thought, said:

"Did you hear that one of the Ferrards was seen last night spearing salmon in Comerford, on my fishing? What am I to do? It's rather an unpleasant position to be in."

Satterthwaite had already made up his mind what to do, but he now took it into his head to ask Perry's advice, so that if his leniency came to be spoken of in Darraghstown, as he expected it to be, Perry, at least, would be on his side.

"I don't exactly like to—punish—" he said, hesitatingly and looking directly at the lawyer.

"I certainly would not advise you to do anything of the kind. I heard all about it. He ran off in one direction, and his factotum, Dirty Davy, grabbed the fish and made off in another—haw! haw! I think you'd best make friends with the young villains. You see"—this in an impressive tone—"the public feeling of the place is on their side; and yet, I swear, they are as bad as a gang of gypsies. In the same way everything is laid on them.

However, it can't last long now. Bruton was in there seeing the old man about a month ago. He had a slight attack of paralysis; but he says his life is not worth a day's purchase, and then the brood must scatter, for they'll have nothing at all when he drops. Oh no! I wouldn't make bad blood if I were you, at all. 'Tisn't worth while; and then, when you recollect who they are —the original lords of the soil—eh? and that sort of thing."

Satterthwaite nearly exploded with laughter at the tone in which Perry pronounced the latter part of his opinion, and the contemptuous expression of his face, as if he deemed it an impertinence on the part of one who merely owned the fishing to interfere with the *menus plaisirs* of these native nobles. His holding the public opinion of Darraghstown as a sort of threat over his head was also an amusing notion. However, he nodded gravely and replied:

"You are right, Mr. Perry, no doubt. The best thing I can do is to make the *amende honorable* for disturbing these young gentlemen last night. I shall make them free of the fishing, and invite them to join me. I am going out to Rosslyne now, and mean to go across to Darraghmore and have a look at the old place."

"Ay, Jim Devereux was here a minute ago. He drove off straight out. You'll find him there, and he will show you all over it. He lives in part of it himself. Remember to look at his colt. May I offer you the gig? I'm not wanting it."

Satterthwaite declined the gig; he had already ordered a vehicle at the hotel and returned thither to see if it was ready. Half an hour's time saw him mounted on a large, heavy outside-car, drawn by a fat, clumsy old mare that no urging could get beyond a deliberate half-trot. It was a lovely spring morning, and the air was fragrant with the breath of the spring flowers, the ditches shone with pale primrose-stars, the thorn was covered as with a fleece of snowy blossoms, and the soft, circinate fronds of the ferns were pushing their way from beneath the blackened, dry leaves of last year. Tufts of yellow daffodils broke the monotony of the level stretches of pasture, and the river, swelled by the rains, tore along foaming to the brim of its bed. The lambs were trying their young limbs in the meadows, and the birds sang from every bough and hedge. The distant mountains were overhung with clouds, and their outline seemed strangely distinct and clear. The buds were swelling, and a pale-green tinge seemed to grow everywhere one looked.

Satterthwaite found a pleasure in contemplating the wild landscape, naturally rich and struggling against neglect, sending out its waste strength in a lush, rank growth of grass and weeds. From the brambles that lined the roadway sprang long white suckers, and the tangled hedges seemed as if the chance nibblings of goats, and cows of perverse tastes, alone checked their exuberance. He passed a farm-steading here and there; the rain-washed walls and air of hideous neglect struck him with a painful sense of the contrast between them and the trim garden-embowered buildings of his native shire. Not a flower had he seen in all Darraghstown. Then he remembered Perry's opinion as to gardens and such accessories to country life, and laughed heartily.

"They require an example. The whole thing lies in imitation. They have no one to whom to look up to in these matters, in fact, to set the fashion. Those girls of his, in the same way, they want some one to keep them alive. What a life they have! They don't read, don't walk!—what can they employ their time with all day?"

He reached Rosslyne and put up his horse and car in time to escape a shower of rain. A body of workmen had come down from Dublin a few days before, and the work was progressing fast. The foreman undertook that in a fortnight the house would be inhabitable. The gardener from Comerford with a batch of assistants was working at the pleasure-ground and the fruit-garden at the back of the house, and Satterthwaite found ample employment for the next couple of hours overlooking and giving directions to his employés. Between three and

12

four he remembered his intended visit to Darraghmore, and ordering round the side-car once more drove off. As he rounded the approach he turned his head, and with a look of real pleasure in his face surveyed his new residence. Rosslyne looked charming against the background of blue sky and sunshine, the dark gray limestone house looked larger and more imposing. The wood was alive with birds. The jackdaws, dispossessed, were holding a court of appeal in the pine trees, whose dark green fingers pointed inexorably upwards. The thrushes almost drowned their hoarse clamor with the sweetest music, and the woodquests' cooing formed a melodious bass. At intervals he could hear the click, click of a mason's trowel, and the voices of the workmen in the grounds behind. There was a soft damp wind blowing, and the smell of the spring was heavy in it. Half-reluctantly, and promising himself to come earlier the next day, he drove out of the entrance gates, which he had to open for himself, into the long neglected boreen and down a gentle slope till the Ballycormack Road, broad and wide, lay before him; then homewards for a mile until the Brophystown Road, on which was the entrance of Darraghmore, opened on his left hand; he turned the horse then and drove on for a mile till a wide gap and a great wooden-barred gate presented itself at the right-hand side.

"This must be the place," said he, looking at it. On the other side of the gate was a cart-track through the grass, and a heap of grass and nettle-grown rubbish showed where a lodge had once been. Half of an old pier still stood at one side; all available stones had long ago been carted away. He got down again and opened the gate for his conveyance, then, having carefully shut it, mounted again and drove on, following the cart-track. He passed innumerable tree-stumps, marking where there had once been a double avenue of trees. Here and there a stray shrub, such as a laurel whose taste had defied the cows, and the broken remains of a fence indicated a plantation.

After twenty or thirty minutes he reached the lawn, and

drove straight up to the hall-door steps. These, of solid granite, had defied the neglect and ill-usage which was so plainly visible everywhere else. But the balustrade was broken off and lay a ruin among the weeds at the side. The hall-door was shut, and had evidently not been open for a long time, for the grass was growing in the chinks at the jambs; overhead was a square slab of marble on which was carved what had once been a bird. The head and wings were gone, and of the motto only a couple of broken letters remained. Satterthwaite could not decipher them. The windows were exactly in the condition described by the driver of the mail-cart, without a whole pane of glass in them. A monthly rose had climbed up to the second story and in at an empty casement there. Nor was it the only out-of-door visitor. The swallows darted in and out undisturbed, and there seemed to be a whole rookery among the chimney-pots.

Satterthwaite looked round and up and down in vain for a trace of human habitation, and marveled much where young Devereux had his quarters. At last he caught sight of a woman's head peering cautiously round the corner of the great rambling old building; he left his car and walked in her direction. On turning the corner he passed before reaching the door at which she stood two windows filled with geranium pots. He obeyed the directions she gave at his request, and after walking across a filthy farm-yard, opened a door in the gate and stepped through into the paddock.

"By Jupiter!" said Mr. Satterthwaite to himself when a full view of the scene lay before him. There were the Ferrards, Miss Helena and her younger brother, assisting Devereux in the breaking-in process now going on. A splendid young bay colt was trotting round the trio, shaking his head and tugging at the long rope by which his owner held him. On seeing the stranger, Devereux, who was in his shirt-sleeves, pulled up the horse and giving him in charge to young Ferrard, advanced to meet him.

Satterthwaite thought he had never seen a handsomer lad: he was tall and slight but had broad shoulders, from which rose a round, short neck, white under the rim of sunburn, below which the crushed collar and careless cravat had slipped. An old felt hat, tossed far back on his head, allowed a broad, smooth forehead to be seen, above which a crop of little fair curls clustered; wholesome red cheeks, well-cut features, and fine, open blue eyes, which met the Englishman's with a glance as honest and frank as his own.

"As handsome a fellow as ever I met," thought he, and he raised his hat. Devereux did the same.

"My neighbor, Mr. Devereux?" asked Mr. Satterthwaite.

"Yes. You are Mr. Satterthwaite from Rosslyne? I am glad to see you, sir." It was not with the tone of an equal that the young fellow replied to the greeting of the new-comer, but there was nothing whatever of servility in his voice or manner.

Helena's first impulse on seeing the owner of Rosslyne enter the field so unexpectedly had been to run off; but she quickly acknowledged to herself the futility of that proceeding, and drawing closer to Isidor stood still, her eyes fixed in expectation and terror on Satterthwaite's face; she felt certain he had come there to look for Char—to punish him—perhaps to take him prisoner.

"These English are so particular and strict," thought poor Hel.

Isi held the colt's head with both hands; his dark eyes fixed on his sister's face, ready for her commands, whatever they might be. He, too, was frightened, but was far more ready to fight than run away. However, this suspense did not last long. His short greeting to young Devereux over, the Englishman stepped forward to her, and with a pleasant look held out his hand. Hel, trembling all over from the sudden reaction, placed hers in it with a smile of relief.

Satterthwaite, who was only too glad to find his overtures of peace so well received, and who, noting her dark, troubled expression on seeing him, had anticipated a different reception, shook hands heartily enough; then turned to Isi, who, puzzled and at fault, was looking at her for his cue.

"This is your brother, of course?"

"Yes. My brother Isidor—Mr. Satterthwaite."

Without a word Isidor took off his hat, his back all the time turned to the stranger; then he began to lead the colt away up the field.

Satterthwaite turned to the farmer.

"I came, Mr. Devereux, to ask your permission to go through the house. You occupy a portion of it I believe?"

"Aye, to be sure you can; but, indeed, I don't know what you'll see. Is the stairs safe, Hel? You were up them last."

"Hel!" repeated Satterthwaite to himself, surprised and amused, a little shocked too to find Miss Ferrard and this good-looking young horse-breaker on such intimate terms.

"Safe enough," she answered, shortly. "Jim, are you going to let us see you leap him to-day?—do."

Another revelation! Satterthwaite was again astonished, and then laughed at himself for being so. Miss Ferrard was leisurely walking down the field after her brother. He looked after her admiringly; her dark beauty seemed absolutely radiant, and the blonde face of Devereux acted as a foil that intensified the deep rich hues of her southern charms.

"What do you think of my colt, sir?" asked the farmer.

"A splendid youngster. How old?"

"Three—over three. I am breaking him for Ballinasloe next autumn. A good jumping horse is always worth his money there; I got ninety for a beast not as good as him last year. He was my father's though, and Freney's mine." His eyes followed the movements of the horse with a glow of pride in them. "Come up here with him, Isi," he shouted.

Young Ferrard led up the horse, and Satterthwaite examined its points closely. His opinion was thoroughly favorable as to the animal's merits, and was given in a hearty, outspoken way that evidently won the favor of its owner.

"Come in now, sir, and we can go through the place.'

"Do you ride, Miss Ferrard?" said Satterthwaite to that young lady, was was walking beside him. Devereux was in front, carrying his coat on his arm; Isidor brought up the rear with Freney.

She turned round and laughed to her brother before answering.

"Whenever I get a chance; that's not often."

"Miss Perry rides, I believe," said Satterthwaite. He spoke in a tone which he purposely tried to render as unconcerned and unrestrained as possible, without being in the least condescending or free.

"Yes," she answered with a perceptible contempt in her voice; "an old garron. I'd as soon ride a chair."

"An old battey," grunted Isidor from behind. "Perry's always trying to sell it. He wanted Cartan to buy it."

Then these two young people, who seemed to be unusually cheerful and expansive, laughed merrily. Satterthwaite was puzzled what to make of them. For a moment the thought came into his head that they were defying him, and he stole a quick glance at Helena's face. Her lips were trembling; and though she laughed, her eyes had the softened light of tears in them. He felt sorry to the heart for her and admired her spirit at the same time. "Evidently," thought he, "this couple are not responsible for Master Char, the elder brother, and he seems to be a thorough-going young scamp, from all accounts. Poor girl! what an extraordinary, impossible position for her!"

He walked back with them into the stable-yard, and waited till Devereux had put up the colt again in his stall, then they went into the house. Devereux, who had put on his coat, led the way into a good-sized room on the ground-floor. This was whitewashed and earthen-floored like the common farm-house kitchens; a fire was burning on the hearth-stone, and a pot swinging from a chain hung over it; a dresser well laden with crockery-ware, plain deal chairs and tables, and a huge old clock composed the furniture of the place.

The servant-woman produced a loaf and butter from a cupboard in the wall, then she went into an adjoining room and returned with a jug of new milk. Her young master took out a key and unlocking a private store, brought forth a jar of whisky, which he proceeded to fill into the blown-glass tumblers. Satterthwaite, who was amused at the idea of drinking nearly a tumbler of potheen, entered a protest, and was desired by his host to help himself. He pushed, as he spoke, one of the glass tumblers in the direction of the boy Ferrard. Miss Helena had filled herself a glass of milk unaided by Devereux, who had seized the loaf and was cutting it in im mense slices.

"I've nothing better to offer you; we ate the last of the ham yesterday. Take a bit, Hel," said he, holding out a great piece to her on the point of his knife.

"What's that you're doing, sir? Oh, come now," said he, catching sight of the tumbler of milk Satterthwaite had filled out, "you mustn't turn your back on Home Rule that way. Take a little more into that," and he pushed the great jar hospitably in his guest's direction.

"Home Rule!" repeated Satterthwaite; "what does that mean?"

"Eh!" replied he; "we never drink a drop of 'the cratur' here now without drinking success to the cause, so we have got into the way of calling it by that name."

"I won't drink that toast, Mr. Devereux; you must excuse me." His host showed a brilliant set of teeth with a good-humored smile.

"We'll make you drink it yet, Mr. Satterthwaite," he said, "before we've done with you—eh, Hel?"

But Miss Hel had left her seat and was amusing herself with the caged linnet in the window. Her brother looked up with a scornful curl of his lip and muttered something, of which only one word—"humbug"—was said distinctly enough to reach their ears.

"Was this the kitchen of the old house?" Satterthwaite asked, looking round at the curiously vaulted ceiling and solid walls, in which iron doors, like those of some cooking apparatus, were inserted at intervals.

"No," replied Devereux; "this was the steward's room, and these are the old safes. There's not much in them now."

"You ought to have a ghost to complete the interest of the place."

"So there was a ghost, your honor," put in the servant-woman. "Lord Claude used to walk them passages regular, till Father Cleary—God rest his soul!—laid him; and that I seen him do with my own two eyes—said Mass on that very dresser."

"On that dresser!" cried the Englishman, astonished, looking at the piece of furniture in question, laden with willow-pattern plates, pitchers, and tea-pots.

"On that very dresser, sir," she repeated, emphatically. "And Misther Devereux paid tin pounds for that Mass. 'Twas rael hard to lay him, 'count of him bein' a—"

"Come along and see the house," broke in her master, impetuously cutting short the speech, which he feared would offend the stranger. "Biddy, did you give the pigs their dinner yet?"

There was a tone of rebuke in his words that Biddy evidently felt, for she left the corner where she was knitting and muttered some unintelligible answer as she moved the great three-legged pot in the chimney.

Miss Helena led the way into a passage, followed by Devereux and her brother. Satterthwaite lingered behind and put half a crown into Biddy's hand.

"Long life to your honor, anyhow!" said she, effusively. "And sure I hope I may meet you in heaven."

There was an accent of doubt, yet condescending goodwill, in the "I hope" that almost upset the donor's gravity. Biddy seemed a thorough fool of the pious, good-natured sort; her manner was perfectly respectful, however, as that of the most uncompromising Roman Catholic somehow always is to the liberal, well-dressed heretic. Satterthwaite laughed as he followed the party through the lower hall into the main building.

The old house was in a fearful state of wreck. The flooring had been for the most part torn up; the staircase was in ruin, and the explorers had to jump over yawning holes in the lobbies. The dining-room was the best preserved; a handsome oak ceiling and paneling still remained, and the chimney-piece was a fine specimen of carved black oak. There had been a conservatory once leading off a pretty room on the first landing, but it was a mere skeleton now, and a tank in the centre that no doubt had once held aquatic plants was filled with rubbish. It was melancholy to see the decay and neglect of everything. A dead vine hung still on the walls, and a monthly rose had climbed in at a deserted casement and shed its soft pink leaflets on the floor. The swallows had built their nests in the corners of the rooms, where they remained from last year; and the wind which swept through the deserted passages caught up and made little whirlwinds of the dust.

The Ferrards strolled about, looking at the ruin of what was their ancestral home with a sort of listless interest. Isi jerked bits of wood at the nests, and his sister plucked the monthly roses from their stem and fastened them in her dress.

"Let me help you," said Satterthwaite, taking out his penknife, for he saw she was scratching her fingers. He approached and stretched out his hand to take the branch.

"Never mind," she said, brusquely; and she snapped off the roses so roughly that a shower of pink petals fell on the floor.

"What a lovely view!" said he, quietly replacing his knife and affecting not to see the results of her self-will. "We have a view of the mountains at this side."

"Yes, I know—the Galtees."

Satterthwaite leaned out of the empty window—the sashes had long ago fallen out—and admired the wide stretch of plain, divided by the Darragh dashing tumultuously between its rocky banks.

"Is that wall, far over, the boundary between this and Comerford?"

"Yes. It's the boundary now, but it was the deer park; all Comerford, you know, belonged to Darraghmore once—yes, beyond the village. Cawth told me,—where's the use talking of it now!" And a flush mounted to her cheek as she turned away and stooped over the bunch of roses in her hand.

The spring sun shone in, lighting up her hair and gleaming in her eyes, and a faint pink shade from the flowers threw its reflection on her pale face. Satterthwaite thought he never saw any one more beautiful or interesting—almost pathetically so—at that moment. Then Devereux and Isidor came back; they had been to the upper rooms.

"It's here you are! I thought you had gone down, Mr. Satterthwaite. Hel! are we going to look for the rabbits to-day? you never fetched the dog as I bid you."

"No! Char has him down the river. Davey and he went out after breakfast.

"Fetch him on Friday then, mind."

"Do you hunt rabbits with a ferret?" said Satterthwaite to Devereux. "I shall have some ferrets at Rosslyne by the end of the week. The place is full of rabbits, and if you would care to have them, you can."

Then they all went down the stairs again and returned to the farm-kitchen. Satterthwaite looked at his watch; it was nearly five, then turned to Helena and said:

"I am going back to Darraghstown, Miss Ferrard; will you allow me to offer you a seat in my car? You had better," he continued, turning to Isi, "let me drive you and your sister home—we shall have rain immediately."

The boy made no answer, but looked at her. Helena seemed undecided what to do.

"Thank you," said she, hesitatingly; "we walked out—I think we can—we had better go back the same way—unless for a part of the road—"

Satterthwaite went on—he saw her objection: "It's a long way, you know, if it rains—six miles. I'll drop you on the bridge if you like."

They took their seats. She and her brother on one side, and Satterthwaite on the other.

"Good-bye," said Devereux. "I'll be glad enough of

the ferrets, my own are dead; and if you come over some day we'll show you how we do them. Hel, remember now—"

There was something in the tone in which this was pronounced that made Satterthwaite prick his ears and glance sharply at the other side of the car. They drove off through the demesne, the car jolting over the rough ground till the rickety springs creaked again. The high road was reached at last, and then their progress was smooth enough. The Ferrards were silent and moody Satterthwaite thought. Isidor leaned back, his chin sunk on his breast, and Helena seemed anxiously looking out for some one.

"Do you care for driving, Miss Ferrard?"

"No! not so much as riding, and I seldom get any of that unless Jim lets me on the colt. I used to ride, in Galway."

"I wonder," thought Satterthwaite, "would she ride my black if I had him here? We'll see about this when I get over the horses;" then, obeying a sudden impulse, he said to her:

"I shall have my horses very soon; there is one that would carry you nicely. Should you care to ride him sometimes?"

She turned and looked at him with eyes wide open, with wonder and pleased astonishment. "Oh! I should like it above all things," she cried; then a doubtful look succeeded the bright glow, and she seemed moody and overcast again.

The gray bank of clouds into which the sunset had melted now spread across the sky in a swift-flying, thick mantle. The mild air became close and oppressive, and the perfume from the hedge-rows was sickly in its heavy sweetness. The distant hills seemed nearer with that gray distinctness that always heralds rain, and the noise of the Rack at the foot of the slope sounded louder. He urged on the horse as fast as possible, dreading a downpour, for which the party were totally unprepared. Ere long they heard the dash of a horse behind them. It was the mail-car from Ballycormack, and in a very few minutes the old gray had overtaken and given them the go-by. Satterthwaite saw Thady the driver eye the off-side of his car with a stare of mingled wonder and amusement. Then he turned to him and roared above the clatter:

"Hurry, yer honor! we're in for it;" and as he spoke he held up his whip toward the sky. The old horse got the whip pretty severely, and by the time they reached the bridge there was a prospect of a speedy shelter ere the rain commenced in earnest, although the big drops had been chasing them for some minutes. Helena and her brother barely waited for the car to pull up ere they jumped off. What they meant Satterthwaite could not imagine, but instead of going home, they appeared to him as he drove on to be climbing down the bank to get under the arches of the bridge—a damp shelter truly. He passed the post-office on his way to the inn, and observed that the knot of idlers collected there stared at him with unusual interest. Doubtless Thady had related what he had seen—the Ferrards driving along the Ballycormack road on his car. This, taken in conjunction with the events of the previous night, seemed to them a most unaccountable proceeding. Satterthwaite chuckled to himself at their wonder.

"A little while and this will be forgotten," thought he; "certainly, I have no intention of punishing these poor children for what is no fault of theirs. I wonder if it will be necessary for me to carry any message to this troublesome Char Ferrard, or is it better to let things alone?"

He mused for a long time over the vexed question. It was plain enough that the Ferrards considered they had a right to help themselves, and the neighborhood in general seemed to favor the notion. As to that matter, Satterthwaite was not inclined, as may be imagined, to agree with them. Still he pitied the boy and girl, and for their sakes wrote that evening a courteous note to Charles Ferrard, to the effect that he, John Satterthwaite, Esq., of Rosslyne, would consider himself under an obligation to Mr. Ferrard, if the latter would avail himself whenever he chose of the privilege of fishing the Rack for five miles above the weir.

To this note Satterthwaite received no reply, and as the river police were instructed that the young Ferrards were to be left to enjoy their sport unmolested, he heard no more of the nightly depredations in Comerford.

A week elapsed and found Satterthwaite still at the hotel in Darraghstown. The Dublin tradesmen seemed to have taken a fancy to their job, and loitered over the work with that ingenuity of dilatoriness so characteristic of their class everywhere, but for which Irish workmen must be decreed the palm. As long as his eye was on them, spades or trowels, chisels or brushes were plied with an industry that exasperated Satterthwaite beyond endurance, for he knew perfectly that the moment his back was turned or his attention required elsewhere it would cease, and the fellows would laugh at him for a fool.

He had not seen the Ferrards since the afternoon on which he met them at the old house of Darraghmore; once, indeed, when riding out in the country he had a distant glimpse of Isidor and Helena, but they jumped over a ditch as soon as they perceived his approach, and since they chose to avoid him he had no other alternative but to ride on without noticing them. As soon as the gang of workmen left him free to devote a little time to other matters, he determined to return the visits paid him by the neighbors. The Reallys, of Buona Vista, claimed his attention first; and one soft, showery April day saw him mounted on his beautiful black horse, ascending the steep, winding avenue which, branching off the Ballycormack Road, led to their residence.

An entrance gate of oak-stained wood, ornamented by well-wrought iron clasps, was opened by a boy from the lodge and gave admission to a well-kept carriage-drive bordered with trees. Satterthwaite looked round approvingly, and Perry's description of the people of the house recurred to him. "'Mrs. Really was brought up abroad, and has a tongue like a knife.' Humph! whereabouts is the telescope, I wonder?" By this time he was at the hall-door, which stood open.

There was a glass porch filled with flowers. A servant appeared at this and led him into a low-ceilinged room, with three pointed windows commanding a full view of the town which lay at the foot of the hill and of the river-course eastward. A fire of wood and turf was burning in the grate, and the slightly acrid smell of the peat-smoke was mingled not unpleasantly with the perfume of a box of hyacinths in the window. A garden lay behind, bare as yet save for a few spring flowers. It was a sunny, bright aspect, and the buds on the fruit-trees were forward and promising.

Satterthwaite sat down and looked about him. "What a contrast to the Perrys' rooms!" thought he. "Is it the foreign training or the Protestantism that is to account for this?" he asked himself, looking at the books and handsome, but more curious than handsome, things that were scattered about. "In Austria they are all Catholics, so it can't be the mere religion or associations in that way." Over the piano hung an engraving of Ary Scheffer's "Dante and Beatrice." "It might have been worse," thought he, looking to another wall; there was the "Light of the World," lantern and all. He smiled and turned away to find himself confronted by "Dignity and Impudence" and the "Stag at Bay." "I wonder does madam read Browning. How does that first chapter of the 'Inn Album' run?

> "'On a sprig-pattern-papered wall there brays
> Complaint to sky Sir Edwin's dripping stag;
> His couchant coast-guard creature corresponds,
> They face the Huguenot and Light o' the World.

"That's it," went on Mr. Satterthwaite, when he had finished his quotation; "here we have it all, 'salubrious acclivity' to boot; but I had not expected this. What did I think to find either? I don't know, and yet I feel aggrieved."

He had no time for further meditation, for the door opened and the lady of the house entered. Satterthwaite looked in vain for some trait or expression of face to connect her with the gossiping description he had had from her neighbors below. A low, deep-lined forehead, close-set eyes of an indeterminate tawny hue, gray-besprinkled brown hair, and a brown but thoroughly healthy skin; the mouth large and full of energy and will. Her manner was good, and, to Satterthwaite's surprise, that of a woman accustomed to society. They exchanged a few formalities. Her bright eyes expressed all the time, as Satterthwaite could see, curiosity as to himself and a sort of wonder. Whether this last was complimentary or not he was in doubt. She sat down in the bay-window with her back to the light, and he, sitting opposite, could feel, rather than see, the half-satiric, half-expectant glance of her eyes upon him.

"Yes," he replied to an indirect question; "it is not the first time I have visited Ireland. I intend to take up my residence here now."

"Indeed! Permanently, may one ask?" There was an undercurrent of amused laughter in the words, demurely and politely as she uttered them. Then she picked up some bit of gay-colored wool-work from a mother-o'-pearl case beside her and commenced it leisurely.

"Yes, permanently—at least, I hope so. If I like it and find the hunting pleasant, I may be here six or eight months of every year."

"And you do like it so far, do you not?"

"Well, I have been so busy—my house is not yet inhabitable, and I have no experience as yet of the people or the place, so I can't say. It's pretty rainy, too."

"Yes, you can see the river from that window; how broad and full it is!"

Satterthwaite rose and went to a side window, from which there was a magnificent view eastward, and looked out. She followed him.

"I can see the whole town; it lies almost under our feet

at this side. You would never believe we were at such a height! Look, there are the Miss Perrys taking their usual walk."

Satterthwaite could see the four figures distinctly. They looked small, but still they were unmistakable.

"I know them," replied he; "I was at their house one evening. What a dull life they seem to have of it! And, by-the-bye, Mrs. Really, do you know their neighbor, Miss Ferrard?"

"Yes, yes," she replied quickly and looking up sharply at him, "I do know her. That's a very interesting young lady."

"Can you tell me anything of them? They are a most extraordinary family. People of title, and so situated!"

"I know her—of her rather. When they came here first my husband made me go down to that den of theirs to call. I shall not forget it in a hurry!" and she uttered a short, amused laugh. "A black-eyed boy opened the door and glared at me through a chink. He did not wait to hear what I had to say, but called out, 'Hoy, Cawth!' then an old woman came out—a frightful-looking crone—and clapped the door in my face, hallooing to the dogs as she did so; and as I drove off I caught a glimpse of Miss Ferrard and the young gentleman who had opened the door to me laughing at my discomfiture from a top window. I was forgiving enough to send her a message afterwards that she would be welcome to sit in my pew in church; but of this she took no notice."

Satterthwaite was silent for a moment, thinking over Mrs. Really's story and picturing to himself the scene she described—perfectly true in every particular, he had no doubt.

"You are interested in them I see," continued the lady, speaking rapidly. "Well, they must be new specimens for you. Don't think all the Irish aristocracy are like these creatures; though, for my part, I find these infinitely more—" she hesitated for a word, then finished, "amusing."

"Amusing!" he repeated, dubiously; "well, yes, it is

amusing, I suppose. But I feel very sorry for that girl and boy, but the girl in especial. Why, she is on the road to destruction! Could nothing be done for them? It is such a pity! and she's a fine creature!"

Madam looked scrutinizingly across her knitting at Satterthwaite and shrugged her shoulders.

"She's a beautiful girl, but untamable—quite untamable, I assure you."

"Mrs. Perry tells me," he went on, "that sisters of Lord Darraghmore who reside in Bath took her in hand; but she ran off home."

Madam Really laughed aloud with a sarcastic ring in her voice. Satterthwaite almost began to dislike her. "She was bitter," he thought, "cold-hearted and inquisitive. Still, busybodies are almost always good-natured —or, at least, officious; there is a distinction between the two, though the people do not always make it. The same feeling that prompts their interest in other people's affairs move them frequently to action in their behalf. Between speech and action there is not always the gulf people imagine," and he wondered madam did not show more kindly feeling to Helena Ferrard.

"Mrs. Fitz-Ffoulke also went to see them several times. She got in once, and the old man behaved rather nicely. She asked the girl to come to the glebe-house and take lessons from their governess; and she promised to get her a situation as companion or governess in England later. The old man seemed inclined to have the offer accepted; but not a word could Miss Hel be got to say in the matter, and Mrs. Fitz-Ffoulke was never allowed in again—in fact, the next time she went there one of the boys threatened to take her life for insulting his sister. She was not gifted with tact, poor lady, and I dare say spoke a little too plainly."

"I dare say," observed Satterthwaite, dryly. He felt angry and amused, too, at the idea of the rector's wife patronizing and no doubt lecturing Miss Helena. It was a wonder she ever left the house with whole bones!

Then the door opened and madam's husband, the exbutter-merchant, came in. He, too, was unlike the idea Perry's malevolent tongue had given Satterthwaite. About sixty years of age, with a weak, submissive expression of face and not too much brains, he yet was not altogether commonplace or unintelligent. They shook hands heartily and sat down. He spoke with a thick, indistinct pronunciation, vastly different from his wife's clear-cut accent. For a few minutes the conversation consisted of repetitions of what had gone before. Satterthwaite explained his motives, if he had any, in coming to Darraghstown, with whose undesirability as a place of residence they seemed both equally impressed, reminding him unpleasantly of the Perrys in that respect.

"You intend to break up the meadows at Rosslyne, I'm told," Really began, clasping a pair of large hard hands on his knees as he spoke.

"Yes; I intend to try farming. I have a fine farm in Bucks. Do you also disapprove of that plan?"

Really shook his head. "If you look sharp after your men you may do well. But I warn you the difficulty of getting laborers is tremendous. They won't do half the day's work your Englishmen will; and they want as high wages—and higher. An honest day's work is not to be had out of them. You can't take your eyes off them from beginning to end of the week." There was no doubting the sincerity of this—Really spoke with real feeling.

"It's the same with Irish servants everywhere. Any other kind think they are in some way bound to give value for their pay," Mrs. Really's sharp voice came in with an odd contrast. "They think work of any sort a disgrace. Positively I sometimes believe the Garden of Eden was situated in this country; nowhere else are they so faithful to the tradition that 'Labor is a curse—a disgrace.' Poverty is nothing so long as they can get on without *doing* anything. Their ideal is, as one of my servants expressed it, 'to live up in state—with her own pig, in her own cabin.' Think of it!" and Madam Really laughed heartily.

"Ah!" said her husband, "but do you remember that story of Teague Brian?"

"Oh yes, that was even better, more characteristic. We had a sort of job-worker to whitewash here recently, and he contrived to dirty the floor of a room so as to excite the wrath of our cook. She told him he should have brought his wife with him to scrub the floor and put things to rights. 'My wife!' cried Teague, indignantly, 'I'd have you to know my wife never went down on her knees in her life, barring it was to say her prayers, and I'm not the man that would make her. She never did such a thing as scrub since she was born.'"

"Biddy never got over that setting down," said Really, laughing loudly; "her pride was terribly wounded."

"I have brought my own servants with me," said Satterthwaite. "Can't bear strangers about me."

Just then a servant announced lunch, and they went into another room—a pretty, bay-windowed chamber with a lovely view of the river and Comerford wood.

"You have even a better aspect here than I have at Rosslyne," said Satterthwaite, standing at the window; "one could never get tired of that view."

"I do get tired of it though," said madam, who was carving a cold fowl with dexterity. "We don't spend more than half the year here usually; indeed, once May is out, I like to get off. I always like to be in London in June. I like the crowd and noise after this hermitage—the strange faces are a variety."

"I am sick of London; the people here are infinitely more interesting to me. They are not as witty as I expected, though."

"Come and take something to eat," said madam, indicating a chair at her right hand.

He sat down, inwardly comparing her handsomely, even tastefully, equipped table with the hideous squalor of the Perrys. A painted china pot in the centre held hyacinths, and slender specimen-glasses were filled with spring flowers. Pretty china and glass, and well prepared though simple food, gave evidence that madam's foreign up-bringing had not been lost upon her.

"Not as witty as you expected, Mr. Satterthwaite? What right had you to expect anything of the kind? You English always fancy that you can buy Irish wit as you buy Irish poplins or whisky. It is not so at all, and perhaps it is as well that the wretches have something left that they cannot sell. I don't know why it is you always expect fun and drollery from an Irishman, and moreover you are angry when you don't get it."

"I do plead guilty to being disappointed in my Jehu."

"There it is—you were disappointed;" she spoke petulantly; "now, what right had you to expect to get wit over and above the mileage in return for your shillings and sixpences? Money never yet bought wit. The historical Irishman has a great deal to answer for."

"What do you mean by the historical Irishman?"

"The Irishman that all you English have in their mind's eye! A wonderful, impossible animal, extinct, thank heaven, as the dodo, bare-footed and ragged, witty as Voltaire and philosophic as Plato, and ready for a consideration to shower his epigrams and reflections on your eager ears. I don't know who is responsible for it, the stage Irishman or the literary Irishman, but somebody is."

"First impressions are always lasting, Mrs. Really, but I allow they may be erroneous."

"True, true. Now I have a theory anent first impressions, and indeed I firmly believe in it. I do think that the cause of the decadence of the stage in these days is due to that pernicious and abominable system of taking young children to see pantomimes. At that stage of life first impressions are really lasting, and you give children ideas of monsters and monstrosities of all sorts in connection with the theatre that they never wholly loose in after life. They cannot disconnect their early ideas of something awful and impossible from the stage; instead of pictures of life they want images in the concrete of their nightmares; anything realistic is distasteful to them. I do wish that a theatrical pre-Raphaelitism might arise and sweep burlesque and extravagance off the face of the earth. They are the illegitimate offspring of pantomime—nothing else."

"I allow it would be a good riddance—"

"Riddance! when we were in London last spring we went to the theatres—I always do—and to see them presenting those odious old heathen gods and goddesses, as if human nature had gone out of fashion and we had got to be transcendental to that degree that the mere sight of our flesh and blood was distasteful to us under any circumstances—pah!"

"I could very well imagine your disgust, Mrs. Really; you are interested in human nature and you study it, whereas I don't study it or care about it one straw. No, I'm tired of that sort of thing."

She looked at him with a curious, undecipherable expression in her dark eyes, and said in a queer, constrained voice,

"I fear you are *blasé*, Mr. Satterthwaite."

"*Blasé*—I don't think I am, but I confess to being disillusioned. No more hock—what capital hock it is!"

"Yes, I never take anything else. My husband, as you see, won't follow my example."

The worthy Really, who was stolidly eating his luncheon, an occasional nod alone showing that he was attending to them, looked up.

"I don't know how anybody can drink those thin sour stuffs; they don't suit this climate at all. I would rather have Beamish and Crawford than a tun of that Hildesheimer. You should always drink the wines of the country, and that's what I do."

Satterthwaite rose to go. Madam Really accompanied him to the hall, and taking a garden-hat from a peg walked down to the lodge gate beside him. He dismissed the boy and led his horse.

"What a pretty creature that is," said she, admiring the glossy coat of his favorite. "You English do get the best of everything in this world."

"An Irish horse, eh, Mr. Satterthwaite?" asked Really with a laugh; "you'll allow us that one merit now?"

He was standing in the porch looking after them.

"Go in, Really—your rheumatism, you know," said madam, sharply.

He disappeared with an obedience that made Satterthwaite smile. They passed under two fine lime-trees; the bud-sheaths were swelling fast, and a sweet growing smell was exhaled from everything.

"My favorites are getting on—my lindens," said Madam Really, glancing upward with eyes that looked the brighter under the shade of the old hat.

"Lindens!" repeated Satterthwaite; "do you know Unter den Linden?"

"Yes!" she answered with a shrug and a quick, sharp look. "I know Berlin well."

They were at the lodge gate now; the boy held back the gate and they passed out. Satterthwaite pulled up Auster to take his leave of her. She stood a moment.

"I am going up the road a bit. Yes; don't be alarmed at my costume. Living in the backwoods has one recompense—you can dress how you like. I hope to see you again soon, and we'll have a chat over affairs in general, and these interesting Ferrards in particular, eh?"

The "eh" was "as sharp as a knife," and so was the glance the lady shot at him. He could not answer for a moment. She went on:

"I am interested in the Ferrards, Mr. Satterthwaite—greatly interested. They are characters. I've met some of the family before. Strange as it may sound to you, *Ober-Hauptmann* Claude von Ferrard was a—an acquaintance of mine in Vienna twenty or twenty-five years ago; so in fact I am a *friend* of theirs on that account."

"A friend of theirs!" repeated he, emphasizing the words and looking at her in astonishment at her speech, which seemed pregnant with a meaning far fuller than the mere words conveyed, and at her own looks, which were in truth odd enough. "Twenty or twenty-five years ago, Claude Ferrard was an acquaintance of mine in Vienna!" The words seemed to ring again in his ears.

Mrs. Really was looking up at him—for Satterthwaite had mounted his horse—and her lean brown face had a red glow in it; the dark, orange-flecked eyes seemed larger and more brilliant beneath the overhanging brim of the garden-hat. Her plain black dress was kilted up for a tramp through the mud—for it had been raining all the morning and the roads were soft—and she was pulling on a pair of wash-leather gloves, which in point of size and fit were to ordinary gloves what easy slippers are to dress-boots.

"Well, well," thought Satterthwaite, "who knows what dead and buried romance we have disturbed the ashes of now! Perhaps she only distrusts me. Does she mean this as a warning or a defiance? I can't make her out!"

"Yes," she answered, "I am interested in them too. Let me see you soon again, Mr. Satterthwaite; *auf Wiedersehn!*" and off she started.

"Yes, certainly. Good-bye, then, for to-day!" And black Auster set out at a smart trot.

His master turned him at the first cross-road he met and rode out into the country, not much caring where he went; for his only object was a ride, and all roads were alike, flowing with water and slush.

It was between four and five in the afternoon, a yellow, watery sun was shining in the west, and the rain-clouds of the forenoon were piled in a black, lowering mass, with huge wool-pack borders that looked like snow-clad mountain tops. The trees, wet and dripping, and with their resinous thick buds almost bursting, were gilded by the far-reaching, trembling fingers of the fast-declining sun. Over the bog eastwards hung a veil of creeping, shifting mist-wreaths, and the red pools were black and silver alternately as the shadows came and went. From the woods of Comerford the birds' voices rose in a jubilant, tuneful chorus; thrushes leading, and their yellow-beaked rivals, less musical but louder, almost drowning them sometimes. The woodquests flapped heavily across the open spaces between the trees, the slate-colored bodies showing clearly against the black tracery of the boughs; and a solitary magpie, bird's-nesting, uttered its hoarse, vindictive screech, as it sailed clumsily overhead.

Every moment the landscape changed; new lights, new shadows fell across it. The Galtees, purple and sullen-looking, stretched like a rampart across the north. Suddenly a breeze sprang up, the clouds stirred and parted, and there they lay bathed in gold. Then it was the Rack, winding like a broad leaden girdle round the woods; in a moment it was a running live stream of molten silver, which gave back the blue overhead and the flying mare's-tails, queerly mixed with pale-green alder branches, gray willow catkins, and here and there the scarlet-tipped head of a water-fowl.

Auster's legs were gray, not black, so splashed and draggled was he; and his rider, who seemed deep plunged in a brown study, roused himself to turn the animal's head homewards, when he caught sight of a horseman approaching at a walk far down the road. At first he thought it was Perry, and he allowed his horse to walk on slowly to meet him. But when he approached a little nearer he saw it was not the lawyer, but the dispensary doctor, Cartan, returning from a visit. Satterthwaite, thinking it would be hardly civil to ride off as soon as he discovered his mistake, drew his bridle and stood till he came up.

"Good-day, Doctor Cartan; I took you for our friend Perry in the distance."

"Perry never rides; he hasn't a horse equal to his weight. How are you, sir? I've been out on one of those cock-robin excursions of mine ten miles away. Lord help me!'

"On a what?" said Satterthwaite, turning his horse.

"Augh! You don't know. Faith, then, you're to be envied! A red-ticket call."

"Ah, indeed! Red tickets; that means no fee, eh?"

"That means no pay, and no thanks either. Ah! Mr. Satterthwaite, these are barbarians of people. I am going five miles round the other side of Tobergeen now to see a rich farmer's wife for the seventh time without a fee. They would do any thing with money before they'd give it to a doctor; and she is seriously ill, too. That's seventy miles without getting one penny. I'll send them a bill; but goodness knows if they'll ever give me half my money."

"What does that mean? Why don't you insist on your rightful due?"

"Where would be the use of that?" replied he, disconsolately. "Doyle is one of the poor-law guardians, and would only do me some mischief. Ah! you see, sir, they're so ignorant here. This very woman let one of her sons die of fever just out of pure neglect. 'They'll die or they'll get well, according to God's will,' and what is the use of the doctor? In fact, the general rule is to send for the priest when they see some extraordinary change in the sick person, and he usually orders the doctor; but, indeed, in too many cases, I'm no use. And look what they'll spend then at the funeral. That poor boy of Doyle's cost forty pounds to bury him."

"How did he cost that sum?" asked the listener in wonder.

"Oh! whisky chiefly. There was a rich farmer in Limerick when I was doing duty there last summer for a friend of mine, and his father-in-law was taken suddenly ill—stroke after stroke of apoplexy. Well, I told him the old man might hold out three days. 'Three days,' said he; 'that will just give time to get the whisky down from Dublin!' And he wrote off to Dublin for a hogshead on the spot. After all, he had to telegraph to them not to send it; for his father-in-law died that night, so of course they could not wait, and they had to get it at the nearest town."

"Is this practice general, Doctor Cartan?" asked Satterthwaite, after a shout of laughter at the matter-of-fact way in which the doctor related this story.

"Ay, it's the rule; but, indeed, the priests are doing their best to keep it down. Sixty gallons were used at the 'giving out' of the last funeral in Ballycormack. Ay," he went on, bitterly, "and a trifle of that cost might have saved the man's life. It is no use trying to get on with such savages; and then, if they take it into their numskulls that my treatment doesn't suit them, off they march to Bruton or MacSheehan and bring them in over my head."

"That is too bad, indeed! Dr. Cartan, I really feel for you." Satterthwaite had great difficulty in suppressing a smile.

"I'll cut it," Cartan continued in a savage tone. "I'll do anything rather than be lost here. They're nothing but barbarians and heathens—nothing. What sort of a place is it for a man to be losing the best of his days in? There's no society—nothing worth staying in it for. There's nothing doing but drinking!"

"Humph! the worst occupation a man could have."

"Well!"—this a shamefaced tone—"what else is there? Do you ever ride out this road? it's the best of the lot, the Dublin Road. I have to go off to this precious Madam Doyle's. I've a mind to put her to the expense of her own funeral. She gave her daughter eight hundred pounds fortune last year; and to hear her you wouldn't believe she could afford herself as much as one pill."

Satterthwaite was laughing so that he could hardly speak.

"Is it that she doesn't believe in doctors or medicine?"

"I don't know if it's that," replied Doctor Cartan, morosely. "All I know is she don't believe in paying me. It all goes by the will of God with them. They'll recover or they'll die according to that, without physic or physicians."

"Why, it's pure fatalism. It reminds me of the Peculiar People."

"Peculiar—oh, faith, I believe ye," replied the dispensary doctor. "They're only too damned peculiar—so they are."

Then he gave his old, worn-out nag a vicious blow of the whip, and set off, trotting heavily through the mud and water of the Dublin Road. Notwithstanding her unpleasant eccentricities, Satterthwaite felt almost sorry for Mrs. Doyle.

CHAPTER X.

"Car les histoires que i'emprunte ie les renvoye sur la conscience de ceulx de qui ie les prens. Les discours sont à moy, et se tiennent par la preuve de la raison, non de l'experience; chascun y peult joindre ses exemples; et qui n'en a point, qu'il ne laisse pas de croire qu'il en est assez, veu le nombre et variété des accidents. Aussi en l'estude que ie traite de nos moeurs et mouvements, les témoignages fabuleux, pourvu qu'ils soiyent possibles, y servent comme les vrais; advenu ou non advenu. Il y a des aucteurs desquels le fin, c'est dire les évènements; la mienne, si j'y savois arriver, seroit dire ce qui peult advenir." MONTAIGNE.

ABOUT a week after Satterthwaite's visit to Madam Really he was able to install himself in his new house. The last of the indoor workmen had been sent about his business, and two rooms were finished and inhabitable—the large sitting-room that overlooked the garden slope at the west side of the house, and which its owner elected to use as a library, and his own bedroom. The furniture was arriving every day in cases from Bristol and Dublin, and Satterthwaite had unceasing trouble about missing parcels. He started one fine day to walk into Darraghstown to inquire at the post-office about a case of books which had gone astray, and, after a long and rather agreeable walk, found himself opposite Madam Really's gate entrance just as that lady was driving out in her basket-phaeton.

"Mr. Satterthwaite!" she cried in a pleased voice, "is that you? I have not seen you about for an age. You have left the hotel?"

She had pulled up the pony and seemed inclined for a chat. He, not unwilling to humor her, stopped too.

"Yes; I am at home now—established in Rosslyne. I was going to the post-office to send a message by the mail-car to the station-master. One of my never-ending consignments has gone astray."

"I am going over to the station. Get in and I'll drive you across. They never do anything right at that post-office."

As she spoke, she stooped sideways and unbuttoned the apron of the phaeton. She had on yellow, gauntleted driving-gloves, and her old hat was tied securely under her chin. Satterthwaite could hardly resist a smile; however, he jumped in and took the vacant seat at her left hand.

"Drive, eh? No, no, I won't let you drive. Max understands me, and then I can talk to you at the same time. How are you getting on?"

"I am pretty well shaken down by this. It seems lonely up there, strange as that may sound, after the town."

"After the brilliancy and dissipation of Darraghstown, eh?" Mrs. Really laughed at him. "I hear wonderful tales of your house-furnishing. By-the-bye, has the parish priest called on you yet? He has come home."

"No. What sort of man is he? Can this be true, what Perry says, that his new chapel cost eleven thousand pounds?"

"Every penny," replied she; "and it is not completed yet. One of half that size and cost would have done very well."

"It is my opinion they wanted a school far more."

"Quite true," she replied, "if they'd only think so. They have the National School in a nice condition. The sister of the priest's servant is mistress of it."

"What about that, if she is qualified?"

"Yes, of course; but she is not—nothing of the sort. The boys' school is not quite so bad. An intermediate school is what is wanted. These people," she went on, pointing to the shops they were passing, "are able to afford a better class of instruction for their children, and it is a pity they should be obliged to send their children to the same school with those of mere laborers and paupers. The National system is utterly rotten and useless."

"The principle of it is sound, though; and as regards the mixture of different classes, I confess I do not see the evil of that. In my mind, it tends to soften the inequalities of rank, and begets a kinder fellow-feeling. I know in the village schools in Scotland the minister's sons often sit on the same bench with the barefooted village children."

"Ah, yes; but the minister's sons are learning classics, and fitting themselves for a university career at the very school where the poor children learn the three R's; that's just the difference, and that's what we want here. These children, poor or not, are all condemned to the same wretched, starved mental food; the consequences are plain to see. They go hand in hand in all their wild political schemes. They are all equally fool-hardy, because equally ignorant."

"I dare say you are right. That system of education must have a leveling-down effect."

"It has; but to my mind that is not the worst evil. Look at all the talent that is lost and wasted; it is positively incalculable. There is ——, the painter; he is abroad, and is very young, so perhaps you have never heard of him. An idle, bright little imp he used to be; one day in the Christian Brothers' school he was found caricaturing the teacher in his copy-book. This sketch was shown to the chief of the institution; he recognized the talent in it, and marched —— by the ear, and sorely against his will, into the drawing-class. The very first thing he ever tried to sell was appraised at fifty guineas!"

"I used to think that the reason that the Irish are so far behind us in art and literature was that all their intellectual energy ran to politics. The English think so, anyhow."

"They are wrong—utterly wrong. If the Irish get anything of a fair chance as regards education, they would soon be—equal to the Scotch, at any rate, and that is saying a good deal. Look at Foley, the sculptor; he belonged to this county, and I could name a dozen more to you. In Carmody's little crockery-shop we passed a few minutes ago is a girl of twenty who has a better and more thorough acquaintance with English literature than many a professor. It's a fact, I think she has Shakespeare at her fingers' ends, and every one of the dramatists since."

"Nonsense! where does she get the books?"

"Buys all that can be had cheap; and she has brothers and cousins in the Queen's University in Cork—these colleges, by the way, are doing a great deal of good—and gets from the library there all that she requires. I can tell you that she is not the only girl here that reads. You must not take those Perry wretches as typical of Irish women. There is a dress-maker who sits up all night reading Carlyle and other books. I believe, indeed, she borrows them from Mary Carmody. They both know history thoroughly."

"Especially the controversial points, I dare say," said Satterthwaite, beginning to laugh. "I have no doubt that the fact of this reading being prohibited is its special charm in their eyes. Why could they not be teachers?"

"The teachers are paid too badly, and it is not a respectable position; in consequence, it is only some one who can do nothing else that would take an ordinary village school like this. Certainly the dress-maker would be a better school-mistress than Miss Magrath, who does not know how to spell. Father Quaide is the patron, and he appointed the chapel clerk to the boys' school and Miss Magrath to the girls'. He rules education and society in Darraghstown as well as elsewhere."

"But the inspector?"

"The inspector is a good Roman Catholic, and he dines with Father Quaide every time he comes here. The whole thing is this, Mr. Satterthwaite: from the first, the priests disapproved of this system, and though they have practical control over it almost all over the country, and have made it quasi-denominational, they will not rest until it is fully so."

"And fully so it never will be; the Government will never suffer it. What the priests want is to get the money into their hands. The idea of handing over the country to ultramontanism and rebellion!"

"There you go," said she, tartly. "The old stock bogy—brass money, wooden shoes, and popery. I did think you had more sense. What do these people know or care about the Pope? just as little as for the Queen; indeed, for that matter they know and see as much of him. The Government has no right to prescribe their education and religion for them, or, since they must have religious education, what complexion it is to take. You allow Scotland liberty in the matter, why not Ireland too? Extend the Act of 1870 to this country; let them have school-boards."

"You think that would settle the matter, eh? But you know the school-boards would be under the thumb of the priests all the same."

"There—begging the question again! If they like to have his thumb upon them, what is it to anybody but themselves? I as a Protestant am not arguing in favor of Papal endowment, you may be sure, but I think the Government is in a false position when it takes on itself the paternal duty of forcing a nation to accept an uncongenial and lop-sided system of this sort. Yet, if it is to remain unchanged, let the Government be true to its own principles and compel them to accept it. The Christian Brothers' schools flourish at the Government's expense; the system is secular, yet the priests are given the control and patronage of the schools."

"Froude was right," said Satterthwaite; "the failure here is due altogether to the Government; they make laws and regulations, and wink at those who break through them."

"I would approve of school-boards on this principle," said Mrs. Really, "that, like the ballot, the very process of election would be a sort of education for these people."

"How about the funds? They are too poor to keep up a school-board in this district. Could they afford it?"

"If they were, the Purgatory rent would be a little diminished perhaps. Look at Mrs. Dwyer's funeral; the priests got forty-five pounds for burying a good, worthy woman. If it cost all that to get her into heaven, how will it fare with the poorer sinners hereabouts? The Harrington's case was the same. When old Harrington died the son went to see the priest and told him he had strong aversion to the burial offerings as they were usually carried out, and asked the priest to forego the usual collection at the house and name a sum equivalent, which he undertook to pay. The priest refused, and the collection was made in this wise: The coffin was carried on men's shoulders out of the house to the nearest cross-roads, and then laid on the ground; the priest stood at the head, and the principal parishioners were grouped round, so as to leave a narrow passage between them and the coffin; up this narrow passage the whole assembly were made to pass, and each person deposited his offering on the coffin-lid, whence the parish priest removed it. When the last penny had been bestowed, the priest pocketed the sum total, and the funeral *cortége* was allowed to advance."

"Why, Mrs. Really, they are worse here than in Naples or Madrid! What sinful imposition!"

"Perhaps so, Mr. Satterthwaite, but I like it; I assure you I can't help almost loving these wretches for that very thing. What would five or ten shillings or a pound be to you—to me perhaps? But remember when these poverty-stricken wretches give that much money, what real hardships and privation it means. The rent is behind-hand—the pig has to be sold, the new coat or new cloak be done without; often—very often—still greater self-denial is practiced. I declare, sometimes I think I would rather see them as they are than that they should become the calculating, selfish egotists that a wider culture might make them."

"I must say I find you a little inconsistent."

"Well, Mr. Satterthwaite, it's the six-guinea sherry and eighty-guinea horses, and moreover the nephews and cousins at Queen's University and Trinity College on the proceeds of the Purgatory rent that make me sometimes inconsistent."

"Oh dear, and do the priests send their own relations to Trinity and to the godless colleges?"

"They do, and they preach against them all the time. Quite recently the bishop declared in his pastoral that those who did not believe in denominational education were practically the same as those who denied the seven sacraments; and moreover they'll pass over the men they have educated themselves and give appointments in their own Catholic University to men educated in the godless colleges."

"It seems a hopeless case, but I have not a doubt that it must be confronted sometime, for the ignorance of these people is a perpetual danger."

"School-boards, properly certificated teachers, and compulsion—they'll thank you for it in the long run. And of this I am certain now, if the school system were placed in the people's hands to-morrow, you would not see the priests at the head of it; and if they were, what harm? They could even succeed if they would modify the present system, create intermediary schools with bursaries attached, and so connect the whole system with the universities. Open a career for the clever boys whom these Diocesan colleges are turning out head-centres and ignorant agitators. Open the door and see if they won't come in."

"And the priests will forbid them, and you will have the intermediate schools stand empty, as the Cork training school is empty."

"Tut-tut! that's because the priests won't give appointments to teachers trained there. This will be quite another affair. There's Jim Devereux; that fellow had brains, and his father had means enough to give him a profession; but of course Father Quaide forbade college training and selected a Diocesan college, where Jim wasted time and money for no better an education than the National School below could have given him. In point of education the boy has very little the advantage of one of his own cow-herds. How can the country improve when such is the case? It is improving as to wealth if you will. I know farmers worth from two to twenty thousand pounds, and you would not find a book in their houses."

Just now a trot was heard behind. Mrs. Really turned her head and saw the young farmer riding his fine colt. He passed the pony phaeton directly, taking off his hat in return to their salutation.

"What a handsome young fellow!" said Satterthwaite; "I never saw a finer face. He has a very winning manner too."

"What a dragoon he would make!" said Mrs. Really, looking admiringly at the tall, straight figure of the rider as he disappeared in the distance. "He and his people are not on the best of terms just now," she went on, with an odd change of tone, half confidential, half satirical. "The Sheahans of Ballybrophy Farm sent 'a message' at last Shrove-tide to old Devereux of Tobergeen. Their daughter Mary has twelve hundred pounds down, and that's quite a fine fortune—rather uncommon—so her people have signified that they consider our handsome young friend a suitable match. He, however, declined to have anything to do with it. And now Father Quaide has stepped in and seems likely to make trouble for Jim. How it will end I don't know. However, as soon as his sister's wedding comes off—and by-the-bye the Sheahans and their daughter are to be at the festival—Master Jim will have to decide the question; both families are anxious for the match."

"It's a regular *mariage de convenance*," said Satterthwaite, laughing.

"Something the same," assented Mrs. Really. "However, although money is the basis of operations, good looks are also taken into account. You would be greatly diverted if you heard the enumeration of a young woman's attractions. Beauty of some sort is indispensable; so many pounds or so many cows and pigs; after that a good complexion, or as they call it a 'clane skin,' ranks first of all, and so on; deformity of any kind on either side is a fatal objection, so is constitutional delicacy. A tendency to consumption, or as they call it 'thisickyness,' is also a hinderance."

"A very wise and proper thing too," he said; "it is to be wished that rule obtained everywhere."

"Yes, and I think it is owing to these customs that the people are so good-looking. You never meet any of the deformities or 'objects' to be seen in villages in England. Long ago here, before the famine, when there were more people, an old lady told me that for beauty of face and form the Greeks of old could not have surpassed the natives of this place. Even yet, though these very safeguards against deterioration are dying out, they are better looking than the average of poor village people."

"That is so. You see few ugly faces. But please finish about young Devereux."

"Oh yes. This message came one Sunday after Mass. A boy trotted across the fields to Tobergeen, and made known to the old couple the feelings of Miss Sheahan's parents. I must premise that Miss Sheahan had never yet seen her intended. The young fellow refused point-blank to hear one word of it. He refused to give a reason either for this unheard-of misconduct; so of course the matter was allowed to drop. Old Devereux made some excuse, and the old people on both sides hope to bring it on again."

"What has Devereux that he is considered a match?"

"He is an only son, and will have the two farms. His parents would give him Darraghmore at once—her money would stock it; or if he had another sister, would 'fortune her off,' as they say, to some fellow or other."

"The Sheahans' money, then, would be used in that way?"

"If you like to call it so. In reality it is buying off her interest in the family property. These creatures, benighted as they are, have got a notion of justice, and admit that their daughters have equal claims on them with their sons."

"That is quite right—in one sense at least."

"Yes; but there is another aspect of the case. If Mary Sheahan has twelve hundred pounds, she has also a very exalted notion of that fact, and the respect and consideration due to herself therefrom. She will be quite above working when she is Mrs. Devereux. She will keep a dairy-woman and a helper, and possibly one or even two servants as well. She will never enter her own dairy, and you can see what a deduction from the profits of the farm you must make for their wages and maintenance. I know farmers' wives hereabouts with hands whiter and softer than a countess's. All round this country-side there is only one farmer's wife who works about her own house and makes her butter for market. She is a Limerick woman, and she is greatly looked down upon by the others on account of that."

"They are very different from Scotch farmers' wives."

"They work hard, I know, and there's a vast difference between their produce and the Irish. It is the same thing all over the country. Anything for a living save—to work for it. Rich and poor have the one ambition; and as the mistress and master are, so are the servants too."

"How do the farmers procure servants? I thought they were very scarce."

"So they are; but you see, sooner than work and do without them, or with a smaller number, they take the plan of subletting cows and pasture for the season to the butter-factors. These provide servants, etc.; so all the trouble is taken off their hands. They have a clear income, and nothing to do."

"In short, these people who are clamoring for land so loudly are the very last who ought to be allowed to have it! They want to get an idle, lazy living out of it. It is all nonsense. Agriculture should not be the calling of the most idle, illiterate classes of society. It is far too important to the world. They think in this country that anybody can be a farmer—no education nor aptitude is required."

"Not any more than to teach the National Schools," said Mrs. Really, dryly. "Believe me, Mr. Satterthwaite, the beginning and the end, the cause and effect, all lie in this education of the nation. Look at Scotland, how all this senseless nonsense of separate nationality disappeared from among them. Their sensible, thorough education did that."

"Well, they won't have it, and don't want it here. Nobody understands what the Irish want, and they don't themselves. Now, Mrs. Really, can you tell me why the Land Act failed?"

"Look about you," she replied with a laugh; "look at that farm-house up there;" and she called his attention to an ugly, bleak, dilapidated house with tumble-down outhouses and ruinous-looking walls. "What compensation can that tenant claim for improvements when he is ejected? There are no improvements to be compensated for. And when there are improvements, the landlord is never deterred from evicting by any sum of claims, because—and this is a vital point—there are always plenty anxious to offer fines three and four times as high as the outgoing tenant's claims to get possession of the farm. You would laugh if you heard the sums they offer in that way. Their appetite for land is something abnormal, and must produce abnormal results."

"How do you account for that?"

"The habit of it first of all; and because there is scarcely any other investment for their money. No business speculations to tempt them. The grocers and publicans in the town behind us all intend to invest their savings in land. For that matter, Tobergeen Farm will soon be out of lease, and the man who keeps the post-office and crockery-shop has money and means to bid against old Devereux. Don't you mention that to anybody. My husband had it in confidence from Comerford's agent. The fellow has asked to get the preference, though the lease has two years to run. Yes, though they are great friends. If Devereux suspected that!"

"What treachery!" said Satterthwaite, disgusted.

"Yes, exactly. I should not wonder if old Devereux would shoot him. Men have been shot for less. Oh, they're a droll collection, I can tell you, here."

"Yes, truly," replied Satterthwaite. "You seem to know them all and all about them." He was amused at the notion of this sharp-eyed dame and her shrewd interest in all the village concerns. "One might fancy," thought he, "that she heard as well as saw through her big telescope."

"They interest me, and I do know them. I am a regular busybody, and love my neighbors and their concerns. By-the-bye, what has become of our pretty friend, that maid of the mill, eh?"

"Who? Oh, you mean Miss Ferrard."

"Oh, I forgot. I didn't finish about young Devereux, that handsome young fellow that went by above there," she went on after a slight pause. "I fancy—it may be only fancy—that he and she are *épris* of one another."

"Indeed!" said Satterthwaite in an altered voice: then he was silent for a moment, as if thinking of what she had said. He was not thinking of it in reality, he was trying to account for an odd, stunned feeling that had suddenly come over him. The news did not concern him in the least, so he told himself; and yet, in spite of himself, he was affected by it. Her face as he entered the paddock that day at Darraghmore, with its frightened, wild expression, seemed again before him. Still he said quietly:

"I am astonished. Are not you?"

"I think it nothing to be astonished at, indeed there's nothing unsuitable in it. He will be able to keep servants for her—what has she ever been accustomed to, a young gypsy?—and then it will be promotion for her."

"But, after all, that a creature like her should marry a mere farmer—a rustic like Devereux. Then her rank—"

"Rank!" madam laughed; "not at all. He is making the *mésalliance;* and Miss Ferrard is certainly a less civilized being, although infinitely more interesting and attractive, than Miss Sheahan. She has been brought up in a convent. There is as much contrast between them as there is between this animal," and she flicked her whip at a huge, old gray goose that barely waddled aside in time to escape from the wheels, "and one of the wild birds in the marshes beyond. Devereux is running a risk; he may find out that she is the undomestic animal I take her for. But *he* would have a good chance of taming her; if any one could, he is the one; as it is, he exercises a good influence over her and Isi."

"Poor things!" said Satterthwaite. "Mrs. Really, could nothing be done for them? That girl ought not to be lost as she is."

"I cannot see that she is lost, or what you mean by saying so. She is very beautiful; but that, Mr. Satterthwaite, is nothing so uncommon here. She is totally uneducated, so far as teaching goes, though, I believe, of late she has taken to study, and has given up rabbit-hunting and shooting. She is not specially talented in any way—none of the Ferrards are. She has fiery passions and an indomitable will, and whoever rules her will do it through her affections only. Woe betide him if he ever forfeits them!"

"She certainly is a wonderfully interesting creature. I can't believe she is not to be tamed."

"Did you ever hear of her Bath escapade?"

"Well, I got an accouht of it from Mrs. Perry, but—"

"I'll tell you the story," said Madam Really in a dry, sententious tone. "The two old ladies sent money for her outfit and passage to them. When I tell you she appeared there almost in rags, you can understand how their behests were obeyed. She remained, I think, a fortnight or so, then slipped off one morning quietly and got home here somehow or other. She couldn't and wouldn't be civilized. It is a terrible misfortune she was not a Roman Catholic. She would have been caught up long ago into a convent and Christianized. Now it is too late. Any attempt of the kind will end in disaster, mind you, to all concerned."

By this time they had got back to the avenue leading

up to Buona Vista. There was a steep hill to be climbed. Satterthwaite jumped out of the phaeton and, going to the pony's head, led him along.

"Fourteen miles; that's not bad for the little fellow," said he, patting the pony's neck.

"Oh, that's nothing for Max! We often do our twenty miles together."

The appearance at her side of an old woman clad in a blue-cloth cloak, the hood of which covered her head, prevented further conversation. Mrs. Really leaned forward to receive a whispered message.

"Yes, Susan; yes;—and wine? All right; I'll send it down to her."

The old woman clasped her hands together with an expression of gratitude, the fervid tones of which left little doubt of her sincerity, and passed on down the hill.

"That's a good old soul," said Mrs. Really, looking after her. "Do you see that blue cloak? Well, every Sunday four different women wear that cloak to Mass, going of course at different hours—four wretches poorer than herself."

"That's like St. Martin of Tours."

"You have little idea how good these creatures are to each other. It is really pure communism—what one has the rest have."

"Ah! that is what keeps them poor. I have not a bit of sympathy with that sort of thing."

"It keeps them poor. Yes, no doubt of it; but does it not show good-heartedness? I like it, though I see the bad side of it too; and I tell them of it; but 'Where's the good?' they always reply, till I've come to think the same for myself."

Then she turned in her gate, and Satterthwaite laughingly walked off home.

As he strode quickly along the high-road he revolved in his mind her talk about the Ferrards, "Helena," for so he always called the girl in his thoughts, and young Devereux. All things considered it was, no doubt, a suitable match. But there was something displeasing in it, nevertheless, to Mr. Satterthwaite. What business was it of his? he asked himself several times. At last he dismissed the subject from his thoughts and, lighting a cigar, began to walk faster. After a time the part of the road lying abreast of Darraghmore was reached. Late as it was Satterthwaite stood a moment to look at the old place. The April sun was drooping behind the wood at Rosslyne, a red blaze marking its decline. The river foamed and sparkled below, the willows, pale gray in the dull light, waved their budding boughs, almost caressing the turbid flood as it went. He leaned on the paling that guarded the steep bank and looked across to the ruined house. It was more desolate and eerie than ever—no sign of life was about; the cows had all been driven in, and not even a dog's bark awoke the echoes. The white line of the far-off road as it ascended a slope towards Tobergeen was clearly visible, and Satterthwaite's keen eyes soon discerned a black speck slowly creeping down it; nearer and nearer it came, and at last he could distinctly see that it was composed of a horse and man: the rider had dismounted and was leading his animal carefully down the steep incline.

Satterthwaite threw away the cigar and, pulling his hat down tighter on his head, started for home in good earnest.

CHAPTER XI.

"A pleasant ill is this disease of love,
And 'twere not ill to sketch its likeness thus:
When sharp cold spreads through all the æther clear,
And children seize a crystal icicle,
At first they firmly hold their new-found joy,
But in the end the melting mass nor cares
To slip away, nor is it good to keep;
So those that love, the self-same strong desire
Now leads to action, now to idleness."

SOPHOCLES (*Fragments*).

THE bright sun of a sweet spring morning shone into the mill-house, and through the two gable windows of Helena's room at the top of the house, lighting up the dingy red hangings of King William's couch, and displaying in strong contrast the gray dust-wreaths that choked its every cranny. It was a queer room, and the bright light seemed to set out its incongruities with double intensity. In the corners of the ceiling were cobwebs of every stage of antiquity and thickness. Long threads, as if for convenience of telegraphic communication, joined the settlements of each angle to one another, while cables and hawsers, which in some places were so numerous and interlaced that they reminded one of the rigging of a ship, depended downwards, and served the families for that aerial exercise so pleasing to spiders. Nor were spiders the only specimens of animal life. The ivy which grew in rank luxuriance up the walls outside and encircled the windows in a thick green training, furnished countless contributions of moths, and a goodly stock of the creatures classed under the comprehensive heading of creeping things; sparrows and rats sometimes were as familiar in Helena's room as in their own quarters without. Despite the sunlight which flooded the room and lit up every chink and cleft; despite the scented wind that poured unchecked through the wide, gaping windows and out at the open door, bringing with it a message from the primrose banks and daffodils in the fields across the river—the room had a dreary, ugly, depressing look. And Helena, who was sitting in a low chair in the window from which the river was to be seen, with a book open in her lap, seemed to have caught for a moment the forlorn, desolate expression of everything. Her arms were raised, and her head rested on the hands which were clasped behind it. Her eyes were straying far out over the landscape; but as they were full of tears, it is doubtful whether she saw any of the brightness or light there.

Helena's eyes saw only a winter landscape, passed away now four months ago. Tobergeen was white with snow, and Madam Really's cottage looked as black as a crow's nest above a huge drift. The Galtees were crowned with a cold diadem that flashed and trembled before her eyes. The river-path to Darraghmore had seven feet of snow-water on it, and Isi and she had scrambled along the dangerous high-road where the bramble and hedge-tops alone warned them from the gulleys where they would have sunk and smothered had they fallen. That was before Clan went, and Clan had been beating and bullying her and Isi (by way of farewell, possibly, for after that day they never saw him again); and they had run away out to Jim Devereux, their friend, for shelter and protection, at least until night.

Hel remembered that day well. The warm, half-dark kitchen where Jim was by himself nursing a sickly calf by the fire. Isi ran off with the dog after a hare, and Hel came in alone and sat down. He made her tell him the whole story. She could see his face redden and his eyes flash with anger; then he came over and seated himself beside her on the bench and wiped away the tears that were running down her cheeks; she could almost feel the gentle touch of his strong hand and the sweet breath that stirred her disheveled hair. They said nothing for a long time. Then he leaned forward a little, and looking straight and close into her face, said in a very low, trembling voice:

"Hel, unless you give me the right to interfere with Clan, I oughtn't to. You understand me, dear?"

"Yes."

"And—and—you do then?"

Hel did not answer at all, but the two faces came somehow nearer and nearer—neither knowing exactly how or why, and they kissed each other once. Then Devereux sat still beside her, both without speaking or needing to speak. How warm it was—the great fire glowed and blazed and lighted up the hams that festooned the ceiling, and the languid brown eyes of the sick calf stretched on a soft fragrant heap of hay. It looked up at Jim, Hel thought, as if it knew and loved him too. So they sat for a while; the ticking of the great old clock seemed as loud as a church bell in Helena's ears, and the whole place seemed for a moment transformed. Then Isi rushed in pell-mell with Rusty, who was yelping and leaping at the dead hare on his master's shoulder.

It was as if only yesterday—the snowy foot-prints on the floor that so soon melted into black, wet streaks—the bright flame of the fire shining in the wistful eyes of the little calf. Now it was far into April, Easter had come and gone, and it was mild and warm. The trees were fast putting on their summer garb. The fields were dotted with the yellow, waving tassels of the cowslip, and the grass was a deeper green and longer. Helena saw none of the rich promise of the summer; the long, undulating reaches of pasture, where the lambs were sporting in the sunshine; the river winding by, shining as clear and joyous as the blue, cloudless heaven that looked down upon it. She lay still, only clasping her fingers till the knuckles whitened, her mouth tight shut yet quivering, and the color coming and going in her cheeks, as of one in mortal terror.

"They'll do it!" she wailed aloud. "They will take him from me! Oh, what shall I do?" Then the great violet eyes, full already, overflowed and ran down her cheeks, and a deep, quick sob shook her chest. But a step made itself heard on the creaking stair without—a deliberate, heavy tread, accompanied by asthmatic groans. Helena with a spring like a cat was over to a basin of water, and was dipping her face in it and splashing industriously when Cawth entered.

"I'll mek yer bed the noo, Hel. Ay, ay"—she seemed to be taking up the thread of some previously dropped discussion, as she began pulling the bed-gear about—"Mary Devereux's weddin' 'ull settle our freen' Jim too; an' he may just as weel marry as not. Twal' hundred pound! my certy, auld Tom Devereux wu'n't let that gae by, and nayther will Father Quaide. He'll hae his bite out o't; and he's richt if the fules will let him. Ah! Father Quaide is just set up on this match too."

"Who told *you* that?" demanded Helena, imperiously, as she turned round a composed face, eyeing Cawth boldly.

"Hech!. must ye hae chapter an' verse eh? Speer at anybody in th' town. I gat it fra' a crony of Jim's mither's—Mrs. Carmody; 'twas she tell't me too Mrs. Fitz-Ffoulke was dead. Ay, an' what think ye o' this? Madam Really—that quare divil!—stopped her powney last nicht and went in to tell the news t' auld Judy Delaney. She's bothered, ye ken, and 'twas in the dark; so sez madam to the dochter, 'Tell yer mither fra' me her guid freen' Mrs. Fitz-Ffoulke is dead.' The dochter went over and bawled it into the auld one's ear, sittin' at the fire. 'Ayah!' sez she, 'dead, is she? Then she's blazin' in hell be this!' Madam by the door heard every word, and off wid her straight. I'll warran' Judy'll come short o' her tay an' wine noo, though Davy seen madam gae up the hill laffin' fit to be tied. Augh! she's a quare one!"

But Cawth, busy inside the great curtains, did not see that she was talking to the empty air. Helena had seized her hat from its nail, and was down in Isi's room, bidding him get ready to go out.

A few moments saw the pair climbing down the garden wall—for Helena of late had chosen that unobserved mode of egress—the sheltered river-path, rough and wet as it usually was, had at least the charm of utter privacy, and she was not compelled to pass the windows of the Perrys, who would be pretty sure to pounce out upon her, or perhaps intrude their unwelcome company upon her for as long a portion of her walk as their laziness would allow. Once, indeed, she and Isidor had played them a trick. The three grown-up ones had pushed themselves on the young Ferrards, and, out of pure idle inquisitiveness and love of excitement, insisted on going with them on a shooting expedition. Helena and Isi planned a piece of mischief, and with much talk of heron's feathers, wild duck's plumage, and such gay spoils, led the trio a ten-mile tramp through bog and mud, and finally sent them home tired, wet and dirty, and cheated. A long coolness ensued after this prank, and might have lasted forever so far as Helena was concerned; but the unstable Perrys came creeping back, and Hel—solitary, proud Hel—consented to endure them again.

"Come away up to Darraghmore," said Helena, as soon as she found herself standing on the soft river bank below the wall. "I'd like to get a word with Jim to-day."

"To-day! Then you won't. He's to go to Limerick about things for the wedding. Didn't you know?"

"I did not," she replied, mournfully; and she stood still a moment as if uncertain whether to go on or not.

What was the use of going if he were away? But to stay indoors with the weight that was crushing her seemed utterly impossible. The only rest from that would be in action; for it seemed as if something was gnawing and biting at her heart, and when she sat still, as she had done since breakfast-time, when Cawth brought in the news, she thought she should choke.

"Let us go anyhow," said she in a despairing tone. "We'll go to Rosslyne woods."

"What if Satterthwaite finds us?"

"No matter. I don't mind him; he's a good fellow, Isi, I think."

"Yes," answered Isi, cheerfully acquiescent; "we won't mind taking any of his rabbits then."

Helena did not reply. She had other and weightier matters than these fine courtesies to think of; and they set out on their journey in silence, as usual.

Isi and the dog found plenty of occupation and matter of observation as they went. It was the third week of April, and even the bleak country round Darraghstown had submitted to the spell of the enchanter Spring. The meadow grass was springing up tall and green; the hideous brown stalks of last year's mullein and wild tanzy were gone, and the red flowers of the early clover took their place. Everything was pushing and elbowing out into life, and it seemed if you shut your eyes for a moment as if you must see a change directly you re-opened them. The fruit-trees in Madam Really's orchard crowned the hill as with a pink and white snow-wreath. The hedges smelled sweetly of the primroses and the tender, resinous odor of the young shoots; tall, thin fern-fronds uncurled themselves and stretched up into the sun-light from beneath the brambles, in whose thickest recesses the nests of the thrushes and blackbirds were yet perilously visible. There had been a fleeting shower in the forenoon, and on every dock-leaf hung a jewel, and the ditches were nearly overflowing. The moss by the river-side was swollen like a sponge with the moisture, which ran out of it as the foot pressed it; and on the least provocation the willows and birches let fall a shower-bath of diamonds. Yet the sun was drying up everything fast. The stones along the river-path were white and dry, though they lay in little lakes of clear rain water; and the crows, busy among the newly-sprouted fields of potatoes, waded deliberately in soft mud.

Helena and Isidor had clearly no objections to the mud

and water, which to anybody else would have been an insuperable drawback to the river-path. Isi tramped through the dirtiest places, heedless of the stones, which Hel, with skirts tucked up, leaped on one after another.

The Darragh was fuller and darker of hue than usual —cinnamon-color almost, between its natural bog-tint and the clay washed down by the rain. Here and there, when dammed by stones and *débris*, the foam and bubbles had collected in great white bells that contrasted strangely in relief with the dark stream hurrying by.

"There's where we got the otter; look, Hel!" said the boy, throwing a stone across at a rank tuft of weeds on the opposite bank—"a splendid skin; Char says he will get perhaps fifteen shillings for it."

Hel only cast a careless glance at the weed-tuft. Two yellow wagtails flew out, trembling, and perched not far off in the shadow of an ivy-grown bowlder. The creatures looked like little living sunbeams, palpitating and watching. Isidor, a veritable *frondeur*, stooped for another stone. Rusty, who was at his heels, watched the act with an uninterested air, as of one despising such trivialities. The sunbeams flew apart, and the stone rebounded off the rock and startled an old water-rat, who was taking his pleasure on a fallen tree stump, into the stream. The little black speck soon vanished into the shelter of its hole. Isi waited a few minutes, but the water-rat did not re-appear, and he followed his sister, who, preoccupied and listless, had got considerably in advance.

"You mightn't splash me so," said she, petulantly. He was walking heavily in huge boots through the mud beside her.

"Very well," replied he, obediently, taking the other side of the path—if, indeed, it deserved that name; in reality it was only a sheep-walk—and they went on for a while without speaking.

Isi and the dog found endless matter for observation. Now it was a nest with a callow brood that opened their mouths and chirped hungrily at the rustle of the branches disturbed by the travelers; or it was a corn-crake, so near that he could almost put his hand on it; or three larks up at once singing in sweet concert in the clouds. Now and again a bird would dart shrieking from the bramble hedges beside them, the wild terror of the poor thing betraying her treasure. Helena never turned her head. All the exclamations of Isi, or Rusty's short, sympathizing yelps, left her unmoved and unheeding.

They had crossed a little bridge at the boundary of the demesne now. Darraghmore lay about a mile to the right across the pastures. The old house was rain-soaked and more desolate-looking than ever; the sunshine seemed to have overlooked the dead-gray walls, and the empty windows gave it a drear, weird look. It was a blot on the bright spring landscape. Helena seated herself on an uprooted tree-stem, and turning to her brother said:

"Go up to the house; if he is not there perhaps he has left a message. But don't let Biddy know I'm here."

She remained brooding beside the river to wait the return of her messenger. Isi set off with long strides through the meadow grass; Helena watched his diminishing figure with heavy, anxious eyes.

"He won't be there, I know. Oh God! what am I to do? how am I to bear it?" Then tears came again to poor, wild Hel's relief, and she sobbed and cried bitterly. Rusty, who had elected to remain with her, came and laid his sympathizing brown head in her lap, but she pushed him aside, and he, finding his overtures unwelcome, went and lay down at a distance, looking at her now and again in troubled wonder. Presently she looked up and saw Isi running fast through the fields back to her.

"Could—no—if Jim were there he would come himself. But why is Isi running so fast? He has a message certainly."

She sat still watching him, and when he came near enough for her to see his face she jumped up and went to meet him.

He had a message, an envelope addressed to himself, and inclosing a folded sheet for her.

Her fingers trembled so that she could hardly hold it,

and her eyes were dimmed with tears, but the round, clear writing was plain enough. Helena with a beating heart read the following:

"My Dear Helena,

"I have to go to Limerick this morning early, about things for Mary's wedding—so I can't be at home till the day after to-morrow. You are invited to the wedding by my mother; Mary made her for my asking—so come. And it will give me pleasure to see you in our house, where I hope you will one day be altogether." (It seemed to Hel that she had not breathed that day until she read this sentence.) "Don't mind anything you hear, and bid Isi look to Freney for me. My dear Helena, with love, yours ever, J. Devereux."

"What does he say? What makes you squeeze it all up that way? Hel, eh, Hel?"

"You're to feed Freney; go away, Isi, and look after him; Jim says I'm to tell you—go."

Helena spoke slowly and distinctly, staring at him with eyes that to Isi seemed double their size.

"Biddy has the key to the corn-bin, and I suppose she'll have fed him. Am I to go back then—now?"

"Yes, and then go out by the entrance gate and meet me on the high-road."

He turned without a word and retraced his steps, and Helena sat down in the grass to smooth out the letter, which in the first paroxysm of delight she had pressed in her grasp till it was a shapeless, crumpled rag. She read it and re-read it slowly, tracing every word with her forefinger, and drawing deep breaths at every interval, then she folded it up carefully and hid it in her dress. Helena had a different face when she looked up; every trace of tears was gone, and the great blue eyes seemed to mirror the new lights and shadows they saw in the day. She pulled a head of red clover that was growing beside her and, plucking out the little florets one by one, bit off the end and sucked the honey out of the long pale tubelet; it was an old childish habit, and she did it in a mechanical, dreamy way, without knowing or caring why. Presently the dismembered head of the clover dropped in her lap, and she jumped up, looking about her eagerly. Rusty got up also and stared at her as if waiting for orders; Hel caught his amber eyes fixed on hers. "Come here, old boy," said she, remembering her past crossness to him.

He jumped upon her, trying to lick her face, and pawing and whimpering with delight. "The falling out of faithful friends renewal is of love;" Hel stooped her smooth pale cheek, and let the brute kiss it by way of atonement. Presently she thought of Isi and turned to look for him. He was standing at the corner of the house watching for her. She waved her handkerchief, and he walked away in the direction she had commanded; then she and the dog set off together by the river bank, and at a point farther down crossed a dam and got up the bank and on to the Ballycormack Road. Here in about an hour's time Isi joined her. They did not take the Rosslyne approach, but passed it by and after half an hour's walking found a broken paling which gave them admission at once to the woods.

"If Rusty isn't to course those things, we'd better keep hold of him, Hel," said Isi; and he took a leash out of his pocket and slipping it around the neck of the dog held him tight.

Helena never answered; she was walking on in front, her eyes dilated and her lips parted—drinking in the beauty and softness of the day in a sort of ecstasy. The new leaves of the chestnuts were spreading their soft, pale fingers to the sun, and their sheaths were dropping every now and then to the ground beside her, where they shone and glistened beside the tufts of long-stalked, wide-flowered primroses growing in wild profusion in the half-dark of the thickets.

Wood anemones were springing, and wild hyacinths were pushing up their little green clusters; dog violets with white, etiolated leaves clustered in the shadow of the trunks, and the ferns slowly unrolled their curled, hairy fronds. Pink catkins hung yet on the pine branches here and there among tiny, hard, green cones, and a fresh aromatic air distilled itself from the young growth all round.

Presently they reached an open place where the surface seemed curiously broken and uneven, and the grass was as short and close as if sheep had eaten it down.

"Stand back a minute, Hel, and you'll see them; do, it's worth while," whispered Isi, pulling her back as he spoke. She obeyed, and they remained leaning against a larch tree and watching; Rusty advanced his head too, and, with his ears cocked, watched intently. Presently a little faint ripple seemed to pass over the face of the open ground—pop-pop! one head, then another, then all the long ears appeared, and at last out came their owners boldly, big and little, tawny, pale gray, of every shade up to black, and with cautious, frightened looks from their soft brown eyes the rabbits began their capers. Some sat up gravely and demurely, but in the majority of instances the white tails were oftener higher than their ears as they frolicked over the grass. Helena stood watching them, careful not to stir and holding one of the dog's ears in her hand—a signal he well understood.

Crack, crack! and then immediately another crack, crack! four barrels while one could breathe. Helena leaped with fright, and the dog yelped and strained at the leash when he saw Satterthwaite, having fired both his guns, advance to pick up the dead. He gave the *coup de grâce* with the stock of his gun to a couple of kicking bunneys, which had only been peppered and frightened too badly to get back, and collecting the creatures in a good handful by the hind legs, advanced to meet her.

"How do you do, Miss Ferrard?" said he, holding out his free hand; he had left the guns to a boy on the other side. "I am glad to see you out in this direction. You spoiled my sport nicely that time you came up first."

"Yes," said Isi; "I saw them just coming out, and we waited to look at them."

Satterthwaite glanced ever so slightly at the dog, and a trace of a smile lurked under his mustache.

"Come round to the foot of the slope and we'll may be get some more there. I have a field of spring wheat behind and they are playing the mischief with it."

"You should have a ferret and nets, that's how Jim Devereux does," said Isi, looking greedily at the two splendid breech-loaders the stable-boy was carrying.

"Take you one of them," said Satterthwaite; "and here, George, carry in those rabbits, and give me the other." The exchange was effected, and they crossed the now deserted feeding ground, and entered the wood again at the other side. "How is Lord Darraghmore?" said Satterthwaite, speaking directly to Helena. He was carrying his gun under his arm, and had fallen back a little so that he could look at her as she spoke.

Helena looked at him too with a mixture of shy wonder and approbation. The Englishman had on a gray shooting-suit that fitted perfectly yet easily to his broad shoulders, and showed his clean-cut, athletic limbs.

What a contrast between him and Isi in his rough, dirty coat, with his black elf-locks and lean, brown face, the chief feature of which was his wild-looking eyes that were keen as a hawk's but gentle at the same time. The Englishman, with his clean-shaved, wholesome face, fresh linen and general look of self-respecting, well-cared *bien aise*, physically and morally, was a new revelation to Helena. How different from Perry, with his unshorn chin and rusty old clothes, or Doctor Cartan, whose dirty smartness was still more objectionable. Jim Devereux was always well dressed and cleanly, but then Satterthwaite was English, and that made a difference. Jim was one of themselves, only much the best of them. Then Helena began to think of Jim, and felt stealthily for her letter. Merely to touch it with her fingers made her laugh for joy.

"Take care," said Satterthwaite, catching a branch which rebounded after Isi brushed carelessly against it, and holding it till she was safe past.

She looked up and thanked him with a glance. His cap, of gray stuff like his shooting-suit, had fallen backwards on his head; the flickering sun rays that came and went among the branches shone in his blue eyes, and lit up the changing tints of his auburn hair. He kept near her, a little in advance, and shielded her from the overhanging branches that threatened to bar their way. He got well scratched in the process, but he seemed not to mind them. He might have come off better had he not been so occupied with his companion. Helena was looking radiantly lovely. Her great eyes glowed and flashed under the shadow of her hat, and when a branch caught or pulled it off, leaving bare her rich, tangled locks, and showing the low, white forehead that the slouched hat so jealously hid, she laughed out with glee, till he asked himself in wonder, Could this be the same sulky gypsy he had seen that night at the Perrys?

Then they reached the field at the foot of the slope. Satterthwaite gave Isi a gun and cartridges, and sent him to the other side to lie *perdu* there till the little people should appear. Helena sat down on a felled tree stump behind a thicket of brambles, and Satterthwaite, who had just loaded his gun, seated himself at the far end on a fork. He remained quiet a moment, looking at her and pulling his mustache thoughtfully. Some crackle as of footsteps made itself heard suddenly.

"Hark!" said Satterthwaite, jumping up, "there is some one in the wood; I hear steps! George! is it you, George?" he shouted aloud, and ran up the slope into the labyrinth of tree-stems. After a fruitless search he returned.

"I heard a foot, I know; who can it be?"

They remained still listening, but no further sound broke the stillness. After a long pause he turned to her.

"Do you shoot?" he asked.

"No," answered Helena with a flush and a startled look; "I've helped with the ferrets, though, sometimes." This was said with a tone as if making some confession, and her eyes drooped with a pained look.

He pretended not to see it, but said rather hurriedly:

"My friends, Miss Seton and Mrs. Trelawney, of Malcombe Abbey, shoot. You know it's the fashion now in England for ladies to shoot. They have guns made specially for them, I assure you, and they almost always go out to see the men at work."

He felt that she was looking at him, but he kept his eyes steadfastly away from hers.

"I don't like it now," answered Helena, simply. "I used to, though."

"What do you like best—walking or riding?"

"I love riding; but I think I like best of all, after that, reading."

He almost started, then he dipped in his pocket and fetched out a little thick book—a pocket "Shakespeare" —in beautifully-clear diamond type, and handed it to her.

She opened it. Use had almost obliterated the name on the back.

"Yes, we have that; but it's a great big, old, torn one."

Hel did not think it necessary to tell him that the greater portion had been used to manufacture gun-wads by the discriminating Clanrickarde.

"Which of the plays do you prefer?"

"I can't understand them," answered Hel, candidly. "That one about the fairies I liked best. You know they say we have fairies here. That was a fort up where the rabbits are, and over there in the middle of that field is another. I don't believe in it, you know," she added.

"You don't believe in them, I am sure," said Satterthwaite. "That fort won't be long there; I am going to have it plowed next autumn."

"Oh, don't do that! Something will happen to you; the good people will be revenged in some terrible way."

The earnestness of her tone made him laugh.

"Ah, indeed! What will they do?—She doesn't believe in them and she's afraid of them," thought he with an inward laugh. "Well, there are plenty such unbelievers in the world."

"Take away the butter from the cows, or send distemper or trouble! It's considered very dangerous—"

"The Irish fairies are more malignant than Shakespeare's, then?"

"Dirty Davy's brother ploughed up a fairy hill one day, and," Helena went on in an impressive tone, "the horse fell dead when he had finished the last furrow."

"Humph! see, there are our friends. Wait till I get a bead drawn on some of those big fellows. St!—"

Then again the reports from both sides of the field rang through the air and echoed with a rattle among the trees.

"Four," said Satterthwaite, laying the creatures beside the log. "Your brother is a good shot, Miss Ferrard."

"Yes," replied Hel in an exulting tone; "he can hit a swallow on the wing."

"I wish he'd come up here and help me to keep down these plagues. There! I've had enough of them for to-day," and, as he spoke, he laid the gun against the log and settled himself lazily and comfortably, leaning on one elbow at a little distance from her.

"What in the world has come to her?" thought he. "She positively looks happy and is almost talkative—almost, for it is clearly an unusual burst. What a perfect child it is!—You like the country?" he said aloud, catching the backward sweep of her eyes, which she had turned heavenwards to search for a lark, whose sweet song reached them, dropping in broken snatches from the white edge of a tiny cloud.

"Yes," she replied, dreamily.

"You would like to live in the country always?"

She answered him with a look only.

"To live here always? Well, not here — near it though?"

"Near it—near here." The words sank in her strangely, and she turned and looked at him with suspicion in her eyes, and something of terror too. Satterthwaite's met hers, and a hot burning flush spread over her cheeks and forehead. Involuntarily she felt for her letter: could it have fallen and betrayed her? No, it was safe. Then her mood changed, and a look of distrust and reserve took the place of the calm, hopeful brightness. She turned half away petulantly, then got up as if to go.

"Don't go, pray—are you tired?" he said, jumping up

too. He repented his all too successful *ruse* now, and was as displeased with its result as she was.

"You must come to the house—do. I'll whistle to your brother across there to follow us."

"I don't think we can," she said, moodily. "There is your book—take it, please."

"Well, come round this way and I can let you out at the gates. It will save you going back through the woods."

He took the book as he spoke and put it back in his pocket, then he shouldered the gun and, taking up the rabbits, walked on as if nothing further was needed. Helena, half unwillingly, had nothing to do but follow. Isi joined them at the other side of the field, round which ran a wooded walk, and ten minutes' walking through a plantation brought them to the pleasure-ground at the west side of Rosslyne. Helena cast a look at the summer-house facing the pond, which had been cleaned out and deepened, as she passed. Satterthwaite looked straight before him, as if he saw nothing or remembered nothing. The slope had been laid out in terraces, and was planted with ornamental shrubs and spring-flowers. A quantity of hyacinths sent up a heavy, sweet smell, and little pink hepaticas and rich, dark wall-flowers were ranged in rows beside the walks.

"How do you like it?" said Satterthwaite. He had noticed her astonished look at everything, from the fine, many-colored gravel underfoot and the velvet-like grass edges to the sloping banks, up to the walls of the house.

"I—I like it," she replied, hesitatingly.

They soon reached the hall-door; but no inducement that he could offer would make her enter. Nevertheless, though she refused persistently, it was almost against her own inclination. She took stealthy, longing looks at the colored awnings and the bright, perfumed flowers, and, past these, at the gilt picture-frames, with here and there a glimpse of rows of well-bound books shining in the half-dark of the shaded rooms. Vague reminiscences of the house in Bath rose in her mind. Yet this was very different; there was restraint, and oppressiveness, and solitude; but here Satterthwaite seemed the incarnation of good-humor and careless sociability. Helena had never yet seen a disapproving look on his face; and it seemed almost incredible to her that wealth and refinement could be so pleasantly connected with the tastes and pleasures that had gone hand in hand with necessity and degradation in her case. He was so good-natured too—nearly as good-natured as Jim, Helena thought. Then it occurred to her that Jim might not like her to talk so freely to a stranger, and she felt as if she had done wrong in suffering herself to admire and almost covet Satterthwaite's luxuries.

"I wanted to show you some books," he said; "and if you would choose some that you would care to read, I could then have them sent down to you. I have a quantity—do come in and look at them."

"No—thank you. No—Isi, come."

"Take this one—you can send it back by your brother. I don't want it, I assure you," and Satterthwaite held out the tiny Shakespeare.

Hel's eyes looked longingly enough at it, but she hesitated. There was something so frank and re-assuring in his manner; there was not the slightest appearance of a desire either to bestow a favor or a condescension; neither was there, what is just as offensive, any effort at seeming equal, or less than equal, on his side. Satterthwaite knew with whom he had to deal, and his own clear and manly sense of what was exactly due to them and to himself prompted his words and manner.

"I—I—" then she held out her hand and took the little volume with a smile.

"Stay, Mr. Ferrard. Your half of the rabbits—you must not forget them. Jerry!" shouted Satterthwaite, "bring out those rabbits."

"I don't want them," said Isi, sulkily, putting his hands in his pockets and frowning: his eyes, however, sought Helena's inquiringly.

"Nonsense! what am I to do with them? You killed

half a dozen, anyhow; so here;" and Satterthwaite sorted out of the heap of gray things the boy had thrown down before them a fair share. Isi in reality had killed eight out of the fourteen. Helena turned away; and left to himself he took the bunch Satterthwaite handed him obediently.

"Now, come up again soon. I must get the ferrets to work at them one of these days. Devereux will lend me his, he says, and you must come up and bear a hand. They ate out all my cabbages in one night. I never saw a place so overrun as it is. Tell me, when may I expect you?"

"We can't come on Thursday," replied the boy; "we have to go to Mary Devereux's wedding."

Helena standing near drew a deep sigh as these words fell on her ear. Satterthwaite saw this, and watched her closely.

"Have you, indeed! I wish I were. This sort of weddings is great fun, I'm told." He was a little astonished at the intelligence, for he thought the Ferrards would have kept themselves above the mere rustics of the place, as he judged the Devereux to be.

"We're going because we know Jim so well,' said Isi, who was in a wonderfully confidential mood; "Hel and I. We never saw the others at all."

This seemed stranger still to Satterthwaite; however, he presently had ample leisure to think the matter over, for they went away, and he went in to take his lunch alone.

The library, his favorite room, commanded a lovely view of the sloping garden, and through a vista, cleverly cut in an angle, of the distant Galtees. The windows were open, and the majolica boxes of hyacinths on the sills perfumed the room, and almost drowned the cigar-smoke which its occupant was sending out in clouds. Lying back in a low smoking-chair, his long legs stretched in their lazy length, Satterthwaite went over in his own mind the events of the morning. "I wonder will they come back? The young fellow—how he eyed my gun!

and can't he shoot too!—is likely to. And what a savage princess that is! believes in fairies, and has read 'Midsummer Night's Dream.' I think, however, that Hans Christian Andersen would suit her better than my Shakespeare. Shall I ever see that again, and when?" Then he laughed, and blew a long curl of gray mist away from him. "What a chance it was to come upon them there! How comes my young lady's temper to be so changed of late? She positively smiled half a dozen times this afternoon! I should like to know what is going on at Darraghmore, and what is that fellow Devereux about? What a queer place it is! I never dreamed of having such neighbors."

He knocked his cigar-ash off on the edge of one of the majolica boxes, and reaching an unopened paper off the table began to read the English news. Two days' old telegrams and leading articles were not very exhilarating mental exercise, so the paper was soon dropped, and Mr. Satterthwaite yawned heartily. Then he mounted one leg over the arm of his smoking-chair, and for a brief space looked musingly into his garden. Somehow the pretty scene that had sprung into being for his wishing, at which he had worked and planned—for he was no mere theorist, but could put hand and foot to the spade with as good will as any son of Adam—seemed to have lost its charm for him. He felt bored and out of sympathy with it. The sun was shining, and he could see that the leaves were larger and the waxy green spikelets of the chestnuts were taller than they had been in the morning, and the branch-tips of the laburnum showed a faint gold-yellow thread here and there. Still, the thing seemed stale. There was not the feeling or the freshness as before. He could not tell how or why. It was just that he was lonely; perhaps for the first time in his life the self-contained Englishman missed something, or felt that there was something more needed in the well-filled cup of life poured out for him by Fate. He was a little puzzled at his own unwonted sensation. But he was not given to indulge in thinking about himself, and his mind reverted again to the early part of the day; and he found himself before long recalling the time Helena's hat was swept off by the beech branch, and the way the sunlight seemed to mingle with the sudden smile that leaped to meet it in her face.

"She's too lovely to be a mere farmer's wife," said he, going out into the hall to take his hat, for it was time he was back to the planting going on behind the house. "And yet it would be a pity she should be anything else. I couldn't fancy that Pocahontas in London. Perhaps madam is right. I begin to believe she is. Eh, what's this?" His eye caught two cards on the hall-table.

"The Reallys; sorry I was out. I'll go down and have another talk with that woman. Egad! she's worth the time."

Then he went off to the kitchen-garden by a walk at the back of the haggard, and coming unexpectedly on his gang of workers, found them all comfortably lying on their backs smoking and otherwise diverting themselves, which agreeable sight soon banished all Mr. Satterthwaite's little tendencies to *ennui* and boredom.

CHAPTER XII.

"N'ayant pas encore l'âge où l'on invente, je me contente de reconter."
DUMAS.

TOBERGEEN, or the Hill of the Geese, lay about four or so miles from Darraghstown. North of Rosslyne and to the northwest of Darraghmore, it formed a sheltering screen that stood between them and the Galtees, and the cold winds that chilled themselves in winter among their snow-clad peaks. It was not very elevated, nor was the path steep or rugged that led up to the high plateau where lay the queer-shaped stones to which the country people's fancy had given the name of geese. All the way up stretched a rich checker-work of emerald meadows and oat-fields where the green corn was waving in uneven drills, and broad acres of fields fresh plowed for root crops.

The farm-house was one of those hideous Noah's-ark erections of plastered limestone, with little mean windows and a bleak, sloping roof of slates, that seem to be the sole possible conception of native provincial architecture. The farm-yard lay before, behind, and beside the house, and the uneven, weedy cobble-stone pavement extended to the one step of the front-door. A large range of farm-buildings and outhouses were built close to the end of the house, and the plentifully stocked farm-yard gave ample token of the prosperity of its owners.

Too plentifully stocked altogether for the comfort of

its inhabitants on such a day as this. The pigs dashed about to escape the kicks and blows so plentifully bestowed by the women, who were rushing to and fro excitedly in the complicated process of preparing the wedding feast. The turkeys had roosted on a sunny wall, and surveyed the scene with dignity from its eminence. The geese, hungry and greedy, invaded the whole territory at their disposal, and now and again with outstretched wings and vociferous gabble made a furious promenade up and down, striking with real or affected terror a band of urchins who were disporting themselves among the conveyances belonging to the wedding guests. The roof was white and blue with the pigeons which kept walking to and fro on the slates, keeping a jealous watch on the door all the while, every exit from which filled them with expectation. The midday feeding-time of the poultry had been forgotten; the great copper in the cow-house, which served to boil their mess of potatoes and Indian meal, was at that moment the receptacle of two hams and as many chickens as would fit in it at the same time, all which were boiling under the supervision of an old woman, who considered herself aggrieved inasmuch as her duties kept her away from the more attractive scene presented by the farm-house kitchen, where the most important items of the *menu* were being cooked. Not only had every fire-place in the house been utilized for the occasion, but, in addition to the farm-yard boiler, fires had been kindled as well in sheltered corners at the back of the house, and three-legged pots and oven-pots steamed and rattled to the delight of the gossoons and hangers-on with whom the place was now swarming. The dinner-hour was fast approaching, and the bustle in the kitchen became more and more intense.

It was a large apartment occupying almost one-half the ground-floor space of the house, and thronged with people, all busy and all talking and laughing and disputing. The whole fire-place was built up with a glowing wall of turf, before which on a horizontal spit roasted a piece of beef that looked like the entire side of an ox.

A little red-headed boy acted as turnspit, and sat on a creepy stool as far withdrawn from the heat of the fire as was compatible with the strict discharge of his function; a function indeed which there was little likelihood of his forgetting, for the roast, which was to be the *pièce de résistance* of the feast, was the cynosure of half the matrons in the place. Just at that moment, however, public attention was arrested by a dispute which had arisen between the dowager Mrs. Devereux, the bride's paternal grandmother—a sturdy old dame dressed in an ancient green satin gown, who seemed to have assumed the position of commander-in-chief in default of her daughter-in-law—and the professed cook who had been hired from Ballycormack for the occasion.

"A turkey into boiling water? augh! Go'bless us, woman! do ye think *I* never boiled a turkey in *my* life before?"

The pitch at which this challenge was proclaimed and the furious tone of it caused a momentary lull; the egg-beating, and pounding, and chopping, and grinding ceased all round, and every ear was strained for the battle.

"Divel cares," retorted the professional, whose fiery eyes betokened the proverbial temper of her class. "I boiled turkeys for me Lord Gormondale and the very hoight of society, not makin' little of you, ma'am," she added with the most delicious condescension of tone, "and into boiling wather that baste must go this minute."

As she spoke she advanced with outstretched hands to seize the cause of contention which was lying in readiness on a dresser by the wall. Mrs. Devereux senior executed a flank movement, keeping her face to the attacking party, and placed herself between her and the turkey.

"I'll not allow it!" she proclaimed. "I've fed him and crammed him with my own two hands, and to go set that before the bishop. Martha! Martha!"

She felt that public opinion was on the side of the professed cook, and that her supremacy was trembling in the

balance, so appealed to her daughter-in-law to re-enforce her.

Jim's mother, who was sitting apart near the window with her daughter's trembling hand held fast in her own, only glanced deprecatingly at the veteran, and said, gently:

"Give Julia her way, now, granny, do; I'll go bail 'twill be equally as good."

Julia, who indeed barely waited for the order, seized the turkey with the scornful remark that she had boiled turkeys for better than bishops in her day; and granny, deposed and discomfited, created a diversion by cuffing the ears of a boy who, incited thereto by his compeers without, had dashed into the kitchen on a voyage of discovery.

The guests began to arrive, and Jim Devereux and his father were busy helping them to bestow themselves, some in the one sitting-room of the house, where the dinner-table for the bishop, priests, and chief guests had been set, and some without in the entry and before the door. A group remained standing in front of the house, mostly men; the chief figure among them was the bridegroom, a heavy but not ill-looking man of thirty; most of them had been drinking pretty heavily. Car after car drove up and deposited its burden at the door. Loud laughter and jest without warned those in the kitchen of the increasing numbers of guests, and their exertions were redoubled. Granny was ubiquitous, and invoked and threatened the bishop at every turn, producing a certain effect in all instances save that of the professed cook, who in her turn appealed to her own deity, Lord Gormondale, and that "better than a bishop," the Protestant Lord Primate from Dublin, for whom she swore that with her own two unaided hands she had cooked a dinner of four courses.

The seventeen-year-old bride sat with her mother and received the greetings of the guests as they entered. Flushed and trembling, and crying now and again, she never raised her eyes, while the mother listened to the noisy congratulations of each batch of new-comers with a strange blending of gratitude and deprecation. Her girl had got the best match of the country-side; but she hardly dared to allow herself even to think so, much less to look or speak as if she were conscious of anything unusually fortunate or enviable, for fear of drawing down envy or provoking calamity by exciting the dreaded evil eye—a timid, superstitious nature, that would forget to enjoy the glad warmth of a summer day while forecasting storm to come. Her husband, who was of a very different spirit, was standing at the door with some neighbors, talking and drinking. He was a lean, sinewy, well-made man, with a handsome but hard face. He was well pleased with his daughter's marriage, but out of respect for himself took a more independent tone in speaking of it.

"Ay, ay, Fitz-Gerald," he said to a neighbor, "I have nothing to say—a clean, decent boy, and, between ourselves, they'll have enough to live upon."

"Why didn't you hold Mary over till Jim here was going off too? Father Quaide 'ud be content with one fifty for the two jobs." Another neighbor asked this, winking as he spoke to Fitz-Gerald.

"Jim's in no hurry," replied young Devereux with a frown, stepping out from the group and away down towards the lane, as if he saw a vehicle approaching that demanded his attention.

As he walked off the old men turned their heads and looked after him admiringly.

"Devereux," said a stooped old man—a Galtee farmer, with keen gray eyes and thin lips, between which as he spoke appeared a set of dazzling white teeth—"what are you doing with that boy of yours? It's time he had a wife. Why aren't you looking after Mary Sheahan, of Ballytrophy? Twelve hundred down, and you could give him Darraghmore out and out."

"He has Darraghmore out and out," said their host, dryly. "And as for Mary Sheahan, a purtier nor nicer little girl never stepped in the county."

"Ay, so!" went on the Galtee farmer. "And, bedad!

Tom Devereux, she won't be long on hand, the same little girl. Thrust Father Quaide to have her settled before —-ay, before Halloween. Money down, and most respectable!"

Jocularly as this was all said, there was an undercurrent of almost savage threatening running beneath. Devereux knew perfectly what they intended. The Galtee farmer, a cousin of the Sheahans, was their spokesman; and Fitz-Gerald, a mountaineer, six feet six in his stockings, was an ally, and was treasuring every word that fell from Devereux.

"Oh! respectable is it?" said Fitz-Gerald. "Faith, yes! Her mother was a Tuohill of Clare, an' a cousin of the Burghos—and every one knows they're next thing to the Knight himself—an' the father is own brother to the parish priest of Ballyhastown. I'm told some of the money will come from him."

"Musha, then!" said old Devereux, in a tone of mingled bitterness and contempt—perhaps the recollection of Father Quaide's fifty pounds oppressed him—"people think if they're connected with a priest they're mighty grand. *I* never could see anything about them, but that they earned their money like other people, only a —— sight easier!"

"Ay, thrath!" assented willingly the facile Fitz-Gerald, whose role it was to play and draw out Devereux. "Sure a priest will do anything for money!"

"Ay," added the Galtee farmer, "barrin' work for it!" And at this old stock joke they all laughed loudly.

However, this was mere by-play. Fitz-Gerald returned to the charge, and, with a big, blustering voice, began:

"Heth! then meself wishes they'd not be in such a hurry entirely wid purty Mary, till I see would me own owld woman thrip up her heels and give me a chance. 'Tisn't long I'd be till I'd be comin' down the mountain to talk to her for meself."

As Fitz-Gerald finished his speech he fixed his cunning gray eyes on Devereux, and so did the old man. They plainly expected a declaration, and Devereux felt extremely puzzled how to give it. He was anxious for the match; it was a suitable one in every way; but of course he owed it to himself, and to his family and position, not to betray the slightest desire for, or appreciation of, the honor they were desirous to confer upon him. That would have been to "belittle" himself, and would, moreover, have been a purely gratuitous proceeding on his part. The real trouble was this: Jim had boldly declared he would not marry the girl; his father's concern now was to keep back this audacious and most disrespectful resolve from the ambassadors, and at the same time give them a broad hint, without absolutely committing himself in the affirmative or negative, or seeming anxious or even overwilling for the match, that a little delay would be desirable. He hoped in time to overcome his son's objections, the real cause of which he was far from suspecting; and he trusted to his own and Father Quaide's influence to accomplish this. To get the negotiations postponed *sine die* was his sole thought. So he replied:

"'Tis no second-hand goods will do Mary Sheahan. No, no, Long Larry," he said, shaking his head. This was a compliment, and went for nothing with both parties. "I've me eye on a boy—I'll say no more; but he's her ayquals in most things, and the rest I dare say wouldn't part the bargain. They might and they mightn't, however. Sure, what's the hurry? There's no one wantin' to run away wid ayther of them."

This oracular speech seemed to close the discussion. The Galtee farmer, with a satisfied expression of face, lighted a pipe, and leaning his back against the wall of the house, amused himself counting the geese and turkeys, which, frantic with hunger and excitement, were making a terrible hubbub.

"I'll go bail those creatures are forgotten," said Devereux, glad of a diversion. Then he shouted in a louder tone than was necessary: "Con, run to the loft—bring down a few sieves of meal; we'll be all deafened if they don't get something."

The boy did as he was desired, and their clamor was

appeased. The next thing was to drive the pigs into a field and latch the gate, so as to preserve the house from their intrusion when the dinner began.

Meantime Jim was walking slowly down the long and steep lane which connected the farm-house of Tobergeen with the high-road at the foot of the hill. He passed the parish priest's covered car containing his own august connection, the bishop, who with the owner of the vehicle completely filled it. Then came the Sheahans' outside-car. Miss Mary, sitting demurely beside her mother, replied with a pleased smile to the salutation of the young master of Darraghmore, and looked a little vexed that he did not turn round to accompany her party to the house. Jim, who scarcely knew her, held his way down-hill churlishly, and when he reached the bottom seated himself on the bank beside the gate-post to wait for the tardy Ferrards. Before long a white cloud of dust beneath the trees that overhung the Comerford wall showed that the expected mail-car was in sight; in a few minutes it stopped and they got down. Isi seemed to have made no change in his apparel, but Hel looked transformed. She wore her black silk dress, which she had carefully preserved since it had been sent to her from Bath; a black bonnet which had only been worn once; and Cawth had produced out of her stores a valuable point-lace mantilla that had belonged to the first Lady Darraghmore, yellow with age and much ill-use, but still with an air of elegance and distinction that somehow suited Helena wonderfully. She looked at him with a smile as she gave him her hand, but to her astonishment he took it silently and gravely; and the trio ascended the rocky lane without speaking to each other. Jim walked close to Helena, a little behind her, and surveyed her changed appearance with a look that became each moment more melancholy and despairing. Helena did not know what to think, but so full of confidence and pleased anticipation was she that she attached no serious meaning to her lover's manner. Simple and straightforward herself in all things, the idea that any complication could have arisen never occurred to her.

When they reached the door and everybody had gone into the house, Jim turned and said to her:

"I'll take you over to my mother and Mary—stay with them; and after dinner, when the dancing begins in the barn, I wish you to go up the hill. I have something to say to you."

Helena was struck by his severe tone, and the cold almost stern look he bent upon her. She was about to speak, but he turned into the entry; and feeling suddenly depressed and frightened she had no choice but to follow, and found herself among a crowd of people, every one of whom immediately began staring at her and questioning each other with astonished eyes.

Helena sat down beside Mrs. Devereux, and in a perfectly composed manner replied to her salutation; indeed, the timid-eyed matron felt far too much awe of her guest to bore her with much conversation, and the bride said not a word. Helena looked at her with wonder; the purple silk dress, white veil, and heavy wreath of orange-blossoms, under which was a flushed, tear-stained child's face, filled her with astonishment and pity. Some of the women brought her cake and wine; she did not refuse it, but the plate lay in her lap untouched.

Then the bishop entered the kitchen; the dinner was ready for him and the *élite* of the guests in the parlor. The cook and grannie had made up their dispute, and their feud was forgotten in face of the common necessity. A living dog is better for all purposes than a dead lion, and Lord Gormondale and the Protestant Primate faded into limbo before the advent of the Bishop of Peatshire. Immediately that his rubicund visage appeared at the door every one knelt down. The Ferrards and the little turnspit alone excepted. Even the servants, with their cooking utensils in their hands, tumbled down higgledy-piggledy; the episcopal benediction did not take long, and his lordship advanced to greet his goddaughter and cousin, the bride.

"Mary, my dear child, so you leave Tobergeen to-day. Ah, well! Martha, don't be crying now; she's not going so far from you after all. Father Quaide, I wonder at your bad taste to be sending all your pretty girls out of the parish that way, though you're not leaving my diocese, Mary."

"Ha, ha!" laughed Father Quaide, who had five filthy ten-pound notes in the pocket of his second-best velvet waistcoat, and felt in very good spirits, "your lordship has nothing to say in these matters at all."

"Take care, take care!" said the Bishop, shaking a warning though playful forefinger. "The Synod may play some of you a queer trick or two."

"Augh, then, my lord," said old Devereux in a bitter tone, "we're hearing of that this long time, and it doesn't seem to be coming off all the same."

This allusion of the Bishop's referred to a Synod which about this time had been convoked for the purpose of re-arranging some trivial matters of church discipline and custom, among them the practice of exacting a percentage on brides' fortunes as wedding-fees—the advisability of priests holding farms, or playing cards, or the quantity of punch which might be legitimately drunk by parish priests and curates, and other small matters of no importance in a political or theological sense, but interesting nevertheless to the lay body at large.

Father Quaide and every one of the priests laughed heartily at Devereux, who indeed joined in the hilarity—though it was, in every sense, at his own cost.

The Bishop had by this time caught sight of Helena, and as he moved in to dinner with Mrs. Devereux asked who she was.

"Ferrard! Darraghmore. Eh, yes, to be sure. I can remember old Lord Darraghmore when I was curate here at Ballycormack; he was on his last legs then, bailiffs in the house, and driving out in a carriage and four—eh, yes, to be sure."

Then he took no further notice of Helena, who indeed was soon tired of the festival, and wished in her heart she had not come. Old Devereux filled her a glass of champagne, and said ceremoniously he was proud to see her in his house. A farmer's wife, Mrs. Sheahan, her rival's mother, good-naturedly helped her to everything within reach. Jim avoided her, and turned away his face whenever she caught his eye, and Hel grew by degrees more miserable and uncomfortable. The loud talk and laughter at sayings and jokes which she could not understand —for Helena with her English blood had inherited a droll obtuseness to Irish humor—made her head ache; the rows of strange faces, the hot, heavy atmosphere, all combined to make the place a sort of purgatory to her, and she eagerly watched for an opportunity to release herself. Presently her neighbor said:

"I think, miss, if you'll excuse me, I'll go, for there are so many waiting to get their turn at this table, and I know what it is to feed such a number. So, by your leave, miss, I'll remove."

"I'll go too," said she, gladly; "no, thank you, I could not take any more." She rose and followed the considerate Mrs. Sheahan, and their places were immediately filled. Helena was delighted to get out of the hot, stifling room; she looked for Isi, but he, less fastidious than she, was enjoying his dinner at the corner of the table, sitting by Long Larry Fitz-Gerald, who was telling him of the past glories of Darraghmore, as he remembered it when a boy. Helena tried vainly to catch his eye, but failed. In the kitchen people were eating and drinking, and everywhere was a bustle of noise and confusion. She went outside and into the farm-yard where the air was fresher and cooler, though the guests were coming and going, and the smell of the kitchen pervaded the air. Every one seemed to stare at her, and there was not one whom she knew how to talk to, or who was not afraid to talk to her. She wished Isi would come out, or Jim—what in the world could be the matter with him? Hel felt every moment more anxious and ill at ease. She watched the entry to see if he would pass by the open door. At last he came out, carrying a huge bundle of candles wherewith to light up the barn in which the dance was to be held. Helena was standing a little on one side amusing herself with a friendly sheep-dog. He did not see her, he was looking round for the servant boy. She heard him order Father Quaide's covered car to be brought round in ten minutes; the Bishop had to go to a mountain parish where he was to sleep that night. Then he went over to the great barn, and having disposed of the candles, came back leisurely. This time he could not help seeing her. He stared a little.

"Oh, you are there, Hel; I'll ask you to wait till the Bishop and Father Quaide are gone—but, come into the house and sit down."

His tone was constrained and distant. Helena, who hitherto had felt no serious uneasiness, turned suddenly cold, a nameless dumb terror took possession of her. What if, in spite of his letter, he was going to marry Mary Sheahan? could it be? No, no, that was not to be thought of. She was scarcely able to reply audibly.

"I'll go up the hill, Jim, and wait for you there; I'd rather." Then, without another word, for there was a perilous tremble in her voice, she turned and walking fast reached the end of the farm buildings, and passing through a gate found herself on a narrow white path that wound past the corn-fields and meadows till it reached the summit of the hill.

It was nearly seven o'clock, and the twilight was falling slowly. The sun was sinking behind the Galtees in a golden flame that yet shone in the little roof windows of the farm-house, while the road which lay far below was in shadow. There was a dew falling thick and soft, and the grass was already damp. Great black slugs crept across the dusty path, leaving little silvery streaks on the stones. From the hedges below the thrushes' nocturns came up to her clear and sweet, and she could hear a faint, far-off echo of the fiddle summoning the dancers to the barn. Helena hastened on, glad to leave that sound at least behind her. At last the little path ended at a great white stone with a hollow in it that formed a comfortable, sloping seat. Hel threw herself into it with a sigh. Round about lay the stone geese, blocks of granite whitened by the weather, and standing out in curious relief against the dark green of the close-cropped herbage.

The valley of the Rack was peaceful and quiet below, and a little band of white mist marked the river course. Darraghstown was hidden by the woods of Comerford, but through an opening on the right hand she could see the lights of Rosslyne. How far off it seemed, and how still. The yellow, glimmering disk of the sun dropped behind the mountain, the farm-house looked a dull, clear gray, and the Galtees stood out above the dim stretch of the valley like a threatening rampart. The sky wall changed from red to purple, and the shadows lengthened and deepened. The corn-crake's monotonous cry rose far below her, and the swallows had ceased glancing and darting above the thatched roofs of the farm buildings. Helena watched the house unceasingly. She saw the black vehicle led round, then it drove off, rocking and jolting down the laneway between the hedges. Still he did not come.

It was a full hour now since Helena had reached the hill-top, and she felt cold and afraid. She did not for a moment doubt Jim, and she was in no way occupied by forecasting any shortcomings on his part. She had seen Mary Sheahan, a pretty, yellow-haired girl, smartly dressed and with a slightly conceited air; and no jealous thought ever entered her mind that he could be engaged with her. She had his letter still hid in her dress, and until he should tell her himself that it was false, she would never doubt what was there set down.

Presently her quick ear caught the sound as of an approaching foot. Through the wet grass, heedless of the dew-drops that his feet shook off the blades, Devereux came striding up, and leaning his hand on the end of the great stone, looked at her for a moment while he waited to take breath.

He had no hat, and Helena thought his face looked strangely careworn. She remained silent, waiting for him to speak first, and watching him expectantly.

"Hel," he burst out at last, "I wonder at you."

"What?" She opened her eyes wide, and if he had seen the expression of her face it might have re-assured him, but he had covered his own with his hands.

"What!" he repeated, angrily; "you were seen with Satterthwaite in the wood on Monday, the day I was in Limerick; ay, by yourself sitting with him. Listen to me, Hel," he went on, making a motion with his hand to command her to listen; "I know he's more your own equal than I am; and if—if—you'd rather have him, I don't want to bind you to me." Then he stopped and looked at her with eyes which were blind with tears, and trembling lips. Helena's head had sunk forward on her breast, and she had covered her face with her hands.

All the remembrances of that day spent in the woods with the Englishman rushed in a flood upon her. She was conscious of the impression Satterthwaite and his beautiful place had made upon her, both when she saw it and since, and the contrast she had drawn in her own thoughts between him and his surroundings and those she was accustomed to. A stinging sense of treachery took possession of her, and then she had his book that he had lent her too. How wicked, how ungrateful she felt her conduct to have been, and now Jim was going to abandon her in consequence of it. She felt rather than thought all these things, and filled with horror and contrition could only sob out his name despairingly:

"Jim! oh Jim!"

In a moment he was leaning over her, and had pulled down her hands.

"Hel, was it a lie? I declare to God, if he lied I'll— Tell me this moment."

"I don't know," said she between her sobs. "We were in the woods, and we met him." She looked up in his face with streaming eyes. He turned away from her, and standing at a little distance, said:

"I'm no match for you, Hel, I know that; and may be you're mistaken. It's some one like Satterthwaite; he's one of your own, and he could keep you like a lady; that would be fittest for you; you're not one of us at all."

The words rang through Helena's ears, and it seemed to her as if Jim were repeating her own thoughts aloud. He paused for a moment, and went on in a hard, dry voice, that sounded strangely in her stunned ears: "That's what they're saying below. Granny says you're the picture of Miss Helena that married Lamont, and that if—if you got your due you might be a duchess."

Hel never answered. She had stopped crying, and her breath came in thick and short gasps, and she gazed at him with wide, dilated eyes. He stood still a moment as if waiting for a reply, then he came close, and leaning again on the rock, said with a despairing cry:

"Will you speak to me? Hel, speak to me!"

Still she did not answer; she could not. He half-fell, half threw himself on the ground, and so kneeling, looked up in her face, now almost gray with pain. Her dumb, frightened eyes met his at last, and as if she read some charm there, her terror and distrust fell from her like an evil dream. Then with a half sob, half laugh she drew his head close to her and leaned her cheek on his hair. He had hardly time to breathe, so quick was her act.

"Why do you say such things to me?" said she in a quick voice shaken yet by a sob.

He put up his hand and loosing one of hers from round his neck held it to his lips for a moment, then he jumped up and lifted her to her feet. They stood looking at each other for a little while; then he drew a long sigh of relief, and stooping forward a little, for he was taller than she by a full head, he laid a hand on each of her shoulders.

"Hel, nothing can part us now; is it so?"

"Yes."

Then, he holding her hand, they walked down the hill to find Isi. Jim had desired him to wait by a hedge farther down. It was almost dark; a brown-red mist still lingered over the mountains, and a tiny cloudlet high up had a faint salmon-colored tinge to one edge, a reflection caught from the Atlantic waves far behind the hills. They passed at the back of the farm-house, and led by Jim found a path round a field that brought them out in the lane at a point near the road. He walked with them to the gate.

"Good-night," said Helena. "Will you be at Darraghmore soon?"

"I'll be there every day from this out," he replied. "Come over on Saturday."

And so they parted.

CHAPTER XIII.

"'Es ist wie mit allen Bitterkeiten,' flüsterte Sophie ihrem Nachbar zu. 'Sie fallen zu schwer auf die Zunge, man kann nicht recht unterscheiden ob es schmeckt oder nur allen Geschmack betaübt, dergleichen ist natürlich für den wahr, der Liebhaber davon ist.'"

TIECK.

SATTERTHWAITE went to pay a visit to Madam Really the day of the wedding at Tobergeen. He got suddenly tired of the gardening and weeding, and decided to take, and no doubt give his men too, a few hours' holiday and ride down to Buona Vista. He was seized with curiosity to hear about the wedding which had suddenly acquired a wonderful interest in this gentleman's eyes since he had heard that the Ferrards were to be there. So his black horse Auster was led round, and he rode off at a trot to catch Madam Really directly she should have finished her two o'clock lunch.

"Mrs. Really is in the garden, sir, but I'll fetch her in to you; the master is in the study," said the servant who opened the door.

"Wait!" said Satterthwaite; "I'll go to the garden; never mind calling her in; show me the way."

He gave the reins as he spoke into the hands of the boy who had followed him up from the lodge.

"The way is open, sir; just go round the house by that walk."

Satterthwaite turned in the direction indicated by the maid-servant and following a gravel path found himself in a few moments in the garden. Madam was invisible, and he looked about vainly to discover her among the closely-planted alleys. It was a large, well-kept piece of ground, covering the whole top of the eminence and falling in a gentle decline all round from the house. A high wall bristling with glass fenced it about, but in no way interfered with the view of the open country without.

"Mr. Satterthwaite—this way, please!" Madam Really's clear voice called from a distant corner where she was busy tying up raspberry bushes in neat bundles. She dropped her knife and bass matting, and taking off one clayey glove shook hands with him cordially. "Why did you not come in time for lunch? Come in with me and have some; that ride ought to give you an appetite. You were not to be found the day we called at Rosslyne. I was disappointed I can assure you; the glimpse we got of the garden was most tantalizing, as you see I only go in for useful things."

"Not altogether," said Satterthwaite, looking at the beds of spring flowers that perfumed the air. "I was sorry to have missed you. I was in the far wood shooting with the Ferrards."

"The Ferrards! so I heard." She burst into a laugh. "Then they accepted your forgiveness in that matter of poaching, eh? Dear me, Mr. Satterthwaite, you are getting on wonderfully with them; what is your secret? Poor Mrs. Fitz-Ffoulke had the door shut in her face and a jug of water emptied on her head, and I was threatened with the dogs and ignominiously ordered off the premises. And here you have not been a month in the place, and behold you on excellent terms with the whole tribe!"

Though she spoke jestingly she really was both serious and puzzled; and she was looking at him with inquisitive, keen eyes.

He laughed.

"You have been told about Charles Ferrard, I see; that very day I went over to Darraghmore and found the younger ones there. Well, we got on pretty well, and I stumbled upon them in my wood on Monday and we had a little shooting, a pleasant ramble, and some conversation together."

"Did Helena shoot?" asked his listener with a smile.

"No; I couldn't persuade her to do so, though she confessed to a liking for it. What a lovely girl she is!"

"Yes," she replied, meaningly; "Jim Devereux may well be proud of his intended wife."

"Intended wife!" said Satterthwaite in a changed voice. "I remember—yes—you told me something of this before; I did not know the affair was settled."

"I cannot say if they are actually betrothed," she said in a careless voice, watching him. "I hope they are, and that the poor girl has some prospect before her. When Lord Darraghmore dies, which must be expected soon, she will be destitute. Isi and she know as much of the world as two kittens. He could enlist, but what is there before her? and she is one whom it would be impossible to do anything for. It seems to me almost providential that this marriage presents itself now; Devereux is a splendid fellow, and they will get on perfectly together."

Her companion made no answer. He walked on silently beside her, with a growing feeling of bitterness and determination. He was debating within himself how far he ought to trust what she said; and what reason, beyond the remote acquaintance she had told him about with the step-brother, she could have for identifying herself with the Ferrards in this manner.

"How do you find your workmen get on?" said Madam Really.

"They get on as long as I am looking at them," he replied. "Their dishonesty is simply incredible."

"I told you so," said she. "Between idleness and petty pilfering, life is a difficulty in this country. Indoor servants are rootedly dishonest; they spoil food to an unbearable degree. It is the same all round; and it is that vice makes and keeps this country so poor. They don't think it a sin to help themselves. So the servants will tell you; and you have no idea of the discomfort they can make by filching everything in the way of food. They all do it. Petty, exasperating thieving is the great curse of housekeeping in Ireland."

"Ah!" said he, shaking his head. "I left these men of mine to themselves for an hour or two one day, and, happening to come upon them from an unexpected quarter, there were the whole gang on their backs smoking and cracking jokes—at my expense, I have no doubt. Didn't I pitch into them!"

"Rule them with a rod of iron. If you are in the least easy-going and tolerant, you will make no hand of them. Come down this way and look at the view of Comerford."

"Your garden is lovely," said he, following her down a narrow walk bordered with fruit-trees. Madam Really stopped at a little young tree and dipped her nose into a cluster of blossoms.

"Isn't that perfect?" said she, turning to him. "It's a Reine Marguerite."

Certainly the garden was exquisite. The summer-snow of the apple-trees was dropping silently beside them, and the sweet, ethereal odor of the ripe blossoms was wafted to them on the wings of the soft west wind. The violets were all gone, but white narcissus and golden-yellow and brown wall-flowers lined the box-edges. An early butterfly flitted weakly hither and thither, trying its feeble new wings in the warmth and light. The sun was shining brightly, but a fleecy bank in the southwest promised another shower soon; and though the gravel was dry and white, the cups of the flowers were overflowing.

When they came to the end of the walk Satterthwaite found himself before three moss-grown stone steps, which led up to a little raised platform, the artificial structure of which was concealed by the rose-bushes and ivy that twined over it. On top was a comfortable garden-seat, and placed before it, on a solid, well-mounted stand, a large telescope. Satterthwaite could not help a smile on seeing it at the thought of Mrs. Perry's resentment.

"This is my observatory," said madam. "I can see the rabbits at play on Tobergeen, five miles away almost.

They have a wholesome terror of this telescope in the town below."

She was adjusting the focus as she spoke, but Satterthwaite stepped over to the crenelated wall to look out. He was surprised at the wide view that stretched away before him.

The two rivers—the Rack and the smaller but more impetuous Darragh—wound for miles behind. The woods of Comerford were lovely. The chestnuts were in leaf, and the pale, soft green looked exquisitely tender against the brown-green of the later oak-branches. The sycamores and beeches were fast changing, and the dull winter-green of the pines formed an almost black background to the soft transition hues of their neighbors. The spring was at that charming transparent stage, when little by little, as of a revelation gradually imparted, does she allow her beauties to appear, charily and grudgingly sometimes, and sometimes snatches them back wantonly—crushing and hurting her own treasures.

"Look at the woods through the glass; you can nearly see the things grow," said she, wheeling the stand a little forward.

He obeyed, and wondered at the clearness and perfection with which every leaf and branchlet, in all their delicate coloring, were visible. Then he turned it towards the village. The mill-house windows were all dark and untenanted—not a sign of life to be seen in it. The green door was shut, and so was the gate of the front garden, which was choked with the overgrowth of the shrubs.

Madam Really stood beside him, watching with a smile, in which bitterness and amusement were oddly blended, the direction in which the telescope was now turned.

"Bruton says any moment may carry the old man off now. He has had a stroke, and seems to be inviting another by every means in his power—lies all day on the sofa drinking whisky, and never takes any exercise. I wonder how it will be with Helena. Perry tells me if they pay what they owe they won't have enough to bury him. They got only eighty-five pounds this quarter-day."

"I did not fancy, from what I had been told, that they were in the habit of paying their debts."

Satterthwaite continued to look through the telescope.

"Helena pays for everything. She cleared off even Clan's scores in the town since he left. Poor child! how does she manage to keep the money from Char? He is a truculent monster, that. Perry says he tried hard to make him pay him the money, but Hel insisted on having it. That's Jim Devereux's doings, I imagine: he has a good influence over her. I really think I'll go down and make another effort to see her."

"If she doesn't refuse the Perrys, why should she you? It is a great pity that creature should be so left to herself. Do try again. Perhaps now she will be more amenable."

"I think I will do it," said madam in a thoughtful tone. "She is enormously changed of late; has got so quiet and stay-at-home. Perhaps she would see me. But, after all, what good could I do her?"

"Something might be done," he persisted. "I assure you I do not like the idea even of her life, and she is such an interesting—"

"Take care of yourself, Mr. Satterthwaite," interrupted madam. "Miss Helena's *beaux yeux* have even won over Perry to her side."

"Perry, indeed!"

"I see you don't like Mr. Perry; neither do I. He is not a good type—though, alas! there are plenty like him. What an idiot his wife is. He married her for her money and connections. What little brains she ever had he has long ago eliminated from her composition. He is a regular bully, of the domestic order."

"So I fancied," said Satterthwaite, carelessly. "Is he well off?"

"Very comfortable. He makes from six to seven hundred a year and his farms bring him in something too."

"Why are they so uncultivated—those girls I mean?"

"Bah! what do they want? I have been told that he

regrets the cost of their education; says the money would have been better invested if put out to interest for portions for them. I dare say he is right, too—according to his lights."

"Come, Mrs. Really, you do not speak your own sentiments, there."

"Quite true. But what social standard have these people? They are forbidden to know Protestants, and it is from Protestants only that they can get any reflection of culture or refinement. Perry laughs at this prohibition—very naturally, for he does business with them as much as with Catholics—but the daughters and their mother are consistent and religious. You see the clergy are not yet awake to the need of higher class education and refinement. Father Quaide, for example—he is an excellent, charitable man; but can you fancy him laying down the laws of society? That, indeed, is a thing no man ever can do. Don't laugh, Mr. Satterthwaite; I am serious. What is wanted in Ireland is a national, patriotic spirit. Yes, just that. Don't mistake me. I don't mean this agitation business in the least—there is too much of that—I mean a common-sense, solid love of progress. Look at Perry; he is making nearly a thousand a year out of this district, and he despises and looks down on it. In Dublin it's the same. They all want to be in London; they ape London ways and London fashions. The real enemies of the country are not the Fenians, nor the agitators, but the Anglo-maniacs—the would-be Londoner set. 'Nothing is worth while in Ireland!' that's their cry. 'It is a charming place to live out of.' The Miss Perrys don't think it worth while dressing themselves because this is Darraghstown, and not Dublin; in Dublin, anybody that has ever taken an excursion ticket to London is the same. Their papa shaves only once a week for the same reason. This is the way with these people all over the country. They have their heads in the clouds. They would be all absentees if they could."

"It is perfectly true. How in the world would you cure this?"

"I'd give them a dose of Home Rule. I would give them a legislative chamber in Dublin, and then you would see them wake up. They'll fight, no doubt; but I would give them a chance. If they prove themselves fit and able to govern themselves—"

"Oh, impossible! This country—England, I should say—has set its face against that altogether. It's absurd. I am really surprised at you!"

"What matter about the impossibility? I do not believe it is impossible. Stranger things have been done. And then as soon as the scheme shall have failed, nobody is any worse off than before."

"I doubt that. You cannot tell what mischief they will be at. Who would the representatives be?"

"Well, I do hope the landed gentry will come forward, and that this perpetual absentee spirit will be put an end to."

"You will have a religious war—that will be the end."

"Oh no! The two religions will work together nicely. Why, the chiefs of the Home Rule party are Protestants. You see that does not affect their position or influence in the least. In fact, I look to Home Rule to restore the prestige of which the Disestablishment deprived the cultured classes. What a blunder that Church Act was!"

"I should like to know upon what grounds you say that. I considered it a disgraceful burden to this country."

"Well, I choose to consider that view of the case to be a purely sentimental one. The established church cost nothing; the weight all fell on the landed gentry; and, moreover, that money was spent in the country, and in return there was the presence of a refined, cultivated family in every parish, in a position to command respect, and with great influence. Now their prestige is gone, their influence destroyed. That measure was a fatal anachronism. It was just, I dare say; but it was inexpedient. As if these barbarians could afford to lose even that civilizing element. But I know what can be made of the same mere Irishry, and I know the talents that are wasted and lost and turned to evil use; and, in short, Mr. Satterthwaite, I have faith in them."

"Yes, you are one of those who look dispassionately on their vices; you find their cause and origin in history, in their religion, or in social and economic causes; in fact, while admitting their wickedness, you hold them irresponsible. Reformers like you, Mrs. Really, are so liberal and so wide of vision one cannot get hold of you anywhere."

"Well, I know my own faults too, I hope, but I tell you what you want to do is to give the people some power in their own hands. London is a long, long way from Darraghstown, though it is far too near Dublin."

"Dear me!" said a voice behind them, "you are at politics, Esther. How do you do, Mr. Satterthwaite?" Satterthwaite turned at the voice. There was Mr. Really, walking with the aid of a stick, coming down the alley. "My wife is a politician, sir; I leave that sort of thing to her. I am content with the newspaper, but she only reads it to contradict it, I think. I don't know how you can be bothered, my dear; and—I don't know any other lady who does interest herself in those things." This was said with a timid primness of tone that did not escape Satterthwaite.

"It's a bad habit I have acquired abroad. Our *salon* in Vienna was always full of diplomats of all sorts; and moreover, what has one in Ireland but politics? We don't read; we don't paint; we are all utterly ignorant and inæsthetic. We are exactly fifty years behind England in culture."

"Oh! Mrs. Really, are you not very hard on your own country?"

"I don't know that! already you have found my prophecy fulfilled in one point—have you not?"

"I met Father Quaide riding out in your direction, Mr. Satterthwaite." This was from Really, who was clearly at sea in the conversation. "He has got his new nag—cost him seventy-five guineas; it's a heavier animal than yours, but fully as handsome."

"Father Quaide must be well off, considering the poverty of this district—"

"He is very comfortable," put in madam so quickly as to finish his sentence for him, "as you will find if he invites you to dinner. Six guineas a dozen for his sherry, and claret to match. Mr. Carrington was astonished the day he dined with him."

"Carrington! by the way I must return their visit; and tell me, then, are the Protestant gentry on such friendly terms with Father Quaide?"

"Well, to tell the truth, this abominable Disestablishment has rather caused an interruption of amicabilities; as long as their reverences were on dining terms with us heretics, they could hardly, without violating the laws of hospitality, promulgate that we were destined for eternal perdition. Before the Church Act there were the friendliest feelings possible between both sects."

"But this bitterness will die out, things will re-adjust themselves, you will see," said Satterthwaite.

"The coolness unhappily has been turned to profit by some people; they have swept it in and included it with other things under the head of denominational education. Mixed marriages have been made impossible, social intercourse discouraged Ah! there is no end to the mischief that measure has brought about. I really think it was the prime mover and originator of the new infallibility dogma."

"*Fiat justitia ruat cœlum*," said Satterthwaite, laughing; "I can only think of the Disestablishment that it was a monstrous, disgraceful anomaly to maintain a Protestant Church at the expense of an enormous majority of Roman Catholics—"

"If that is the principle you go upon, Home Rule has the very same recommendation to your favor," she interrupted him in sardonic tones.

"I don't believe in Home Rule," said her husband. "Esther, I believe you'll end as a Communist; would you believe it, she actually took the part of the Reds in that last insurrection in Paris."

"It wasn't that I sympathized with their mischief," said she, "but there must have been some idea among them—some sentiment, now, and I've got an eye for a sentiment, though you might not believe it of me."

Satterthwaite laughed. Mrs. Really amused him thoroughly; the sharp voice and keen, cynical countenance had a flavor for him that was both novel and interesting. He wished she were a little softer, and that she would show a more womanly, kindly feeling to poor Miss Ferrard. There was something harsh and cruel in the idea that, because the girl was in such desperate circumstances, she should be allowed to drift into the position of a mere boor's wife. She was young enough to learn, to be trained yet to take the place in society which belonged to her rank. And how pretty she was—what a wild, interesting face! Satterthwaite as he rode home began thinking of his encounter in the woods, treading his way in the undergrowth with Helena, and watching the sweet flitting shadows as they fell upon her face. It was only a few days ago, but already he felt it too long, and he began to ask himself with impatience when he was to see her again and how. She was at Tobergeen that day. Things could not have gone so far, he thought; for if Devereux's parents knew of his entanglement with her, they never would have invited her to the feast—that was clear enough. He determined to be at Darraghmore early next day to meet her. There was no time to be lost.

Satterthwaite rode over to Darraghmore the next day, in the hope of finding some news of the Ferrards there. The door was opened after a long delay by the servant Biddy, who looked sleepy and answered rather crossly, "that himself was at Tobergeen, and she didn't know if he'd be back before night or not; he didn't come back from the weddin' yesterday."

"If he does come home to-day, say that Mr. Satterthwaite of Rosslyne will be here to-morrow afternoon."

There was nothing to be done now but ride back, and feeling disappointed and baffled, he returned home. Close to his own entrance gates he overtook Lawyer Perry driving along in his dirty gig.

"Good-day," he cried. "What has become of you lately? I was just driving up to ask for you."

"Come along," said Satterthwaite, riding on before the gig, "I was going back to lunch." Perry drove after him, and they soon reached the house. A man led away the gig and his master's horse, and they ascended the hall-door steps. Perry stared round him with an amazement that made Satterthwaite smile.

"My word!" he cried, "but you have improved the place; you English have taste surely; but then 'tis you have the time and money to gratify it too. I never saw anything so pretty; it beats Lord Comerford's to fits."

"I cannot imagine living in the country without a garden."

Satterthwaite felt in a mischievous humor. He was disappointed in his expedition to Darraghmore, and now had a malicious inclination to get some fun out of the worthy attorney.

"Can't you? ha, ha!" laughed he, "how well we do it! What's the use of spending money on things of that sort? Madam Really has a garden too, I believe; I dare say you and she are the only ones who have. Who is to see them, and where's the good?"

"H'm! that's a matter of taste, Mr. Perry," replied Satterthwaite, dryly; then to himself he repeated, "Who's to see them, and where's the good?" noting Mr. Perry's unshaven chin and tumbled linen; "I wish madam were here to enjoy this confirmation of her opinion. I begin to believe what she says, and that there is something needed to keep these creatures from lapsing into their original barbarism; it was not enough to have conquered the country, something should have been done to civilize the natives. Fancy a well-to-do country attorney in England shaving only on Sundays, and behaving in general like this fellow."

"How is your neighbor, Lord Darraghmore?" asked Satterthwaite, when they were in the study.

"Faith I don't know; if he doesn't keep alive till next quarter-day, I can't tell how it will be with them for money. Eighty pounds was all I had for Miss Hel last time."

"Miss Hel! she seems to be the manager."

"Since Clan went I give her the money. That other young villain, Char, as they call him, wanted to get it, but I always give it to Hel. Ha!" went on Perry with a chuckle, "she's a well-plucked one that—a splendid girl. She rules that house now—has them well in hand. I wonder how it's going to end with her and young Devereux here?"

"Eh! how do you mean?" asked Satterthwaite, not ingenuously, but he felt some morbid eagerness to get the particulars from Perry.

"Bah!" went on Perry, who was eating ham in huge mouthfuls, "he'll never think of marrying her, he'd never be that fool. There's lots of farmers' girls hereabout with their seven or eight hundred, ay, and twelve hundred pounds, would be well off to get him."

"If he would only think so," said Satterthwaite with a faint smile. "Take a little more spirits."

"Augh!" said Perry, speaking in his tumbler, "that'll turn out all right yet."

"What do you think will become of that girl? The income dies with the old man, does it not?"

"It does! I don't know; the boys can enlist, anyhow. What a lot of books you have, Mr. Satterthwaite!" He was standing before some half-filled shelves. "Pretty picture! A Madonna that now, hey! you're High Church?"

It was a good copy of the famous Beatrice Cenci that Satterthwaite, who had inherited an artistic taste, had picked up at a sale in London. He was astonished at Perry. However, he replied gravely, ignoring his first question:

"I am not High Church; in fact, just now I don't attend church."

"Don't you now!" said the lawyer, with a grin; "that wouldn't do for me. I'm a business man." Then he took up a beautiful copy of Faust and opened it. "Ah, a French book I see. You have been abroad?"

"Yes, I've been on the Continent. Every one goes nowadays, you know."

"Do! do they indeed! I've never been farther than London. These girls of mine are persecuting me to give them a trip on the Continent. I think really I'll send them to Lourdes" (pronounced Lowrds) "on one of these pilgrimages. Have you ever been, Mr. Satterthwaite? Ah, no! I was forgetting. Not indeed but they're dearer than Cook's tickets, but they seem to be all the go."

"They do indeed!" replied Satterthwaite a little absently. He was thinking of what had been said rather more than of the answer it required. Perry was now standing looking at the gem of Satterthwaite's small but valuable collection—a Turner—which he had inherited from his father. He was amused to see Perry put on a knowing air as he surveyed it.

"My daughter Ellen, Mrs. Sheedy, did that sort of thing at school. Water-colors, isn't it?—one of your own?"

Satterthwaite, who had his weak points like every one else in the world, got almost angry at what he thought must be deliberate impudence on his friend's part; he answered, however, composedly:

"It belongs to me, I am happy to say. That picture is worth two thousand guineas."

Perry stared at him as if he thought him mad—no doubt he did.

"Good Lord! And that Blessed Virgin on the stand by the books?"

"The C—oh! I paid thirty-five only for that."

"I don't know anything about pictures," said he, turning his back on a fine sea-piece; "they are things, like horses, a man ought to know something of before he goes buying or even looking at them."

Perry uttered this truism with the voice of one announcing an original discovery. He was staring now at a quantity of splendid blue Nankin only that morning unpacked, and which was piled on a pretty oak buffet. "Is that a new set, may I ask you? They're very queer shapes."

"Well, they are not new. Oh no! They're curiosities, too."

"Oh, indeed! Curiosities, too, are they?" said Perry, dryly, with a contemptuous grin at a blue dragon vase. Satterthwaite had a good mind to tell him the cost—it would have shocked him as much as that of the Turner—but he judged that his friend had had lesson enough for one day.

"Won't you look at the horses?" said he, "and see the new fittings of the stables? Come along. Light a cigar first." Then he handed him an excellent cigar, and having helped himself they set out for the stables. Once arrived in the newly-paved yard, Perry assumed a very different manner from that he had displayed in the study. He spoke in a loud, authoritative voice, and pulled the horses about in a way calculated to show that of them at least he knew more than his share. He discovered an incipient spavin in one of the best horses, and traces of firing in Black Auster before he had looked at them for ten minutes. He directed all his criticisms to the groom, ignoring Satterthwaite altogether in the conversation, except when he had any disparaging remarks about the horses to make; he then gave their owner the benefit of them. Satterthwaite was thoroughly diverted. He saw Perry was taking his revenge, and with a mixture of good-nature and mischievous fun, resolved to allow him to rehabilitate himself in his own good opinion.

"Handsome screws, Mr. Satterthwaite! very nice, elegant beasts for easy ridin' and drivin'; but law bless you! those horses would leave their legs after them in the mud here in winter. That brown horse, now, he's something like! I'd enter him for Punchestown if I had him. But Lord, man! it's a stronger brute than that you'd want here. Less blood and more bone." Then he pinched the windpipe of the poor horse as he spoke. The animal did not cough—to Perry's evident chagrin. "Ay, ay!" went on the audacious lawyer, speaking in a sort of depreciating, cheapening tone, as if Satterthwaite were wanting to sell the horse. "Sound enough—yes, I dare say he's sound; stands well too! but he's a bad head. Worth eighty now, I dare say."

Perry was standing with his legs apart and his hands in his pockets, leaning a little back, and with a malicious sparkle in his cool gray eyes. Satterthwaite shook his head and laughed good-humoredly. The horse had cost two hundred pounds, and was well worth the money, but he did not choose to tell Perry so. He signed to the man to put back the animals in their stalls.

"I'll tell you who can ride," Perry went on; "Miss Hel. I saw her fly over the paddock on Jim Devereux's colt the other day; it did me good to look at her. She sits as well as himself. Did you see the colt?"

"I had a look at it—a fine, well-bred beast. I've a good mind to bid for it. He would be worth a venture."

"Everything's in the education of him," said Perry in his usual didactic tone. "He's clever, but he wants careful riding and education. If he's well broke I wouldn't say but what he'd fetch his two hundred in a year or so. Jim had always a wonderful hand with a horse."

"Come back to the study and have something before you go. Jenkins can send round your trap to the front door."

"That little horse of mine, now," said Perry, raising his strident voice for the groom's benefit, "is more use than any one of these fine-breds of yours. I ask you what work will you get out of them here?"

"Wait till you see those hunters after a run on the grass." Satterthwaite began to get impatient of the fellow, and had had enough of his boasting. "I hope to have some good riding next season here."

Then Perry swaggered indoors after him. Once in the library and removed from the tempting field of display he was subdued and deferential again—at least, comparatively so. He did not remain longer than was necessary to swallow another dose of brandy and water; the dirty gig and ill-groomed horse were waiting without, and he had already overstayed his time.

CHAPTER XIV.

"Habitual associates are known to exercise a great influence over each other's minds and manners. Those whose actions are forever before our eyes, whose words are forever in our ears, will lead us, albeit against our will, slowly, gradually, imperceptibly perhaps, to act and speak as they do." BRONTE.

"TWO of the finest ewes and a lamb! It is a bad job for us, Hel, I can tell you that. However, they don't know it was Rusty did it; and what you have to do now is to shoot him immediately. Once a dog begins that work he'll never leave it off."

Jim Devereux got no answer to this speech, and as he was lying in the rich grass of his meadow at Darraghmore with a thick tuft of buttercups and long-stalked clover between his face and Helena's, he did not see the rebellious frown that gathered in hers.

"Cawth says"—this was from Isi, who was sitting a little farther off—"he came in this morning between four and five. I never knew him to go out at night that way before, and he certainly had blood on his shoulder."

"Rusty!" called Helena, suddenly, "come here, sir!"

The old dog obeyed, slinking across to her with drooping ears and tail, and stood beside her while she ran her hands over the curly coat and examined it for the stains of his cruel sport. The brute looked conscious and sulky, knowing well that he was the subject of discussion.

"Oh! it's he did it; you needn't be in the least uncertain," went on Devereux. "Since Fitz-Gerald's dog was shot two years ago, there hasn't been a sheep worried in the whole district, and that fellow had killed a hundred before he was stopped. Twelve pounds worth in one night is no joke. You may as well shoot him at once, for my father is going to watch for him to-night himself, and he knows whose dog he is well."

He raised himself on his elbow as he said this and looked at her fixedly. Helena let fall Rusty's ears and pushed him away from her.

"I'll do it—if you wish, Jim," said she, submissively and sadly. Then she sat silent for a while, looking in wonder at her disgraced favorite, picturing him in her mind's eye harrying the defenseless, frightened sheep from end to end of the field in the dark quiet of the night, tearing their throats, one after another, till they bled to death or fell dead from exhaustion and terror, and only giving over the cruel sport when day-break warned the marauder, almost human in his cunning and malignity, that it was time to withdraw.

Devereux lay quietly in the grass, watching her face at his ease.

"Are you fretting for the dog, Hel?" he asked at last, seeing that her eyes were filled and ready to run over. "I'll get you a nice young terrier instead of him."

"No—no," she replied.

"What is it then—eh?" He crawled over nearer to her and looked up into her face.

She bit her lip, but did not reply.

"What ails you? Have you been hearing more of Mary Sheahan—eh, is that it? If she'd the Bank, let alone twelve hundred pounds, I'd never marry her. And when I say a thing I mean it; they may say what they like."

She looked at him in an absent way. She was thinking of his words, and was occupied in picturing to herself the different kind of family life they suggested. Jim's father and mother seemed so interested in, so careful of his prospects. It seemed odd and puzzling to her, for whom no one, save Isi, was concerned in the least. She came and went, lived and acted as she chose—at least, since Clan's departure; and the indolent Char had found that her strength, united to Isi's, was more than a match for his. Cawth grumbled as usual; but Hel had subdued her too, and the old man was now almost imbecile. She felt some curiosity as to the way of the household at Tobergeen. Save the Perrys, she had no experience of domesticity, and their ways were anything but mysterious. The mother and daughters made common cause against their lord and ruler, to circumvent whose tyranny by every kind of deceit was the business of their lives. She despised them heartily. Open warfare was her mode of encountering all opposing forces; and the falsehoods and petty cunning of her friends seemed to her as useless as they were ridiculous and cowardly. Jim's mother, on the contrary, agreed perfectly with his father. Helena could see that for herself, and she was wonderfully puzzled to understand how it came about that Mrs. Devereux, while remaining on good terms with her husband, could preserve an almost neutral position in the dispute as to the Sheahan match. This complication was a standing puzzle to Hel. She knew that Jim was his mother's idol, and on that account she thought she should be altogether on his side. To remain neutral while having a bias in either direction was an impossibility to her. She could not even fancy herself looking on dispassionately at a dispute between Isi and Char.

"You see," went on Jim, nibbling the pink head of a daisy as he spoke, "Father Quaide has such a pull on her. There's always the way. I was at her there after Mary and Delahunty went home. She was crying in the kitchen, and she said to me, 'Jim, if you'd bring home that nice girl, now, instead of Mary, I'd have some one with me to look to me.' 'So,' I said—"

But at this point the daisy's head had been all nibbled away and a new one had to be selected. Perhaps it was this operation that made him pause a full minute before he finished his speech. However, first clearing his voice, he began again:

"I said, 'There isn't any use deceiving yourself. You know what my mind's on,' for she does know, Hel. This week back, since he," nodding his head in the direction of Darraghstown, "got so bad; and then—'Well,' said she, 'do you think you could turn [convert] her?' 'I never asked her,' said I; and Hel, I never will."

Helena looked at him with eyes that spoke only of dumb, loving trustfulness. She hardly understood the drift of what he had been saying. She could appreciate his magnanimity, but was far from conceiving its extent. She knew nothing of the intense religious feeling of the woman who, next to her now, had the best right to him. Hel's own religion had as little meaning to her as the faded crest and motto or empty title of her family, which she hated and felt in a way ashamed of, just as the boys did. And she, too, was beginning, like them, to feel a hungry desire to be away from where their barren distinction only served to bring on them a galling notoriety. She had so keen an instinctive sense of her incongruous position that whenever she met any well-dressed people or carriages on the road, her first impulse was to conceal herself. The comments which she felt they must make were unbearable, even in her own imagination. To live as much out of sight as possible, to avoid every one, had become her practice; and since Devereux had fallen in her path this had seemed easy and pleasant, and all difficulties and troubles had come to an end. She never thought of the future. That care was left to him, and Helena, fearless and sturdy to all besides, was pliant as a reed in his hands.

"There's Satterthwaite—look!" called Isi, excitedly. "There, he's riding up to the house."

They could see the black horse and his rider approach the house at a rapid trot; then, after a moment's parley with the servant, the animal was turned and urged at a gallop across the fields in their direction.

Devereux sat upright, and began to whistle carelessly. Helena looked a little downcast; perhaps the remembrance of Satterthwaite's pretty little book, and the undeserved ill-treatment it had met with at her hands, pricked her conscience somewhat. She had hurled it under her bed the evening of the wedding at Tobergeen, where it lay, crushed and dusty, along with a heap of rubbish, the accumulation of years. Isi, who liked the friendly Englishman, got up and walked to meet him.

Satterthwaite was not long reaching the trio. The black horse took great bounds through the grass, and, panting and foam-flecked, drew up a few paces off. Devereux had risen and was standing near. Satterthwaite stepped forward to Helena, and with a frank, pleasant smile, held out his hand. She took it in a hesitating sort of way and without looking at him; she glanced instead to Devereux, just as her brother, when in doubt, sought her eye.

"How are you, Mr. Satterthwaite? We were waiting for you," said the young farmer, heartily. "Freney's not been out these two days, so he will be as fresh as a daisy."

"Indeed! My horse is not too hard-worked either," replied Satterthwaite. "We can try them at the hurdle if you like. What do you think of him?" said he, turning to Helena. "Don't you think he would suit you nicely? He is as gentle as possible; my cousins have ridden him."

Helena smiled; but she would not look at the horse, scarcely at its owner, who was walking along beside her. Satterthwaite was puzzled by the change in her demeanor, and was half inclined, in his masculine vanity, to attribute it to coquetry. He caught a glance or two that was intended for Jim—who marched along stolidly with Isi, far more occupied with the points of the horse than anything else—and began to put Hel down in his own mind for an arrant little flirt. He thought of the day in the wood, and her smiles and unembarrassed talk; and now, because this handsome lout of hers was with them, she could not spare him even a look. He made an inward vow to drag an answer out of her.

"You have not told me how you liked the little Shakespeare, Miss Ferrard; which of the plays have you been reading?" A sudden glance, quickly followed by a hot flush, ensued upon this. He went on: "My favorite is 'The Tempest,' I think you spoke of 'Midsummer Night's Dream.' Did you not?"

"I had no time to—to—" Helena felt really guilty. "I must send you back the book."

"I wish," said he, walking a little closer to her, and pulling his four-footed companion with an awkward lurch after him, "you would do me the favor to keep it—do, please. I have a couple more of them, and it is a handy little thing to carry about."

Hel, who had a strong suspicion that the back of the "handy little thing" was broken, looked confused while relieved.

"I will, thank you," she managed to say.

By this time they had reached the paddock. A hurdle was erected in the middle of it, and Devereux and Isi hastened to bring out the young colt. Helena and Satterthwaite remained together. She was looking admiringly at the horse, which stood obediently beside him.

"He is handsome," she said at last, and, stretching out her hand, she stroked Auster's forehead gently.

"I have a side-saddle at Rosslyne," said Satterthwaite, feeling encouraged; "and I should so much like you to try the horse. I know you ride. Will you?"

Helena's eyes sparkled with delight, and she looked up into his with unfeigned pleasure.

"I will," said she, enthusiastically. "I do like it."

Then the others came up, and with them Freney, bridled and saddled, and evidently full of spirits, tossing his head and snuffing. Satterthwaite ran his eye over him with a satisfied air that did not escape young Devereux.

"Yes, Mr. Satterthwaite," said he; "but you wait till Freney's as old as your horse, and he'll look as well; he isn't got up quite such a dandy either."

This was true, for the black horse was shining fresh from the hands of his careful groom, whereas Freney had been merely rubbed down with a wisp of straw.

"Will you try a jump with me?" said Devereux. "Or I will give him a trot round first, to take the impudence out of him."

As he spoke he laid his hand on the pommel and sprang into the saddle—an old, worn-out thing, pieced and stitched in ever so many places. That he was a practiced rider could be seen at once from his Centaur-like poise. He had thrown off his hat, and with his yellow, curly head, and broad-shouldered, handsome, shapely form, looked like a picture in the sunlight. Satterthwaite glanced from him to Miss Ferrard, and saw that her eyes were following his every movement with something more than admiration. He felt, without knowing it almost, some dull sense of discomfort. The leaps and curvetings of the wild creature, chafing at the restraint of the heavy bit, feeling all the odious weight upon his back and debating how it were best to get rid of it, were delightful to Helena. She turned her back on Satterthwaite and encouraged Devereux at the pitch of her voice.

"Take the gate, Jim!" she cried, excitedly. "Over with him!"

"No, not yet," he replied. Then, after a turn or two, he rode up to them.

"Let me up, Jim—do!" begged Isi.

"No; I'm to ride him!" said his sister, imperiously.

"What!" cried Satterthwaite. "Ride on that saddle, Miss Ferrard! How can you venture—"

Devereux was off, and seizing her, swung her lightly up. How she fixed herself in the old saddle he could not tell; but there she was, sitting up straight and to all appearance quite comfortably.

"Give me the whip—oh, Jim, do!" She stooped over, pleadingly.

"Not a whip; I don't want an inquest on you."

She pouted, and shortening up the rein, dealt the colt a slap on the neck that started him at a wild gallop down the field. Satterthwaite with difficulty repressed a cry of alarm, but the young farmer and Isi burst out laughing when they saw first her hat and veil, then her comb, fall to the ground, and, last of all, her long twisted hair all fly in a loose cloud on her shoulders. She galloped up and jumped off, without waiting for the aid proffered by Satterthwaite. Her eyes were dilated and sparkling, and a rose-flush lighted up her face.

"I'm shaken to pieces," she panted. "Isi, come and look for my comb. Now mind, Jim, when I've tied up my hair I'm going to jump the hurdle."

"That you won't," he muttered; he was angry, though proud at the same time, of Satterthwaite's admiring glances, and he thought the girl's wild spirits, innocent and spontaneous though they were, out of place. He mounted the colt and rode away; slowly Satterthwaite followed, leading his horse still, to aid in the search for Miss Ferrard's missing gear. Presently it was found, and Hel twisted up her long, glossy hair in two tails and stuck it in.

"Ride Auster instead," said Satterthwaite, coaxingly. "Do, please, try him; he is as gentle as a lamb, I assure you."

She cast a doubtful look at her lover, who seemed to be sulkily contemplating the hurdle, then at the tempter beside her. Satterthwaite read consent in her eyes before she spoke, and in a minute he had lifted her up and was placing the reins in her hand. He led the horse forward a little, then handing her the whip, let go his hold of the bridle. She rode straight over to Devereux, who said something to her in a low voice that made her hang her head. She took two turns round the field, then back to Satterthwaite.

"I will get down, please," said she, coldly.

"Doesn't he go nicely?" said he—he was eager to hear her praise his horse; "don't you find him easy to ride?"

"Yes, very—very nice," she answered, constrainedly; Satterthwaite was in the act of lifting her down as she said this. He held her for an instant in his grasp, and, leaning forward, said, looking into her eyes as he did so:

"Would you like to ride him always, to own him? tell me?"

But Helena, with a little movement, slipped away without answering, and, as if afraid to remain or to trust herself longer, ran across the field to where Jim was. Perhaps this girl, who was as unsophisticated as a savage and as truthful as only women of the very highest and most cultured stamp are or can be, did not understand his meaning. The Perrys would not have been in the least puzzled by it.

Satterthwaite sprang into the saddle and was after her directly.

"Come and leap the hurdle," he cried to Devereux. He was eager for the contest, and with Helena there to look on and act as umpire, felt himself capable of putting Auster at the side of a house. Devereux too was excited and disputatious. He had got the advantage over Satterthwaite; the position was his beforehand—to keep it was now his care; and this rich, elegant, well-dressed Englishman, with his glossy, prancing horse was no mean rival.

"I'll go first," shouted Satterthwaite, moving down the field so as to give himself a run. Auster cleared the hurdle like a bird. Hel, who was standing well away on one side, clapped her hands with enthusiasm. Then it was Devereux's turn, and he too did well.

"Jim, Jim!—let me try; do!" she cried; "I won't fall off, you'll see."

"No!" he said, gruffly. "You couldn't jump without the crutches."

"Let me send up to Rosslyne for the side-saddle. Do, Miss Ferrard!" pleaded Satterthwaite; "I'll be back with it in half an hour."

She would have liked dearly to give the permission And it was with her eyes fixed on Devereux's face tha she answered no.

Satterthwaite saw this, and it nerved him to further effort. "I will go for it without your leave," he said; "I know you would like it, and why should you not? You are free to do what you like?"

This last sentence was more a question than a statement, and was uttered stooping down almost to her face.

He began to turn the horse's head to go, but she said, imperiously:

"Don't, Mr. Satterthwaite. I will not ride your horse." Then she called to Devereux: "The hurdle is too low—take him at the gate."

The gate was a rickety old structure, with a hollow filled with mud on the other side. A soft fall if the animal did not leap far enough. Satterthwaite, who was feverishly excited now, sent his horse at it, and cleared the whole thing with a leap wide enough to have taken him across the Rack. Devereux followed, the colt jumped short, and slipping in the mud, fell heavily with his rider. Jim utterred a cry—moved purely, he said afterwards, by terror for his horse; but Satterthwaite never heard it in the agonized shriek that burst from Helena. In a moment, before he could dismount, she had flung herself over the gate and was dragging the luckless rider from the confused heap in the hollow.

"Oh, Jim, Jim!" she wailed, pitifully; "are you hurt? Oh! say you're not!"

Isi lent his aid, and Satterthwaite, and the fallen hero was soon upon his legs. Except for a shake, and a good deal of mud, he was none the worse. Then the colt was pulled on his feet—he too had escaped with a dirty coat; and Devereux, sitting on the ditch-side rubbing his pate, felt bound to make some acknowledgment for their trouble.

"You thought I was killed, eh?" said he, addressing Helena, who with white face and lips was trying to laugh as she supported herself against the gate. Satterthwaite was watching her with a feeling that was gradually deepening into despair. She did not answer, but raising her head a little looked at Jim with her splendid eyes.

The other man turned away and began to tighten the straps of his stirrups. He would go home straight, he thought; the sooner the better. Then the gate was opened; Isi took the colt and led him on in front; Helena and Devereux walked together; Satterthwaite followed, walking along beside his horse. Everything looked different to him now, the warm spring air had become choking and oppressive, the stable-yard was an ill-kept, offensive den, and the dreary, tumble-down old house had suddenly lost all its charm. He could see the mountains through an opening in the trees; and a sudden whim took him to go away and ride to Kilnacronan, a village perched on the side of the hills, just to pass the day, and to get off out of sight of them, and try to reason himself out of the depression that had grown upon him. So he mounted and rode out past the kitchen-door without even looking for his companions. He had not got far when a shout came after him.

"Mr. Satterthwaite, don't go! Please wait!" It was Devereux; he ran after him and besought him to come in.

"Oh no! No, thank you!" he replied. "I should be only in the way," he added, bitterly, to himself; "I have been for a long time."

"Do come in, sir—if only for a moment," went on Devereux, looking up to him.

Satterthwaite could discern nothing of exultation or triumph in his rival's eyes. And the thought flashed upon him that after all, since he was beaten in the game, he had better resign his part with a good grace. So he consented; and they entered the farm-kitchen. Miss Ferrard was sitting in the window, apparently quite at home.

"Oh, we were afraid you had gone." Her eyes met his perfectly unconcernedly. He was astonished.

"Thank you! I was about to go. I thought he might like to rest after his fall, you know."

"Oh, that was nothing. I was frightened though, you know," she added, candidly. "I think you were too—you are paler."

Then Devereux ordered the servant to get something to eat. A great piece of cold beef and bread and butter were produced; and the Ferrards and their host did justice to their repast. Satterthwaite drank some whisky, but would eat nothing. Helena talked to Devereux, and laughed over the performances of the animals.

"I like Freney best, Jim. I can stick tighter in the old

saddle—yours is too new and slippery," she said, turning to Satterthwaite.

He assented mutely, and sat watching her face with a bitter longing. She was sitting in half shadow, for the kitchen window was choked with flowers and bird-cages, and the panes were thick old glass that let in but a greenish, faint light. The projecting black chimney of the fireplace obscured the place too, and Helena was sitting facing it. The reflection of the few red embers in the grate glistened in her deep, soft eyes, and lighted up the black, shining coils of hair she had carelessly twisted up in her comb. Devereux's handsome head looked like a pale cameo beside her.

"They are a well-matched couple, so far as beauty goes," thought Satterthwaite, unwillingly; "she idolizes him; and pride alone ought to make him good to her. May be my friend is right; and it is wrong as well as useless to interfere between them. And yet he is only a farmer, and she a nobleman's daughter, and beautiful as an angel! How she looked that time on the horse's back!" He leaned his head on his hand for a minute in a fit of half-angry impatience. It seemed so foolish—so unnatural that things should be allowed to go on in this way. He had wealth and position to offer her—merely what was her due and right in the world; and was the girl to condemn herself to such a life as this mere boor could give her because an unlucky accident had determined his precedence in the field? He felt half inclined to resist, to make some fresh effort. Something ought to be done to save Miss Ferrard from herself. Then he looked up again. There was Helena talking away in a low, sweet voice, and looking and smiling into her lover's eyes. It was beyond bearing; and Satterthwaite pretended he had forgotten something that had to be posted, and tore off at a fierce gallop that soon left Darraghmore far behind him.

They hardly noticed his departure. Isi started on a ramble through the old house and left Helena and Devereux sitting together in the kitchen. They did not lack for material for conversation—the doings and prospects of the colt occupied them both fully, and invidious comparisons were instituted between him and Satterthwaite's beautiful horse. This had lasted nearly an hour when the servant Biddy came running in breathless, and called to Helena:

"Miss, Davy's outside—Dirty Davy, ye know! Cawth has sent him everywhere looking for ye. The lord's had another stroke, and ye're to go home at wanst."

Helena leaped up with an inarticulate cry and seized her hat.

"Isi, Isi!" she shrieked; but Isi was too far off to hear. "Jim, send him home after me by the river road."

Then away she ran as fast as her feet would carry her across the pastures. She had not got far after receiving Dirty Davy's message when she was overtaken by Isi. Jim had found and dispatched him after her almost immediately, and she had barely reached the river bank when he came up with her, breathless and panting.

"Oh Isi, Isi!" she cried, "let us run, it will take us so long to get back."

"Jim told me he'd come down to-morrow night; he can't to-night for he has to go up home."

"Very well," she replied.

"And he told me to remind you about Rusty. What am I to do?"

"Do you or Davy shoot him, or drown him over the bridge when we get in," said Helena, casting a sad look at her favorite who was trotting along beside her, his long, thin red tongue hanging pendulously from his mouth and his brown eyes seeking her face for guidance at every turn of the path.

Hel paid him scant attention, though at any other time such an occurrence would have called forth a burst of grief. She strained every nerve to reach home as quickly as possible, and a wild terror lest all should be over with her father ere she reached him lent her additional energy.

At last the bridge was reached. They crossed the piece of waste ground and again climbed down the bank behind the parish priest's house. A few moments' splashing among the mud and stones brought them to the mill-house garden. Isi leaped up first and dragged Helena, who was by this time utterly exhausted, after him.

Cawth was standing at the back-door watching for them.

"Bruton's here—I thocht ye'd never come—he can dae naething for him. Sae just come richt in."

He was alive at least, and Helena breathed freely again. She pushed past Cawth and went into the house.

A week passed without any change for better or worse in Lord Darraghmore's condition. Satterthwaite called every day at the mill-house door to inquire for him; he saw no one but Cawth, whom even golden bribes could not seduce into civility, not to speak of communicativeness. He rode up to Buona Vista one day, feeling more than usually exercised on Helena's account, to inquire from Madam Really if she had gone as she intended to visit Helena. The servant told him that Madam Really had driven out some twenty minutes before to Rosslyne to visit himself. He rode away as fast as possible to try and overtake her.

Max, the brown pony, must have been in good order that day, for Satterthwaite only came up with madam as she drove up the approach to his own hall-door.

"How do you do?" she cried back to him; "we were playing at hide-and-seek, it seems. I am lucky to find you, even though you are out."

Then they followed the course of the sweep, Madam Really uttering ejaculations of surprise and admiration at the change and improvements she saw. Her clear, sharp tones rang above the noise of the wheels and the horses' feet. She seemed to be, as usual, bright and in good spirits; and Satterthwaite, who had been somewhat dull of late, felt invigorated by the mere seeing and hearing her. She was delighted with the place, which was looking its best that day. The large bay-windows of the house were open, and under their colored awnings there was a vision of cool shadow, perfumed by the rich-colored flowers of the majolica boxes and the parterres of the pleasure-grounds. The woods in all the lovely richness of their May foliage resounded with the voices of the birds. The undergrowth and brambles were gone, and here and there an opening made so that through the long aisles of the beeches and firs you got a distant view of the Rack valley winding towards the mountains.

"It's a paradise!" almost screamed madam as she drew up before the hall-door.

"Glad you like it," said its owner, flinging his rein to a groom and hastening to help her out. "Come in for a few minutes, then I will take you all round."

They went into the one sitting-room—the library; she cast an appreciating glance about her before she sat down in the low chair which he placed for her in the side window.

"Pah! smoke!" she said, curling up her nose; "what a desecration! you men respect nothing. Oh! what a lovely—"

Her eyes had caught the sloping garden beneath. At the other side of the pond, which lay in clear shadow, was a group of beautiful trees; a horse-chestnut in full bloom, covered with superb spikes, which looked like snow against the dark background of a copper-beech whose leaves were fast ripening to a rich brown. Farther back a laburnum, like a gold cascade, dripped brilliant flowerets on the grass. Some of the chestnut blossoms had fallen and floated on the water, quivering as did the shadowed trunk in its glassy depths.

"Fancy Perry wanting me to drain that pond, and recommending the slope for potatoes."

"Like him!" said madam with a chuckle; "has he seen it since you got it in such order?"

"Oh yes!" replied Satterthwaite. "He was here a week or so ago."

He glanced around with an involuntary smile at the recollection of Perry's performance on that day.

"Isn't he a savage, that character? Anything of this sort," nodding towards the garden, "is simply incomprehensible to these people. If he saw it in England he would admire it and talk about it, but the idea of having such things here would seem ridiculous to him. I can't understand it. They know what is nice—they can appreciate it thoroughly, but they would never imitate it or dream of having it for themselves. They want example, you know. This is the consequence of their being left to themselves, of absenteeism; society is disintegrated—disorganized. Look how the Perrys dress; if Lady Comerford were to come here now and again and invite them to an annual ball, give them a glimpse of civilization, the creatures would have some respect for themselves and conform to modern ideas a little more than they do."

"Well," said Satterthwaite, "I was going to say they are to be pitied; but they at least do not know what they lose. What I cannot understand is that their manners are so utterly vulgar. Why should that be? Perry is not a Chesterfield, and Mrs. Perry's comportment leaves much to be desired; but the girls are much worse than both."

"You are right, Mr. Satterthwaite; and the rising generation of Roman Catholics all over the country are infinitely less tolerable than their parents. I will prove to you the reason, taking this one place for a type of the rest. The Misses Perry, the Hollahans, Miss Fair, and some others of the same social class were all educated at the same convent-school, and with them the farmers' daughters, the shop-keepers' and petty traders' of the district, in fact the two inferior social grades. You can imagine how that amalgamation would result. The inferior class, because it predominated numerically, impressed its stamp upon the others. If you were to talk to Devereux's sister, or any of the shop-keepers' girls in the town, you would find them precisely the same as the Perrys. There is a distinction, but not a tittle of difference between the various classes of Roman Catholics. Professionals and traders are all the same as to manners and culture; and their own obtuseness as to the importance of early association is to blame."

"Roman Catholic society is new. It must be new, for they have only legally existed, so to say, very recently. And since you say the Disestablishment removed a means of culture from them, you ought not to be too hard upon their shortcomings."

"Bah! I'm not. It's their conceit with themselves that I ridicule. They shut their eyes to everything that is æsthetic, that is intellectual. Look at their faces; infallibility is written all over them. If they can play or sing so as to torture every one within earshot, they are 'highly educated;' if they have a drawing-room, or two or three, crammed full of looking-glass and gilding—catch them with pictures or books in their possession!—they are elegance itself; and if they have been presented and have furnished the Castle with matter for ridicule and laughter for a season, they are fit to adorn the peerage forthwith. I give them all credit for their good intentions; and, considering the means at their disposal and the drawbacks that they labor under, they have already accomplished a good deal."

"Assuming that the Protestants in this country are the exclusive possessors of culture, refinement, etc., do you not think the ecclesiastical prohibition and discouragement of social intercourse has had a certain effect in checking the downward progress of class improvement?"

"Well, isn't that what I told you before? The Disestablishment threw the Protestant party on its own resources. They gathered themselves together, and of course the *narrow*, anti-liberal section in it, finding the spirit of the hour in accordance with and ready to lend itself to their views, showed a hostile front to the Roman Catholics, whose leaders in turn were not slow to seize their opportunity, and, as you know, have been consolidating and advancing their claims ever since. It will take half a century to recover the mischief of that measure."

"I still believe you are mistaken—you must be! How could an Act, proclaimed just and necessary by the whole world, have brought about a state of things such as you describe?"

"The whole world doesn't know Irish society or the peculiar condition of the people," snapped madam. "This is the mischief of having philosophers for rulers. They fix their eyes on a principle shining somewhere in the distance, and trample over all manner of expediencies and usefulness till they haul the thing down and make a present of it to people that never wanted it, and now that they have it find it no matter of use or good, but quite the contrary."

"Come down into my garden—come, Mrs. Really. I want to talk to you about something. We'll come back here when you have seen the improvements I have made."

They went out together and down the broad steps of the hall-door. Satterthwaite felt glad to get out again; he wanted to speak of the Ferrards, and it seemed somehow easier to talk about Helena in the fresh, open garden. It is possible that madam, foreseeing his intention, desired to stave it off as long as possible, for she kept up a constant string of questions and exclamations.

"Japonica—yes; but it won't flower for you till next spring. The plant will be all the better for it too. You say *improvements!* Yes—I call it a *neue erschaffung*—a creation all over. It is exquisite! The idea of this being made out of that wild slope. Are those the water-lilies you spoke of coming up?"

They were standing on the top of the terraced slope now.

"Yes," said Satterthwaite. "There are a few leaves of nymphæa showing, but they take a good time to strike. I don't know whether or not to root out that clump of reeds. From the window it looks well enough, but from the seat it hides the water completely."

"Leave it," said madam; "it would look too artificial without it. You see the pond is so small."

"Yes, it is small. I wish it was large enough for a swan; it would make a pretty sketch. Look at the flowers shadowed in it."

The tall chestnut with its snowy armor seemed doubled by its reflection in the pool. They could hear the hum of the bees above their heads, and even on the ground they were busy among the fallen blossoms and the sticky, brown sheaths of the leaves. Suddenly the shadow was broken by a little water-hen, which ran down from beneath the trees and swam fussily across the pool to her nest among the reeds. The shrill cluck of the little creature broke the stillness, and the shadow-tree in the water moved as though a storm were blowing.

"You would fancy the leaves would be shaken off," said Mrs. Really, laughing. "Don't disturb her. I would rather have that than a swan."

"Yes; your taste lies that way," said he, meaningly. He saw an opening now, and was determined to follow it out. "I must say I do not agree with you. No, no—that may be carried too far."

"Hum! no amount of training, education, or care would make anything of that wild bird but what she is. She would be perfectly capable of biting the fingers of any one who tried it, either."

All this was uttered in a tone of lightest persiflage by Madam Really. She had plucked a red oxlip and was twirling it with affected carelessness in her fingers, watching Satterthwaite with eyes that shone like topazes beneath their drooped lids.

Notwithstanding what he had seen that day at Darraghmore, he had done nothing since but think of Helena, and felt impelled to make one more effort. He persuaded himself that her emotion was natural—the outcome of mere nervousness. She had some affection for Devereux—that was perhaps excusable, natural, considering how much they had been thrown together. But it seemed to him impossible and wrong that such a union could take place. And now he had a wild hope of being able to enlist Madam Really on his side. It was a last chance; but drowning men catch at straws, and though he had a half-perception that this was but a straw, he intended to try it.

They were passing by a little rustic seat and he stopped, and turning so as to face her, leaned both hands behind him on the rail and said:

"How is Lord Darraghmore to-day? I could not make up my mind to face that hag again. She looks as if she thought I was coming to steal something, and I want so much to see Miss Ferrard."

"I don't think you will see her again," replied Mrs. Really in a measured, cold voice, and taking no notice of his start of surprise. "Doctor Bruton says the old man cannot last more than twenty-four hours now. I cannot do anything for them. I went, of course, and saw Helena, who seems to be nursing him most devotedly. Poor child! how pale and worn she looked! but there is nothing to be done."

"Not now," said Satterthwaite, almost irritably. "I mean, when he is dead."

"I may be wrong, but I believe that the very day the old man is buried will see Hel and Devereux on their way to Canada." And as Mrs. Really finished this she raised her eyelids and looked straight into Satterthwaite's eyes as if defying him.

"Mrs. Really," said he, driven to bay at last, and desperate, "I do not think Devereux a suitable match for Miss Ferrard. I think that girl is fully capable of filling the place in society her birth and beauty entitle her to; and—"

"And you propose to take this risk, this charge upon yourself." She finished his sentence for him. "No, no, Mr. Satterthwaite, I think too much of you and of her to stand idly by and see such a folly perpetrated. You do not know the Ferrards. They are not in their present position for nothing, believe me; they have fallen by their own fault. People are like water, they find their own level sooner or later in this world; and if you, my dear sir, were to interfere here between this girl and her lover, you would rue it, and Helena too, the longest day you lived. You talk of educating her. Not a Ferrard that ever lived was susceptible of education. They are splendid animals; make excellent soldiers, as I have seen, but that is all. Believe me, Mr. Satterthwaite, Helena is utterly devoid of intellect. Energy and will she has plenty of, like the rest, and Devereux has almost civilized her, but 'so far, and no farther.' You could no more tame her permanently than you could a gypsy; take my word for it, and do not wreck your life and hers in a fruitless attempt."

"You ought to know them; still—" He turned away his head with a determined movement.

She looked at his downcast face with a glance that was half pitying, half admiring.

"'Convince a man against his will, he's of the same opinion still;' is that it? Well, I like your spirit. She is dazzled a little by your superior appearance, your beautiful house, etc.; but tell me, do you think that Hel Ferrard, as she is at this moment, could ever move in your circle in London? could you present her to your lady friends? No, Mr. Satterthwaite, do not wrong yourself and her; don't spoil her life—and she has longer to live than you—leave her to Devereux. She is his first love and he hers. She is a woman and weak, and your refinement and superiority may have momentarily caught her eye. Perhaps, like all daughters of Eve, she is a coquette. She is beautiful, and she may have thrown you some crumbs of encouragement; but, Mr. Satterthwaite, you are not what I take you to be if you prove yourself now a blind egotist, if you step between these two young creatures."

He did not hear what she was saying. He was plunged in deep thought, and with a pale face walked along beside her. He had never fully realized the position until now, and certainly Madam Really had in no way beaten about the bush in placing the affair before him. She was sincere; that he could not refuse to believe. The whole expression of her face had changed; the tones of her voice were different, and he began to feel a strange, and to him a novel, sensation of self-doubt and distrust. What if he should have been wrong after all? If, instead of Helena's good and advancement, he had been seeking his own gratification? Had he not acted treacherously to Devereux? mere farm lout, boorish rustic as he might be, he was yet a man, and the girl was his promised wife long before he, an interloper, had appeared in the field at all. Madam Really's keen tongue seemed to have stripped every fibre and laid bare every nerve of the affair in glaring black and white. She almost accused him in plain language of seducing Helena's affections willfully from her betrothed husband. She was a wild creature, no doubt; but what other than a pure object could this woman have in appealing to him against himself as she had done?

They walked back to the house in silence, and re-entered the library. Mrs. Really sat down and looked about her at the well-filled book-shelves, the pictures and china, and the open piano.

"The idea of wanting to add Hel to this collection!" said she to herself; "I could never allow such a thing! The idea of that wild bird beating her wings in such a gilt cage!"

"The dining-room is not carpeted yet, and I have not decided whether to use the drawing-room as a billiard-room or not," said Satterthwaite, forcing himself to speak in his customary cheerful, sonorous voice again. He wished now that his visitor would leave him. He wanted to be alone with his thoughts, and madam's talk somehow began to pall upon him. He wanted to think over all she had been saying, to debate what he was to do. Helena was not to be given up so easily. And he felt a dull sense of discomfort and *malaise.* However, he exerted himself to the utmost to entertain his guest.

"This is the room of all the house to live in," said she; "I like your pictures. That is a good Cenci; what a difficult expression it is to catch—that of the mouth, I mean. I have only one or two pictures. My husband bought me all those engravings you saw, while I was away at Buxton for my neuralgia, and there the things were hanging when I came back. He wanted to surprise me—"

"Look at this, please," said Satterthwaite, walking over to the window with a small painting, done on a piece of board, in his hands. She rose and placing herself in the proper light looked at it long and earnestly.

It was a study of an Hungarian peasant girl. A singularly wild, beautiful face, sibyl-like and weird, with great, terrified blue eyes. Dark curls were blown sideways and floated like a veil from her head. The soft-lipped but determined mouth seemed parting for speech. It was not a child's face, neither was it a woman's. And yet it had a fire and character of its own—one of those unforgetable expressions that, when a real painter catches and fixes it, lives longer in our memories than the mere living face.

"Dear! how like," she cried, "it is—"

"Yes, is it not? The brow here is narrower though, than Helen—" Satterthwaite stopped suddenly, and placing the little picture—it was not more than a foot square—on a velvet bracket near the window, stood back and scrutinized it searchingly. After a moment or two he seated himself opposite to her, and in a business-like, indifferent tone asked:

"Where will Devereux get the money to take them to Canada, and to establish them there?"

"He has some money of course—people like him have always money. I should not be surprised if he had five or six hundred of his own; that is, provided his father allows him to keep the farm produce; if it is otherwise, I cannot tell."

Satterthwaite stared thoughtfully out of the window, pulling the end of his mustache.

"I never asked you to take anything. I insist you do not go until I get you something."

Mrs. Really had risen and asked for her carriage. He rang the bell hurriedly.

"No, no! I shall be back to lunch. Now, Mr. Satterthwaite, when are you to be in Darraghstown again? I hope," she added, "that you will think seriously of what I said. Don't think me impertinent or interfering, pray. I know I am incurring a risk."

She was going down the steps now. Satterthwaite handed her the reins, and shook hands with her cordially, ignoring her last speech save for a smile. Then she shook the reins, and the pony started off down the sweep. Satterthwaite remained standing on his hall-door steps, and watched the little phaeton circle the lawn among the trees. The crackling of the gravel ceased at last, the gates swung to with a crash behind it. For a few moments he could hear the trot of the pony going down the lane. Then all was still again; the cawing of the rooks and the soft murmur of the young leaves alone disturbed the stillness of the sweet spring day.

He remained still for a few minutes, then walked absently into the wood by the path that skirted the pleasure-ground; it was the same route that he had come with the Ferrards the day they were shooting in the wood, and Satterthwaite began to pace it up and down moodily. He never dreamed he could have felt anything of the kind so much; and he could not explain to himself how the feeling had grown upon him. He remembered the first time he saw Helena in the Perrys' house; he had been interested in her, of course; who would not have been? Then the day they met at Darraghmore and explored the old house together. So far from encouraging, she had avoided him; certainly he had no complaint against the girl on that score. Then came the day in the woods. That handsome Devereux had had the start of him—that was all, he told himself, gnawing his mustache. But the fellow had his rights too; and even if Helena were inclined—"inclined to," he repeated, with a bitter laugh, "after what I saw that day at Darraghmore? No! she idolizes him. If she consented to marry me, it will be, as my friend hints, for my house and horses. No, no! Devereux is her first love, and she his. I'm a fool!"

He had leaned his back against a pine tree, and was looking away up a long, green aisle in the woods. A scented wind swept lightly down the long open, shaking the catkins of the pines and rudely kissing the wood-primroses. The honey scent of the furze blossoms on the mountains hung upon it yet, and Satterthwaite removed his hat and let it play upon his burning forehead; for a minute only; then he turned towards the house, walking quickly.

"I'll go back to London," said he to himself; "things here are sufficiently in train for me to leave them for a month or so; and first to see what I can do for my friends at Darraghmore."

He went into the library and unlocking his desk, spent a few minutes searching among his papers. Then he came out with his whip in his hand and shouted an order to a man who was raking the gravel before the coach-house door. In a few minutes Black Auster, saddled and bridled, was led round; his master mounted and rode away.

It was between three and four in the afternoon. The trees began to throw long shadows across the dusty road, and the distant Galtees lay bathed in a pale gold color, as Mr. Satterthwaite trotted his black horse up to the old entrance of Darraghmore. The grass on the deserted drive was rank and long, and tall nettles and docks were springing up at the side; the cows were browsing almost knee-deep in the rich pasture; and young Devereux, their owner, sitting on a broken granite pillar by the edge of the old steps, was engaged in mending a whip, the leather of which was all unplaited. He had thrown off his coat for coolness' sake, and, tired after a morning's hard work with his colt, was now taking his ease. He did not see the approaching equestrian until he was close upon him, for the horse's hoofs made hardly any sound in the soft grass.

"Good-day, Mr. Devereux!" said Satterthwaite, pulling up. "You are surprised to see me. I shan't keep you long, though. You were telling me you intended selling your colt, eh?"

Devereux opened his blue eyes and looked at him in astonishment, and a crowd of fancies rushed into his brain, crowding on top of each other. The colt had been a sore thought to him for some time back. How was he to go to Canada without disposing of it in some way? He could leave him, like the rest of the stock and chattels—the cows and pigs, and the well-plenished dairy; but it was a hard thing for him, when he had reared and trained the animal, to turn his back and let some one else step in—even though it was his own father—and take all the credit and gains away from him. To dispose of him by private sale was not a thing to be done in the twinkling of an eye, and a couple or so of days was all the time he had now. Could it be that the Englishman wanted to buy him? His face flushed up, and he answered, stammering:

"I—I'd sell him—yes."

"Well, Mr. Devereux," said Satterthwaite, speaking in a dry, hard voice, "you said, if I recollect rightly, that you expected to get eighty or so pounds for him at Ballinasloe; that's six months off; and, taking into account his keep and so forth till then, will you take seventy-five for him now?"

Satterthwaite, in his first generous impulse, had intended to offer a hundred for the horse, but on reflection he concluded to put on at least the appearance of driving a fair bargain.

"Seventy-five—I'd have given him to you, sir, for fifty. When will you have him sent home?"

"Any time," said Satterthwaite, absently. "This evening, or to-morrow—when you like; and I will leave you these notes now; I chanced to have Bank of England notes for the amount or near it."

He put his hand in his pocket as he spoke to take out his *portemonnaie*. Devereux was standing near the black horse's shoulder; his eyes were turned in bewilderment away towards the open field, and the oblique rays of the declining sun gilded his crest of yellow curls like a glory, and shone in his soft blue eyes. Satterthwaite counted the notes mechanically, then handed them to the young fellow with a somewhat dreary smile. He was no longer at the white heat of self-sacrificing resolve, and Helena's face and eyes, as he saw them when he lifted her off the horse, seemed to float with mocking persistency before his own. He held out the clean, gray notes with a slow, grudging feeling, and for a moment a terrible sensation of envy and disappointment, mixed with indignation, took possession of him. Devereux, who seemed too surprised even to thank him, took the money and began to count it slowly, reading the signature on each bank note and turning them over deliberately.

"Well," said Satterthwaite at last, "is it right?"

"Yes," replied the young fellow, stuffing the bundle into his pocket. "I'm greatly obliged to you, sir. I'll have him up to-night to your man Jenkins, for I'll have a deal to do these next few days."

These last words were uttered rather more to himself than to Satterthwaite, who was looking at him in an earnest, abstracted sort of way, as if he thought of something he would like to say but could not. They remained standing thus awkwardly together, neither speaking. At last Satterthwaite drew up his reins to go. "Good-bye," said he, curtly, and with one more glance at the young fellow, he turned his horse and rode back to the gate entrance. As he took the course to the left, on to the Tobergeen Road, he looked back once more at the old house of Darraghmore. The nettle-grown carriage-drive wound away to the front, which lay in clear, gray shadow now, for the sun had got round to the west. The swallows were flying in and out the empty windows, and he could see the tall climbing-rose, the flowers of which he had aided Helena to gather. The cows were all standing at the yard door, lowing to be milked, and above the deep musical sound rose the cawing of the rooks in the trees. Satterthwaite drew a deep sigh as he looked. "One could live contentedly enough like that," said he to himself. "What can a man want more?" He was thinking of the man whom he had left standing in the field, amazed and happy—not of himself, to whose felicity he now deemed an important ingredient lacking.

He rode on between hedge-rows, out of whose tangled green, pale stars of wild-honeysuckle were shining. Their ethereal perfume was lost in the strong bitter-sweet of the hawthorn. Tall, dusty nettles bordered the ditches and hid the fern leaves and one or two late-staying primroses. A little running stream bubbled and muttered below, and from the distant woods came the cuckoos' and the thrushes' even-song. After a long ride he rounded the slope of Tobergeen and a sudden whim took him to climb the hill and make some excuse to get sight of the old Devereux. So he passed through the white wooden gate, hospitably open, and on up the rugged lane between two wild hedges, where alder blossoms and hawthorns, sweet-brier and wild-honeysuckle united in one lush bouquet, and out of which the thrushes flew with a wild alarm-note at the clatter of the now tired horse among the stones. At last they reached the top and stood before the door of the old farm-house. A man presented himself at it suddenly, calling hurriedly almost before he appeared:

"Jim—is it you, Jim?"

"No," replied Satterthwaite; "it is I, Mr. Satterthwaite of Rosslyne; and will you be good enough to give my horse a drink of gruel? He is tired, and I have a good piece to go."

"Certainly, sir. Con, Con!" he called. "Come in, sir, and sit down. Do, if you please. I thought it was Freney's foot, with my son from Darraghmore."

"Freney is not unlike my horse," said Satterthwaite, swinging himself down. "I won't go in, thank you. I never touch whisky, either. No, much obliged. Yes, Freney's a fine brute."

"Ah!" returned the farmer in an exulting tone, "Jim has a wonderful hand with a horse. I never saw anything like the way he can manage beasts. He'd tame anything."

Satterthwaite smiled bitterly at this encomium. "What if I were to tell him that his son had sold me the colt? That would play the deuce with his new project. No, no, that would not answer."

Then Jim's mother came out—an amiable, mild-eyed woman—pretty still, but timid and anxious looking, and joined her entreaties to those of her husband. Satterthwaite refused, and mounting the refreshed Auster, wished the couple a pleasant good-night, and began to descend the hill.

The two old people stood looking after him.

"Do you know what," said Devereux, turning to his wife, "I'd never be surprised he'd buy the colt, he speaks that warm about it. He's terrible rich. To see the drains, and buildings, and gardens he has there at Rosslyne—'tis wonderful, I'm told."

"May be he would then after all! These English are so rich."

"Ay, and don't know what to do with it. They're all quare—I never met one of 'em was like other people. Look at that jobber came here last October with Jim O'Brien; he'd drink straight on till he'd fall, an' then to sleep with him like a log."

"I don't know but what it was a peaceabler way, then," said the wife in a dubious tone, as if not unwilling to allow that this especial phase of English "quareness" was not without its redeeming feature in her eyes.

The horseman was out of sight now, so they went back to the house.

Satterthwaite held his way down the lane slowly. The view of the valley was beautiful. The gray and purple of the barren tracts that alternated with the chess-board-like squares of green corn and meadow on the mountain-side were varied here and there by a gold fleck of furze-bloom or the white wall of some mountain shieling, and the river ran still and white between its two pebble-strewn banks.

Once down on the road, he took the Darraghstown direction at a quick trot; he wanted to hear how Lord Darraghmore was, and to see Perry on some business. The demesne wall of Comerford was soon reached, and in the shadow of the great overhanging chestnuts he slacked his rein again. He was wondering how it was with Helena in the sick-room at the mill-house. "How white and worn she looked." Mrs. Really's words that morning came back to him. Poor Hel! poor child! He would have given the world to have been able to assist and console her. Then he fell into a half-melancholy reverie, and letting the reins fall on the horse's neck left him to take his own way. The honey-laden blossoms were dropping from the boughs, and the road was carpeted in pink and white. The bees were still at work, and a sweet, drowsy hum filled the air. The low of the cattle across the Rack came over the open water with a distant, home-like sound, and he could hear a girl's fresh voice lilting some old tune as she returned with her milk-pails from the field. Little by little the sun was sinking to the western edge of the horizon. The tops of the trees were bathed yet in a pale gold light. A red mist was gathering round the eagle-haunted peaks of the Galtees, and their sharp profiles showed more and more distinct and black. The red deepened to crimson, then purple shading into a pale yellowish mist, in which here and there a tiny sparklet was visible. Soon he had crossed the bridge and rode down to the Perrys' door. Two dusky figures were standing on the pavement before it—Perry and old Doctor Bruton.

"Hillo, Mr. Satterthwaite!" cried Perry in his big, loud voice; "how are you? Bruton, our new neighbor from Rosslyne."

"I am told," began Satterthwaite, "that Lord Darraghmore is dying."

"Sinking fast," said the old doctor, a queer, lean old man, with a figure and face like the presentments of Don Quixote, dressed in an old black dress-coat, and with a great satin stock that came up to his chin. "He cannot last till morning."

Satterthwaite cast a lingering look at the gloomy old house as he turned to ride off. How were things going on there? he wondered to himself.

"I'll send in to-morrow to know how he is."

"Humph!" said Perry, "I'll let you know about that. I dare say," he added in a lower tone, "you'd like to attend the funeral?"

"Yes. Where could we get a carriage?"

"Why, they'll all walk. Sure it's only up there on the slope. Yes—I'll tell you to-morrow."

There was some impropriety in discussing these details while the poor old man was yet alive, and Satterthwaite was moving on in order to put a stop to the conversation.

"Very well—good-night. Good-night, doctor," he replied over his shoulder.

CHAPTER XV.

"Und der Tod ist unser Arzt. Ach! ich will nichts Böses von ihm reden, und nicht Andre in ihrem Vertrauen stören; denn da er der einzige Arzt ist, so mögen Sie immerhin glauben er sei auch der Beste, und das einzige mittel das er anwendet, seine ewige Erd-kur, sei auch das Beste." HEINE.

"But religion, they tell us, ought not to be ridiculed, and they tell us truth, yet surely the corruptions may; for we are taught by the tritest maxim in the world that religion being the best of things, its corruptions are likely to be the worst." SWIFT.

DOCTOR BRUTON was right; his patient died just eleven hours after he had spoken to Mr. Satterthwaite, and foretold the time the old lord had to live.

The mill-house was darkened, and a bunch of crape hung on the door. The wolf-dog was walking up and down the deserted parlor, whining and scratching at the door of that inner room where his master was lying, alone and in the dark. The parlor had been swept and garnished in some rude sort. The windows were closed and the curtains drawn, but a stray sunbeam came in through a chink and lighted up the bleared eyes of the old dog, and a whole evensong of thrushes and blackbirds poured in the broken panes so as almost to drown his piteous moans. The dead man in the little back room, with the sheet drawn over his worn white face, had heard the birds that morning, when in the first flush of dawn he had waked out of the sleep which was indeed but a sort of prelude to the great sleep which soon after overtook him. But now the sunlight and the birds were closing the day together merrily, a day which for the poor old man had never closed, hardly begun, at all. Pale-faced Helena, sitting all night beside him, had given him a drink and smoothed the pillow, and he looked at her once—she often thought of it afterwards—then stretched down his weary limbs and closed his eyes again—for good and all this time.

So now the door was locked and the curtains drawn, and there he would lie till the time should come to take him to the Abbey church-yard. Had he been a Catholic things would have been differently ordered. There would have been wax candles lighting night and day, and watchers praying, and the house would have been open to all who chose to come and pay their last respects to him, that odd—savage if you will—but intensely human Irish fashion, according to which all joys and sorrows are common property. Irish human nature, wishing rather to take cheerful views of things, has contrived to suppress the element of grief as much as possible, in many cases to put it out of sight altogether.

Helena however determined to uphold the colder tradition of her own class, which indeed seemed to her just now not only more decent, but more convenient.

The towns-folk were in some sort of commotion over the event. A good many, even of those to whom he owed money, shut up their shop windows, nearly all drank something extra, and there was much talking and comparing notes with the good old time when this man's father was "waking," and two hogsheads of whisky were drunk by his sympathizing adherents. There was no "giving out" on this occasion. Dirty Davy had reported that Miss Helena had barred the doors with her own hands, and dared him or Cawth open them to anybody, and added the astounding, incredible news that there was not a drop of whisky in the mill-house. A death in Darraghstown and no whisky, no wake! It was unaccountable. The bridge was thronged with malcontents all day, and some walked in couples past the door, casting curious glances at the front of the house. The ill deeds of the

Ferrards were the chief theme of their talk. Later on Davy bruited it abroad that Miss Hel had got money from England, and meant to pay all that was owing in the town; whereupon a sort of revulsion of feeling took place. Some more shops closed their shutters. The antiquity of the family was remembered, and Miss Hel's beauty and breeding descanted upon. The inherent and ineradicable virtues of "rael owld blood" and "owld stock" occupied their minds and tongues; and Mr. Satterthwaite, from Rosslyne, who rode up to the post-office in the afternoon to post his letters, could hardly get anybody to hold his horse. A few women ventured to the yard-door on some officious kindness ostensibly, but Cawth reconnoitred them cautiously from a hole in the wall, and sent them coldly about their business.

Char was in his own room writing letters. One must be sent to his step-brother Claude, of the Imperial Hussars, at Vienna; one to Bath, to his aunts; to San Francisco, to another step-brother supposed to be there, but shot in a brawl nearly a year before. Clanrickarde was also at Vienna, and Claude, now Lord Darraghmore, would inform him of their father's death. For that matter Char could do it in person, for he expected to be in Vienna himself ere the week was out; he would not be sorry for that, for, after all, Darraghstown was a stupid hole, and since this wretched Englishman had come more unbearable than ever. Then he dropped the pen and ran his hands through his curly black hair, yawning at his ease. Writing letters was not to his taste, and, moreover, something had occurred that afternoon that had discomposed him seriously. Hel had got all the money in her possession—she always kept the money nowadays, since Clan's departure—and had said she intended paying the family debts in the town. So Cawth in mingled rage and grief had informed him, and this too when they were going to leave the place forever and wanted the money so badly. Char concluded that Hel must be mad; there was no other way of accounting for that sort of nonsense. She had eighty pounds, and their aunts in Bath had sent a check for fifty, one hundred and thirty pounds, and she wanted to waste such potentialities of luxury. He would not allow her to do it. So he told Cawth, and confirming his resolution with a vigorous oath, he jumped up from the table and followed her down-stairs. Cawth walked on hopefully before him—she could not understand Helena's mood—and led the way into the kitchen, where the two younger members of the family were sitting together.

The evening was warm out of doors, but the old house was damp and dark. Helena, chilled and dispirited, was crouching over a tiny peat fire on the hearth, holding out her hands over the dull-red glare, partly to warm them and partly to keep the light out of her eyes, sore with crying and with want of sleep. Isi stood beside her, with his back against the wall and his arms folded, looking at her thoughtfully.

When the kitchen-door opened and Cawth appeared, Char tramping heavily behind her, Helena looked round a moment, then resumed her pose apathetically. Isi raised his head and looked defiantly at Char, his dark brow frowning, his eyes sparkling and angry. Neither of the defensive party spoke. Cawth finished rattling among some of her cooking-gear in the corner, and flung herself on a chair with a groan of rage.

"Ma word, but we's a' to turn oot and beg for Miss Ferrard's airs; giv' a' the money to they fules! I'll ha' my wage. I'd warran' ye years and years of wages; it's no the work-house I'd be facin' noo if I'd taken my ain siller lang—"

Char cut her short.

"You'll give me fifty of that money. I'll have my share. Do you hear, Hel? It's I who have a right to it, and not you." Char blustered and stamped.

Helena had folded her hands in her lap, and, without even looking at him, was blankly impassive. Isi stood forward a little, his fists clenched.

"I say you must hand it over," vociferated Char. "I will make you; see if I don't! and you, you pup" (this was to Isi), "interfere if you dare!" He caught Helena's arm as he spoke, and was swinging her off her seat, but Isi was too quick and jumped at him, striking down his arm with a quick, hard blow. Char was a bully, and a coward like most bullies, but he was in a fury, and the two boys were grappling with each other directly. Helena caught Char's arms from behind his back and held him. In obedience to a glance from her Isi drew back, his lip set, however, determinedly, and watching his opponent's eye.

"Listen," said Helena in a distinct, hard tone. "I have not got the money here. Jim Devereux is keeping it for me, and you dare not take it from him. I shall pay every farthing we owe in the town; and, Cawth, I'll punish you if you dare to speak of it again as you have now. I'll punish you, do you hear?"

Cawth, who had advanced, and was beginning to utter a fresh volley of insolence, shrunk from the fiery glance the girl shot at her and sat down again appalled. Helena turned again to Char.

"You shall get your share, and so shall Isi, of whatever is left—not a penny more; and if you say more now you shall not have anything at all. You can't make me give it to you."

Char's eyes fell before hers, and he quailed at the threat which he well knew she would and could put into execution. He muttered and grumbled below his breath, and slouched across the kitchen to a dark corner, where he sat down and brooded in dumb sullenness. Cawth lifted up her voice and wept aloud. She hoped to soften her ruler by this means, but she was mistaken. Helena remained for some ten minutes or so stolidly impassive, then abruptly ordered the old woman to prepare supper. She obeyed sulkily, and they partook of the meal together in unbroken silence. Helena ate scarcely anything. The excitement had passed away, leaving her weary and crushed in body and mind. The supper over, the two boys went upstairs to smoke or sleep as they inclined, and Helena returned to the creepy stool before the hearth. Cawth, who was watching her stealthily, proposed to make tea;

it was a peace-overture, and was accepted as such, and the old woman and she sat in the half-dark and drank the tea together.

"Perry sent in word he had settled everything—the funeral, ye know—that time ye war asleep. 'Twill be on Wednesday; an' Mrs. Really brought the message. She wanted to see ye badly, and asked if ye'd let her in the morn."

"What does she want?" said Helena, wearily. "I'll speak to Jim about it."

Then she laid aside her cup and saucer, and resting her elbows on her lap, leaned her aching head on her hands and remained a long time without speaking or stirring. She could not go to bed, for she had to wait to see Jim Devereux, was was to come in by the river-road and the back gardens of the houses, so as not to be seen from the road, to arrange some matters with her. She was worn out and exhausted, and before long her head drooped lower and lower, and at last in that uneasy posture she fell asleep. She had not been so long when the back door opened noiselessly and the young farmer entered. He cast a rapid glance round. There was no one but Cawth dozing in an old arm-chair she had fetched out of the sitting-room. He stepped lightly across the floor and seated himself in a vacant chair beside the sleeping girl, and without waking her, remained a while looking at her pityingly. Then seeing by her fitful starts and moans that she was uneasy, he half lifted her up, half drew her, as softly and gently as if she were an infant, till her head rested against him. Her face was upturned now to his, and the firelight fell upon it, showing the paleness of her cheek, on which the long eyelashes rested in dark contrast. A lock of tangled dark hair had fallen over her brow; he stroked it back with rough but reverent fingers tenderly. For more than an hour Helena rested, guarded thus. At last he looked at his watch, and deemed it necessary to awake his charge.

She started and stood up.

"Oh Jim, why did you let me sleep so? It must be

awfully late. Oh dear! how tired and dazed I am! And I was dreaming—"

Then poor Helena sat down again suddenly, and burst out crying and sobbing. He took her hands in his and stroked and pressed them; still she did not cease. He knelt down beside her, and put one arm round her and drew her closer, and leaned his cheek on hers till she stopped, soothed and quieted like a child.

"What ails ye, my bird Hel, eh, what? Was it Char?"

"Oh no; that's done now. That was nothing."

Then she drew away from him, and he sat down again, watching her gravely.

"No," she continued, "it wasn't that, it's everything together, I think," and she sighed and her lip quivered.

"Listen!" said Jim; "imagine Satterthwaite coming down and buying Freney from me. He did, and I've the money at home—seventy-five pounds."

Helena turned round suddenly, staring at him with bewildered eyes.

"Satterthwaite!" she repeated, flushing suddenly, "he bought the horse?"

"Bought and paid for him, and he's home in Rosslyne stables now."

"Ah, Jim," cried she, effusively, "he is a good fellow. I always knew it."

"Yes, if he had prosecuted Char that time, where would we be now?"

Helena did not reply. She had rested her aching head in her hand and was looking into the fire in a sort of dream. It was to her so wonderful that just now Satterthwaite should have performed this second act of beneficence. How good he must be and how amiable! She remembered the day in the wood, his care of and courtesy to her, both of them a new experience to Helena. She had his book too that he had given her up-stairs; this time it was carefully laid aside among her most valued possessions. Then, too, in a mist of doubt and regret there rose before her his face and the words he had said when he lifted her off his beautiful horse that day they were at Darraghmore together. But Jim Devereux pulled down her hand and made her look at him.

"Ah, Hel!" said he with a sigh, "I wish this was all over. I was up at Tobergeen and we had a dreadful row. It's all Father Quaide's doings, but for him things would go all right; but he's so anxious about that fifty pounds. I declare I don't know what he wants with all this money. Look at Mrs. Dwyer's funeral; I gave them a pound then—and, faith, I'm sorry for it now."

"You did! to whom did you pay it?"

"Augh! when it was all over and we were going away there was a table in the hall with a cloth and a lighted candle, and Dwyer sitting at one side and two of his children at the other to take the money for the priests. It was enough to make one sick to see them. However, every one gave, and I'm told that they made their forty-five pounds. I can't understand them preaching about purgatory and the tortures of it, and they won't say a mass for a creature's soul till they are paid first."

"He wouldn't marry us then?" said Helena.

"No, nor any priest in Ireland; we'll just make the journey. Satterthwaite's money will take us over well, and we needn't break the three hundred pounds. So I'm ready for the road. Isi and you and I will get along first rate—eh, Hel?"

He stooped towards her, leaning his hand on her shoulder and looked with his bright, confident glance into her dimmed, tear-stained eyes.

Hel looked up at him, a faint smile for a moment flickered on her lips, to be followed by a sigh, however.

"You are not afraid, are you? Hel, are you as true as I am?" He held out his hand to her, and she laid hers, now warm and trembling, in it. There was a silence, broken only by their breathing, for a while. Then he spoke:

"I'll be round to-morrow night if I can. There's no use setting them talking. Do you want any money before Wednesday?"

"No," said Hel, firmly. "I'll want it all on Wednesday, though, to pay the bills and give Char his share."

"Ay, that's right, Hel; leave them nothing to say against you—pay every one of them."

Helena's face lighted up and flushed a little at this expression of his will. She said nothing, however; only glanced at him meaningly.

"Well, I must go; I've plenty to do. I wanted to say to you, if I don't get down to-morrow, the funeral will be at eight, in the Abbey burial-ground. Is that so?"

"Yes, Perry settled it so. Are you going home by the river-walk?"

"Yes, of course; the quieter the better now; come down as far as the garden wall with me."

Helena got up and followed him out of the back door and down the narrow path leading to the wall. It was late now, nearly ten o'clock; the twilight was gone and a mild summer's night, balmy and soft, reigned in its stead. Helena felt it warmer in the open air than in the damp old kitchen, and, without knowing why, she felt suddenly almost happy. They were out of the black shadows of the old house now. The river stretched away before them, winding in a broad silver band between the waving banks of reeds. Above, the stars shone through a warm, luminous haze. There was no moon, yet it was clear and soft, and a tiny breeze, scented with yellow whin bloom, that seemed to follow the Darragh in its course from the mountains, lifted and stirred the little loose tresses on her temples. There was not a sound but the running murmur of the water, and the soft rustle of the new-leaved branches as the night wind passed through them.

"I wonder will it be like this in Canada, Jim?" said Helena, dreamily. "One fortnight more—imagine it."

"I don't care what it will be like," answered he. "You and I will be there together, and that's enough for me."

She was looking up at the sky, counting the seven white stars of the Plow, in a sort of dreamy languor. At his words she turned her face towards him and smiled. All the beauty of the sky and earth seemed reflected in it at that moment.

"Good-night, my jewel," said he, slowly. "Go in now—I don't want you to be seen."

She turned obediently to go, but he stretched out his arm, and, drawing round her face, kissed her cheek and pressed it one moment to his; then lightly leaped the wall and was gone.

CHAPTER XVI.

HELENA was in her own room sorting and preparing her miscellaneous stores for the packing-boxes which encumbered the floor. An old leather valise was full already, and she was making strenuous efforts to make the hasp meet and catch in the lock. It would not shut down; the leather cover refused obstinately to yield to pulling or pressing. Hel even sat on the top, but the cover only bent in with her weight, and the hasp was farther from its place than ever. So she jumped off impatiently and sat down in the window in her accustomed place. She was tired with her efforts and drew a long breath as she leaned back and curled up her feet in her favorite attitude to rest herself. It was warm in the room besides. The sun beat on the slates and on the attic windows and there was very little air stirring. There was no blind on the side window and it was half open. The swallows and the swifts darting by in the sunshine cast sudden, fleeting shadows on the floor. Everything was still and quiet; the faintest possible ripple was borne upward from the river, and a few old men lying on the bridge wall seemed overcome with sleep.

The street was silent and deserted, and the blue turf-smoke from the little moss-grown cabins shimmered like gossamer-threads in the sun. Tiny white clouds floated high up in the clear, limpid azure. In the fields just before her a lark had risen and was singing its sweetest and strongest, beating the air with its wings. It looked no bigger than a bee, Helena thought, as she followed it with her eyes and watched it till it dropped weary to the grass again. Then all was once more mute. Even the geese crouched languidly in the sunniest places on the sloping bank of the river and preened their feathers at their ease. Helena sat still for a good time in her chair, twisting her long fingers thoughtfully. At last a bell roused her from her reverie. It was the twelve o'clock Angelus ringing from the convent. She jumped up quickly, for she remembered suddenly all she had to do. Stepping over the litter of books and clothes to the toilet-glass, she seized her long plaits of hair, which were loosely wreathed round her head, and began to untwist them. The thick locks soon hung loose on her shoulders, forming a strange frame for her pale face. In a few minutes she had plaited and coiled it again and stood for one moment looking at her own reflection in the little mirror. The fine straight brows were now no longer sullen or overhanging, and the beautiful half-melancholy, half-thoughtful eyes were clearer and more serene of look. The skin, pallid but soft and fine as an infant's, was like ivory in contrast with the surrounding mass of hair, and her ears looked like little white shells among the tiny rebellious curls which broke loose from their restraints to caress them. Helena put up an impatient finger to push them back, but started round on seeing Cawth's wrinkled visage, looking now twenty years older, mirrored beside her own in the glass.

"Here's Mrs. Really below. She says she will na go till she sees ye."

Helena threw back her head with an impatient gesture and set leisurely about finishing her toilet. She poured out a basin of water, and plunged her hands in it. They were hot and tired, and she splashed them to and fro in the cool water. Cawth waited humbly.

"Show her in," said Hel at last. "I'll come down and see what she wants."

Then she threw down the towel, and began to speculate as to what madam could be wanting her for. The other day she had been again, asking to be allowed to do something, and when refused had said she would come back. Perhaps Mr. Satterthwaite had sent her. If that was so, Hel certainly would go to her. She seemed to be a friend of his, so on that account she should be spoken with at least. Then she crossed the room and opening the drawer of a queer little old escritoire, took out of it Satterthwaite's pocket Shakespeare. She looked at it and laid it back again. Helena intended to keep that book always. Then she took out a tiny packet of silver paper, much crumpled and a little dirty. She unrolled it by degrees and then laid the inclosure in the palm of her hand, turning and looking at it almost reverently. It was a gold ring, a thick circlet of frosted gold. Helena slipped it on her long white finger, and holding her hand a little way from her, looked at it again. A long thin ray of sunlight had crept through the shutters of the front window, and as it fell on the outstretched hand, the new gold frosting glittered and shone like particles of diamonds. She smiled and gave her head a little determined shake, then hastily pulled off the ring and folding it up in the silver paper again, turned away and down the stairs. She passed Char's room and looked in. He was lying on his bed smoking, his saturnine countenance turned so that he could look out of the window which commanded a view of the river and bridge. He too had been making preparations for his departure. His double-barreled gun had been taken to pieces and was lying on a table, and the floor of the room was littered with miscellaneous property scattered about in the process of selection. Helena said nothing. The tobacco smoke made her cough, and she pulled the door impatiently to and ran down the stair.

Cawth was standing in the hall and signed to her to go into the parlor. Helena stood one second on the mat, and pressed her hands to her temples. Then she opened the door wide, and walked in with head erect to meet her visitor.

Madam Really, when she told Mr. Satterthwaite that she had seen Helena, had given him, perhaps unconsciously, to understand that she had paid the girl a friendly visit. In reality, she had been admitted for a few minutes to the hall, where she exchanged a few words with Helena, who, indeed, had far too much on her mind to be willing to endure the well-meant officiousness of the elder lady. Helena had never been accustomed to receive attentions or civilities from people of Madam Really's class. She had a sort of dread and dislike of strangers, springing chiefly from a morbid sense of her own anomalous position, but resulting also from the unsocial habits in which she had been trained. However, Satterthwaite's friendship for madam was a protecting ægis. But for it she would have been driven off, as heretofore, with something more than incivility.

Madam, however, had no suspicion of the cause of her unwontedly civil reception. She set it down to the score of the improvements which Devereux's influence had effected in Helena, and added it also mentally to the sum of self-gratulation at her own wise selection and well-planned manœuvres. She identified herself, as people will, with the success of her *protégé*, Jim, and took much credit to herself on this account, and sat quietly in the dark parlor waiting for her appearance and inwardly praying that it might not be long delayed. There was an indescribable odor in the room—the damp that always is in ground-floor chambers, the smell of the tobacco-soaked curtains, and the mouldering furniture all mingled horribly together, and though the windows were open, nearly stifled her. The sofa was wheeled away from the fire-place, and on it lay the old man's inseparable companion, his faithful wolf-dog. She went over and looked at him; then held out her hand to caress him. He snapped at her feebly with a cross snarl. A plate of food lay on the floor untouched. She picked her way back to the window over the rags of carpet on the floor, and sat down again, wondering how long Miss Helena meant to keep her, and wishing her vinaigrette had not been forgotten in the phaeton.

Then she heard the quick, springing step on the stair. The door opened and Helena walked in, looking at her questioningly and distantly, but not defiantly.

Madam Really was almost taken aback. Hel seemed to have grown taller. Her long black dress fell gracefully round her slim, well-poised figure, and her face only looked more beautiful for the fatigue and paleness it showed.

"How do you do to-day?" said Mrs. Really in a sympathetic voice, holding out her hand. "Are you rested? I hope you have not been ill."

She continued to hold the girl's hand in hers, waiting for an answer. Helena withdrew her hand, answering composedly that she was quite well. She looked fixedly at madam with her great eyes, somewhat tear-stained, but brilliant and deep.

"Sit down, dear; I want to speak to you—to ask you to let me do something for you."

Helena sat down, frowning a little, but patient and dignified.

"First of all, my dear child," began Mrs. Really, "I want you not to look on me as a mere stranger interfering in your affairs. I was at one time a great friend of your step-brother Claude, now Lord Darraghmore." She paused to see the effect of her words.

Helena's eyes had kindled with a sudden interest at the mention of Claude, but they wavered and filled with tears at the words "now Lord Darraghmore;" her head drooped a little, and the hard set look left her face. Mrs. Really was touched—infinitely more touched than she had expected to be—and it was in a more feeling tone that she continued.

"Yes, my dear," she said in a gentle voice that called up in poor Helena an odd remembrance of her aunt Elizabeth in Bath, "it is so. You won't look upon me as a stranger, then, and you will believe that I am really interested in you—is that agreed, now?" She took the girl's hand in hers; it remained passive enough in her grasp, but the head was turned aside and her eyes averted Mrs. Really went on:

"I know your circumstances well, and believe me, I am really interested in you—willing to help you, too, if you will let me. You are no more than a child yet, dear Miss—dear Helena."

Helena sighed and moved uneasily in her chair. Then she looked at Mrs. Really and said in a hurried but gentle tone:

"Well?"

"I have been thinking," said she, "that it will be so difficult for you to get everything arranged, and you are so isolated here now; will you come and stay with me at my house, and let me assist you for a few days until you are rested and able to start? Do, please," said madam, entreatingly. She was really in earnest, and she would have added more, but that the expression of her listener's face warned her it was of no use. "You are not without friends and well-wishers. Mr. Satterthwaite also would like to serve you in any way he could."

Helena's face flushed and a deep frown came on her forehead. It was more the expression of pain than anger, as her friend acknowledged when she heard the tone in which Helena repeated his name.

"Mr. Satterthwaite is very good, but he has nothing to do with me. Jim Devereux and Isi and Cawth and I are going away to-morrow." Then the long eyelashes drooped till they rested on her cheeks, as she turned her head aside so as not to meet the other woman's eyes. And again a hot flush dyed her brow, her cheeks and neck.

"Be it so!" said Mrs. Really to herself; "I might be only doing the mischief I have been trying to prevent. Jim is her mate after all. If she were with me, Satterthwaite would insist upon seeing her. She has a regard for him; and there is no telling how things might turn out —it would not be for Helena's happiness, certainly not for poor Jim's. And what ought their happiness to be to me?" thought she, as a wave of bitter, envious feeling swept through her. She thought of a scene long years ago, a ball-room, with bare polished floors and long mirrors that reflected the gay uniform-coat of a tall hussar, who was holding her hand for the last time and looking at her with sad, despairing eyes. What had the world been to her since? And now here was this creature with Claude's own blue eyes looking at her: certainly, if she could help her to what she had herself missed, she would do it. She put up her hand to her brow and pressed it hard, and something like a tear—was it regret, or was it envy?—dimmed her bright eyes a moment.

"You are right. Tell me now, dear, can I do anything for you? Do you want money? I would lend it you, you know," she added, hurriedly; she feared to offend her.

"I shall have enough when everything is paid," answered Helena, proudly. "Thank you," she added on meeting the eyes of her new friend.

Mrs. Really pondered a minute with her hand on the door, watching her.

"Helena," said she, impressively, "if you are not happy with Jim it will be your own fault."

"I know that," answered the girl, quickly, and with a tone that plainly came from her heart; her violet eyes kindled and her cheeks glowed.

Mrs. Really often thought afterwards of the picture the beautiful creature made as she stood in that hideous, sordid room that moment. She stooped forward suddenly, and taking her head in both her hands, kissed her cheeks twice.

"God bless you, my child! be a good wife to him and obedient always." Then the door shut, the pony-carriage drove off fast, and Helena wiped a tear off her cheek wonderingly.

It was not her own.

At eight o'clock next morning the funeral *cortége* left the mill-house. The coffin was carried on the shoulders of half a dozen men. Isi and Char walked behind it, each holding a corner of the rusty black pall. Isi was sobbing, and Char walked with his dark, sullen face turned resolutely to the ground. Behind them came Devereux and Perry, Satterthwaite and the old doctor; Blake, the inn-keeper, and Doctor Cartan walked in couples. A little crowd of shop-keepers and towns-folk tramped after them. They had not far to go; the old grave-yard on the other side of the river was almost within stone-throw of the mill-house, and it did not take long to deposit their charge in the family vault. He was the last Darraghmore that would ever lie there. The burial service was read by a clergyman from Ballycormack, whom Perry, at Mr. Satterthwaite's instance, had sent for. Satterthwaite it was also who had ordered that the church bells should be tolled until the ceremony was over. He was disgusted with Perry's indifference and coldness, and had with difficulty refrained from giving him a piece of his mind. The Ferrard boys were too young and ignorant to superintend the arrangements. Their sister of course could not, and Perry, who had been their business man always, should have seen that a respectable funeral was provided. The lawyer, however, characteristically represented that there was no use going to expense; everybody knew who and what Lord Darraghmore was, and "the quieter the thing was got over the better." As to bringing a clergyman from Ballycormack, he pooh-poohed the idea; it would cost a guinea, may be two. Satterthwaite qualified Perry in his own mind as an indecent savage, and undertook to bear the cost of the ceremony himself, adding that considering who Lord Darraghmore had been in the parish, it looked ill not to show his remains somewhat of respect.

The funeral over, Satterthwaite followed Blake to the hotel to have breakfast, and the rest dispersed. Char and Isi, with Devereux, returned to the mill-house. They were to leave that afternoon—Char for London alone, the rest to Queenstown. So, though everything was packed up, there was enough to do before twelve o'clock, at which hour they were to start for the Darraghstown station.

The hall-door was ajar when they reached it. Char pushed in first and led the way to the kitchen. Helena was standing at the window reading over a list of figures. She turned round with a slight shiver as they came in.

"Oh, Jim! I hadn't seen you. I didn't know you had come."

"Of course I came," said he in a low voice. "What are you doing? Perry bid me tell you he would be in presently when he had done breakfast. Satterthwaite wouldn't go to breakfast with him. He has gone up to the hotel."

"Oh, Jim!" said Helena, "I should like to see Satterthwaite again to bid him good-bye and thank him, you know." She looked wistfully at him as she said this.

"Yes," said he; "I'd like to shake hands with him too. I think he's going somewhere; his gig is at the hotel, and his portmanteau and hat-case are on it. I saw him drive up just as I came here."

"Hel," said Cawth, who had suddenly sat down at the other side of the fire, "ye must get them their breakfast. Aw'm no able."

Helena turned round. The old woman looked indeed to be seriously ill. A sudden faintness had taken her; her cheeks were pale, and her usually bright eyes dim and clouded. She spoke in a feeble voice, very different from her usual harsh tones.

Helena poured out strong tea in the cups—the boys were already eating cold meat and bread—and carried Cawth her breakfast to where she was sitting. She ate nothing, and turned querulously from the plate of food Hel offered her. Grief and fear of the change and the long voyage before her had been more than the old woman could bear. Helena was frightened, for Cawth had never been ill in her life; and she looked at Devereux to call his attention to the change in her nurse's face. He whispered something to Isi, who went to a press and brought out some spirits. Then they made her swallow some, and she revived sufficiently to drink her tea.

"Will you be able for the journey, Cawth?" said Devereux, anxiously. "Hel," he added, turning to her, "I don't believe she will."

"Yes," said the old woman, looking up suddenly and imploringly into Helena's face. "Eh yes, Hel; ye won't lave me alone now? I'll not trouble ye lang."

"No," said Helena in a kind voice; "I'll not go without you, Cawth." Then they all sat down to table.

"I wonder," said Helena after a time, "where Davy is. I want him to go messages. If Kelly and the baker would come soon I could settle with them. There's a good deal to be done."

"Davy's outside," said Isi. "Shall I tell him to go for them?"

Helena replied in the affirmative, and having finished her own meagre breakfast, went with the boys into the parlor. Devereux remained with Cawth.

It was not long before the creditors arrived and were paid in full of all their demands, to their surprise; for though a rumor had gone abroad of the young lady's intention to do so, they never expected to get more than an installment on account. That done, Helena, after a consultation with Devereux, sent Davy to the hotel to ask Mr. Satterthwaite to come and speak to her. He had scarcely been dispatched when Perry walked in. He grinned when he caught sight of the young farmer, and laying his hat on the table sat down and stared at Helena. Devereux walked out of the room, and Isi ran up-stairs to Char.

"Well, miss, so you're leaving us for good and all—hey?" said the attorney.

"I am going away to-day, Mr. Perry," replied she, gravely. "I should like to settle your account, if you please, and I am greatly obliged to you for your kindness and attention."

This speech, an unusually long one for the laconic Helena, took Mr. Perry rather unawares, and he turned his eyes aside, as if the gaze of Helena's disconcerted him.

"Never mind that, me dear child," he mumbled; "neighbors are neighbors, ye know, and—"

Whether, owing to the working of Mr. Perry's long-disused conscience, or that the sight of Helena, pale and worn-looking, sitting there in her heavy black dress moved him, cannot be determined; but he did feel an unwonted sensation of pity. He turned a little to one side, and dipping into his pocket, produced a folded blue paper.

"That's it—yes," said the lawyer, recovering himself as soon as he got to business. Then he opened the paper with a flourish and began to read:

"'Helena Ferrard to'—hum—'debtor'—This is the—the funeral this morning, you know, and etceteras—nine pounds, two pounds two—it comes to eleven pounds two."

Perry had purposely overcharged two pounds. He intended to return Helena these two, for to do him justice he was above cheating her, now at least—and to give himself thus a magnanimous air at no expense. He credited Helena with being a good woman of business, by which he understood that she knew when she was cheated and could take care of herself, and if opportunity offered cheat too; and he would have thoroughly relished a last bargain with her—a bargain in which he was to cede his point in a considerate, delicate way without being, at the same time, one farthing out of pocket. So he repeated the total—eleven pounds two—staring hard at Helena to see how she was going to take it.

She said not a word, though the amount did shock her, and it was a serious deduction from her little store. She only looked at Perry with troubled eyes, and her lips moved slightly and got a little paler as she opened the lid of her desk and began to count out the required number of sovereigns. Had the sum been double, Hel would not have disputed it. Perry, who had never been able to calculate on this reception of his manœuvre, sat dumbfounded, and stared when Helena, having counted the sum, laid the sovereigns in a heap on top of his account, and dipping her pen in the ink gave it him to sign. He took the pen from her mechanically. Then some other idea came into his head. His face turned suddenly very red, and he affected to find fault with the nib of the pen. He looked once more at Helena, who was waiting to see him receipt the bill. A sad white face it was that met his eyes. Perry muttered something that had a very profane sound, scribbled a horribly blotted signature, then, crumpling up money and bill, jumped up, and stuffed the whole into Helena's hands.

"Keep it, me dear—keep it from me. It'll buy you black things. Good-bye, now. Don't say anything: I'm in a hurry."

The hall-door banged before Helena had realized what ne had done. She ran out to Jim and told him Perry's extraordinary conduct.

"Ought I to send it back to the house?"

She ended her narrative with this question.

Jim laughed.

"Don't," said he; "he meant it kindly, and anyhow it will be 'before him in the next world.' Certainly I never thought it of Perry."

Neither did Helena, and this, to her, unaccountable development of character afforded her food for meditation until she was again summoned to the parlor, this time to see Satterthwaite.

It might have been his unusual dress—for Satterthwaite always wore some light-colored suit—a black frock-coat and tall hat, that made him look so pale and gloomy, but even Helena, who was naturally unobservant, noticed his altered looks. He shook hands with her and Devereux. The boys were up-stairs finishing their preparations.

Helena spoke first:

"I wanted to see you, to thank you and bid you good-bye. We," with a glance towards Devereux, and a quick, fleeting blush, "are going away now."

"So I am told," replied Satterthwaite. "I wanted to ask your permission to accompany you as far as Cork. Pray don't refuse me, Miss Ferrard—I am bent upon this."

"It is really kind of you, sir," said Devereux in a moved tone, "to take so much trouble on yourself. I assure you we are grateful to you."

Helena cast a surprised look at him, but did not speak.

"You go by the —— ship, do you not? I know that line: the boats are excellent, and very comfortable. You meet the Cork mail at the junction there to-day. You have not very much time."

Satterthwaite spoke in a voice which he endeavored to render as cheerful as possible.

"Oh, we are ready," said Jim; "the trunks are in the hall since last night, and the cart will be here directly for them. Then they'll go over in the mail-cart. I am going to ride by myself."

"I can give you a seat in my dog-cart. The man can come over to the train for it. Do take it," said Satterthwaite.

Jim had no time to answer. The door opened with a crash, and in rushed the Misses Perry and fell upon Helena with tearful embraces, protesting their sorrow and desolation at the prospect of losing her, and upbraiding her in unmeasured terms for keeping her projects a secret. Satterthwaite and Jim made their escape unnoticed in the excitement and ungenerously left Helena to cope with them unsupported.

"I'll be at the station before you, till then—"

Satterthwaite hastened away in terror lest the Perrys should sally out and fall upon him. Then the cart came to take away the baggage which lay ready in the hall. It was all carried out and loaded. Devereux wanted to see Helena to tell her he was going. His effects were at the station already; they had been conveyed there by a trusty man the previous night; but the Perrys, who were embracing her by turns, and literally reveling in demonstrative grief, were not to be got rid of.

At last the red mail-cart, with Thady Conlon, drew up to the door. Helena disengaged herself, and ran out to take her hat and shawls and help Cawth out. The boys came down ready dressed for the road, each heavily loaded, and exclaiming loudly against Dirty Davy, who had long ago walked across to the station with the avowed affectionate intention of seeing the last of his masters, and at the same time getting out of the way of any extra labor which the exigencies of moving heavy baggage might entail.

Thady Conlon, with laudable foresight, had allowed himself nearly half an hour as margin against possible delays or accidents, and having got the hall-door open and a stir created inside the house, assembled a little throng of lookers-on and proceeded deliberately to enjoy the excitement. A grocer's wife, one of Cawth's chief cronies, crossed the road, carrying a parcel in her hand and walked into the mill-house unchallenged. She was to lock the house and keep the key for the landlord and was in no danger of forgetting her task. She went straight into the kitchen where Helena was tying on her hat.

"Oh! Mrs. McGonigle—sarvice, miss;" she saw Helena, and dropped a reverential courtesy—"'tis come to this wid us, is it? I made bowld to bring you a small present; it might be useful one day." She handed Cawth her parcel as she spoke. This plainly consisted of whisky and tea, which Cawth, having verified by an experimental squeeze, tucked under her arm approvingly. "Oh miss, jewel, if you'd happen to meet my boy out in those parts, if you'd only let me know. Mrs. McGonigle, you never seen my Larry; but sure you'd know him out of me."

"Ay, ay!" croaked Cawth; "the keys are all in the dures, an' mind Davy does not get in to sleep till she comes. Div ye hear me?" she added, for Mrs. Carmody, between real and imaginary grief, was weeping noisily. They picked up their parcels, and went into the hall. Isi and Char had piled all the small packages on the car and stood in the front scowling at the sympathizing mob without the railing. The Perrys dashed out and stood on the pavement in sight of every one and in the way of the travelers.

"Curse it!" growled Char. "Here, get up, Hel, do!"

He pushed and lifted the old woman into her seat; then went sulkily round and took his own.

Hel, stunned with the noise and longing to be away, was turning to mount into hers, when Mrs. Perry, her cap-strings flying, appeared at her own hall-door. She had merely put out her head to see them go, but discovering the scene that was going on, she realized suddenly the amount of excitement she was losing, and forthwith, beginning to weep sympathetically, scuttered down the pavement.

"Wait, Thady," ordered one of the Perrys; "here's mamma."

"Oh! good-bye, good-bye, darling child! good-bye! Oh! won't you write us a line?" sobbed Mrs. Perry, embracing poor Helena, who was almost unable to answer, so bewildered was she. "No! to me, Hel! won't you write to me?" cried her daughter. "'Twas me you always liked best. Ah, Hel, do! Only one bit of a note!" pleaded the girls in chorus, as Isi, thoroughly out of temper, lifted his sister bodily up beside Cawth, who, sick and feeble as she was, was relishing the whole scene thoroughly.

"Go on, damn you!" Char roared to the driver, who he saw was prolonging the scene.

Thady unwillingly cracked his whip, and amid a tornado of blessings and lamentations the mail-car at last started. A number of people ran after it, sending messages and recommendations to relations "out there"—all wishing the travelers God speed!

Even Doctor Cartan, forgetting how often Char had cheated him at billiards, ran up alongside and shook hands with him. Perry watched the whole scene with a grim smile from his own hall-door. Then he came down as he saw the car drive off to rally his wife and daughters on their exquisite sensibility after his own peculiar fashion.

"My stars! Mrs. P., who's dead? Gad! I thought you had a telegram from O'Malooney Castle at the very least. Julia, yes, I hope Hel will write to you. Have you forgotten the day she made you see stars for giving her impudence? Go in out of this, and don't be making me sick with your foolery. Crying, indeed; much else you ever did for her!"

Then Mr. Perry recollected how very much more he had done for the Ferrards, and stepped into the bank to regale the manager and Doctors Cartan and Bruton and the clerks with the history of his own generosity in the morning. He had no doubt it would astonish them as much as it did himself. But it is only right to say, in justice to the characters of the worthy lawyer and his listeners, that the recital only provoked a unanimous burst of derisive incredulity.

The mail-car drove off, hurrying to make up for lost time, along the straight highroad and the town was soon left behind. Helena, now they were all out of sight, put back her thick crape veil and drew a deep breath of thankfulness. The boys were silent and Cawth seemed to be dozing. Thady, the irrepressible, kept up a monologue of talk, chiefly accounts of the wonderful fortunes made in America by his own relations, which were good-naturedly meant to encourage the travelers.

"Now, miss," said he, "when we get to the top of this hill, look back and you'll get the last sight of owld Darraghstown, and that'll be Comerford Bridge and your own house."

Helena did as she was desired, and she could see, as he said, the bridge and beside it the end wall of the mill-house. One window of the top room, which had been hers, was visible. It was open, as she had negligently left it, and the blind had been carried out and was flapping in the wind. Then the car turned the bend of the slope and descended the hill, and Hel had seen the last of Darraghmore forever.

At the station Satterthwaite and Jim were in waiting. Devereux lifted Helena down, and leaning on his strong arm she ascended the steps to the platform. Satterthwaite had arrived the first and made use of his precedence to buy first-class tickets for the whole party.

Their train came up almost immediately, and taking their places they found themselves without much delay on the first stage of their long journey. They had an hour to wait at the junction for the American mail. Here they parted with Char. His luggage was extracted from the van, and after a hurried farewell—for the Dublin mail only waited for the branch train to arrive and deliver passengers and mails—the youth parted from them on his journey to Vienna. Cawth cried bitterly, and so did Helena, but Isi did not attempt to look upon it otherwise than as an unmixed deliverance. The hour of waiting was spent dully enough. The two women went into the dirty, cheerless waiting-room, and the men sauntered up and down smoking. At last the mail arrived. They bestowed themselves nearly all in different carriages, for the train was crowded; and until Cork was reached they were pretty well left to their several meditations.

Once there, however, there was plenty to do as well as think of. Satterthwaite found some large packages waiting for him at the terminus of the Passage railway.

"Why, one would think you were coming with us," said Devereux with a puzzled look, which intensified when he saw his friend pull off the labels and affix his (Devereux's) name to them instead.

"These are some things you may find useful on your journey. I got them for you and Hel"—he checked himself—"Miss Ferrard."

"You have been too good to us, indeed you have, Mr. Satterthwaite. I never could thank you—never."

Then they found themselves with the rest of the American passengers in the railway for Queenstown. They had a compartment to themselves, and Satterthwaite contrived to place himself next to Helena. She was looking out of the window at the river, and thinking of that gray morning she had sailed down there by herself last September. What an age it seemed since! And then she thought of her aunts in Bath, and determined to write, as she had promised, and tell them how she and her husband got on. Helena turned her head then with a flickering smile and blush to look at Jim, who was talking with Isi at the other end of the carriage; her eyes met those of Satterthwaite, fixed with an expression at once sad and kind upon her face. His hand rested on the partition between the seats. Helena suddenly took it in both hers and held it.

"Ah, Mr. Satterthwaite," said she in an earnest, low voice, "how good you have been to us! Never—never was anybody so—"

Helena's face was very close to his, and she suddenly let go his hand and stopped speaking.

"Helena," said he in a hoarse, broken voice, "if you would have let me be good to you—if you would have been my wife, I wanted to—"

But he never finished—she started violently, and with an involuntary and almost angry glance to the other end of the carriage, put her hand suddenly on his mouth.

Satterthwaite seized and pressed it passionately to his lips, then he threw himself back in his seat so that he could not see her even, and lay motionless and silent till they reached the tender. Having collected everything of theirs and obtained permission to accompany them to the steamer, which was lying farther out in deep water with her steam up waiting for them, Satterthwaite took his seat on one of their packing-cases, and with a brave effort talked cheerfully to Devereux. But his eyes would wander to Helena, who was crouched on a bench beside her nurse. It was cold and he noticed her shivering, for she had not thought of providing herself with wraps.

"Open the small case when you get on board," he said at last to Devereux; "you'll find a traveling-rug and shawl for her in it;" then turned away, biting his lips hard, and asking himself with a bitter, envious feeling, would these two men take care of her and comfort her as he thought he would have done?

They were in the blue water now, and, as Satterthwaite saw with a pain that grew every moment keener, fast nearing the huge ocean steamer. The passengers who had gone on board at Liverpool were collected on the deck-rail next the tender, watching eagerly for new-comers and newspapers to enliven their already monotonous existence. The tender swung to, ropes were thrown out, and the party climbed up the ladder and on to the great ship. The mails were being passed in speedily, and Satterthwaite had now but a few minutes. It was almost impossible to hear a word. The steam of both vessels was escaping, that of the tender with a hideous, half-strangled whistle. The multifarious steamboat smell—dinner, bilge-water, oil, and close air—poured out of an open door beside them.

Then a bell rang. The mails were all in, and the floor began to throb significantly under their feet. Helena's eyes, running over with tears, were fixed on Satterthwaite's. A woman was weeping aloud near them, parting from a husband.

"Good-bye!" said the Englishman, wringing Isi's brown hand; "stand by your sister, my boy."

"She won't want him to," said Devereux, holding out his, and looking straight into the other man's eyes.

"I believe you," said Satterthwaite, giving him his right hand, and with the left taking Helena's.

"Good-bye!" he said.

The man who was taking leave of his wife beside them had lifted her down to the deck of the tender and returned. The gangway was in the hands of two sailors, who were watching the captain on the bridge for orders; he indeed was giving them fast enough.

"Shore! shore!" he was shouting, with his red, angry face bent on the little group.

"Go, sir, go!" cried Isi, pushing him.

Satterthwaite had both her hands in his, and was looking his last at Hel. She said not a word, but he could feel the hands he held in his tremble and burn.

"Let go!" screeched the captain. "By the heavens I'll take him!"

The sailors did let go, and the gangway was being pulled in. Satterthwaite cared not; he had lifted Helena in his arms, and was straining her to him in one firm embrace.

"You won't grudge me that," he said as he placed her in Devereux's arms. Then he laid a hand on the edge of the taffrail, and was standing on it, measuring with his eye the gulf of foaming green water that lay between.

"Catch him! stop him! ho-o-o-ld him!" came from the dancing maniac on the bridge in a prolonged howl. "He'll be drowned. No," in a disappointed *sotto voce* tone, "he's safe; this is always the way. Mr. Chizzle, full steam on! and, God bless my eternal soul, how's her head?"

"I wonder I am not indeed," said Satterthwaite, shaking his feet, which were stinging from the concussion on the deck of the tender, and looking at the width of the boiling chasm that now separated him from the great vessel. "If I were I don't think I'd care."

Then he caught the eye of the captain, who, now restored to good humor, showed a set of white teeth at him, and he went down to the stern of the tender to try and get a last glimpse of Hel's sweet, pale face.

Neither she nor Devereux nor the boy appeared, and after a while he felt glad it was so. Little by little the great ship diminished. He could see, following her course with dim, sad eyes, the long white furrow that stretched in her wake rising and falling with the Atlantic rollers. The cloud of black smoke was driven southwards and floated like a dark shadow above the laughing crests of the waves; but in a few minutes the tug swept into the harbor, and Satterthwaite with a sigh bid adieu to even that consolation.

One week after the departure of Lord Darraghmore's family Mrs. Really met the groom belonging to Mr. Satterthwaite of Rosslyne. The man was mounted on Devereux's cob, Freney, and led his master's own riding horse, Black Auster, who, wrapped in blankets and with bandaged knees and hocks, had the air of being out of sorts or going to travel. Such an occurrence could not fail to attract her attention.

"Mr. Satterthwaite's man, eh?" said she. "Is not that Devereux's horse?"

"*Was* 'm; master bought him last week, 'm."

Mrs. Really remained so long silent that the man, touching his hat, was about to ride on, but she stopped him with a sign; then, first clearing her voice, she asked:

"That is your master's own horse, eh?"

"Yes, 'm; I'm taking him to Cork. 'E's going to London to master."

"Good-day." But as she was driving off a sudden thought struck her and she pulled up again. "Er—when is your master coming back?"

"We don't expect 'im back, 'm. Mr. and Mrs. Lewis

Satterthwaite, master's cousins, are coming over with theii family for the summer, or till master decides to come his self, and has 'e's going to Russia with Mr. Carew's family we don't know when that'll be."

NERVOUSNESS
FAREWELL!
BHUD TEA
CEYLON
35 CENTS PER QUARTER LB
Tiffin 25¢ per Packet
Bungaloe 18¢ " "
CAUTION.—This tea is very much stronger than any other, hence carefully ascertain the quantity your taste demands; and to preserve its full strength and flavor keep it in an air-tight jar.

THE SEASIDE LIBRARY.

POCKET EDITION.

LIST OF AUTHORS.

[When ordering by mail please order by Numbers and state Pocket Edition.]

E. About.

1467 A New Lease of Life 20

Mrs. Leith Adams.

1345 Aunt Hepsy's Foundling 20

Author of "Addie's Husband."

388 Addie's Husband; or, Through Clouds to Sunshine.................... 25
504 My Poor Wife............ 10
1045 Jessie.................... 25

Max Adeler.

1550 Random Shots.......... 20
1569 Elbow Room............ 20

Author of "A Fatal Dower."

246 A Fatal Dower.......... 20
372 Phyllis' Probation....... 10
461 His Wedded Wife......... 25
829 The Actor's Ward........ 20
1373 The Story of an Error... 20

Author of "A Golden Bar."

483 Betwixt My Love and Me. 25

Author of "A Great Mistake."

244 A Great Mistake.......... 20
588 Cherry... 10
1040 Clarissa's Ordeal. 1st half 20
1040 Clarissa's Ordeal. 2d half 20
1137 Prince Charming......... 20
1187 Suzanne........... 20

Author of "A Woman's Love-Story."

322 A Woman's Love-Story.. 10
677 Griselda.................. 20

Author of "For Mother's Sake."

1900 Leonie; or, The Sweet Street Singer of New York.................... 20

Author of "He," "It," etc.

1916 King Solomon's Treasures.................... 25

Hamilton Aide.

383 Introduced to Society... 10

Gustave Aimard.

1341 The Trappers of Arkansas..................... 10
1396 The Adventurers........ 10
1398 Pirates of the Prairies... 10
1400 Queen of the Savannah. 10
1401 The Buccaneer Chief.... 10
1402 The Smuggler Hero..... 10
1404 The Rebel Chief......... 10
1650 The Trail-Hunter........ 10
1658 The Pearl of the Andes.. 10
1672 The Insurgent Chief.... 10
1688 The Trapper's Daughter 10
1690 The Tiger-Slayer........ 10
1692 Border Rifles............ 10
1700 The Flying Horseman... 10
1701 The Freebooters......... 10
1714 The White Scalper...... 10
1723 The Guide of the Desert. 10
1732 Last of the Ancas....... 10
1734 Missouri Outlaws....... 10
1736 Prairie Flower........... 10
1740 Indian Scout............. 10
1741 Stronghand 10
1742 Bee-Hunters............. 10
1744 Stoneheart............... 10
1748 The Gold-Seekers....... 10
1752 Indian Chief............. 10
1756 Red Track................ 10
1761 The Treasure of Pearls.. 10
1768 Red River Half-Breed... 10

Mary Albert.

933 A Hidden Terror 20

Grant Allen.

712 For Maimie's Sake...... 20
1221 "The Tents of Shem"... 25
1783 The Great Taboo......... 20
1870 What's Bred in the Bone 20
1908 Dumaresq's Daughter... 25

Mrs. Alexander.

5 The Admiral's Ward.... 20
17 The Wooing O't......... 25
62 The Executor............ 20
189 Valerie's Fate.......... 10
229 Maid, Wife, or Widow?.. 10

286 Which Shall it Be?...... 20

339 Mrs. Vereker's Courier Maid.......................... 10

490 A Second Life............ 25

564 At Bay................... 10

794 Beaton's Bargain......... 20

797 Look Before You Leap.. 20

805 The Freres. 1st half.... 20

805 The Freres. 2d half.... 20

806 Her Dearest Foe. 1st half 20

806 Her Dearest Foe. 2d half 20

814 The Heritage of Langdale 25

815 Ralph Wilton's Weird... 10

900 By Woman's Wit......... 20

997 Forging the Fetters, and The Australian Aunt.... 20

1054 Mona's Choice........... 25

1057 A Life Interest........... 20

1189 A Crooked Path......... 20

1199 A False Scent............ 10

1367 Heart Wins............... 10

1459 A Woman's Heart....... 20

1571 Blind Fate.. 20

1582 An Interesting Case..... 20

Alison.

194 "So Near, and Yet So Far!"..................... 10

278 For Life and Love........ 10

481 The House That Jack Built..................... 10

Hans Christian Andersen.

1814 Andersen's Fairy Tales.. 20

W. P. Andrews.

1172 India and Her Neighbors 20

F. Anstey.

59 Vice Versâ............... 25

225 The Giant's Robe......... 20

503 The Tinted Venus. A Farcical Romance...... 10

819 A Fallen Idol............ 20

1616 The Black Poodle, and Other Tales........... 20

G. W. Appleton.

1346 A Terrible Legacy...... 20

Annie Armitt.

759 In Shallow Waters....... 20

T. S. Arthur.

1337 Woman's Trials........ 20

1636 The Two Wives.......... 20

1638 Married Life............. 25

1640 Ways of Providence..... 20

1641 Home Scenes............ 20

1644 Stories for Parents....... 20

1649 Seed-Time and Harvest. 20

1652 Words for the Wise...... 20

1654 Stories for Young Housekeepers.................. 20

1657 Lessons In Life.......... 20

1658 Off-Hand Sketches...... 20

Sir Samuel Baker.

267 Rifle and Hound in Ceylon...................... 25

583 Eight Years Wandering in Ceylon................ 20

1502 Cast Up by the Sea...... 20

R. M. Ballantyne.

89 The Red Eric............. 10

95 The Fire Brigade......... 10

96 Erling the Bold.......... 10

772 Gascoyne, the Sandal-Wood Trader........... 25

1514 Deep Down............... 20

Henore De Balzac.

776 Père Goriot................ 20

1128 Cousin Pons.............. 20

1318 The Vendetta............ 25

S. Baring-Gould.

787 Court Royal.............. 20

878 Little Tu'penny.......... 10

1122 Eve...................... 20

1201 Mehalah: A Story of the Salt Marshes........... 20

1697 Red Spider.............. 20

1711 The Pennycomequicks... 20

1763 John Herring............ 30

1779 Arminell.... 30

1821 Urith..................... 20

Frank Barrett.

986 The Great Hesper...... 20

1188 A Recoiling Vengeance.. 20

1245 Fettered for Life........ 25

1461 Smuggler's Secret....... 10

1611 Between Life and Death. 20

1750 Lieutenant Barnabas.... 25

1828 Under a Strange Mask.. 10

1940 Olga's Crime............ 25

J. M. Barrie.

1896 My Lady Nicotine....... 20

1977 Better Dead............. 10

Basil.

344 "The Wearing of the Green"..................... 20

547 A Coquette's Conquest.. 25

585 A Drawn Game.......... 20

G. M. Bayne.

1618 Galaski.................. 20

Anne Beale.

188 Idonea.................. 20

199 The Fisher Village....... 10

Alexander Begg.

1605 Wrecks in the Sea of Life........ 20

E. B. Benjamin.

1706 Jim, the Parson......... 20

1720 Our Roman Palace...... 20

A. Bearimo.

1624 Vic 20

E. Berger.

1646 Charles Auchester...... 20

W. Bergsol.

1445 Pillone.................. 20

E. Berthel.

1589 The Sergeant's Legacy.. 20

Walter Besant.

97 All in a Garden Fair.... 20
137 Uncle Jack............. 10
140 A Glorious Fortune..... 10
146 Love Finds the Way, and Other Stories. By Besant and Rice.............. 10
230 Dorothy Forster......... 25
324 In Luck at Last......... 10
541 Uncle Jack.............. 10
651 " Self or Bearer "....... 10
862 Children of Gibeon..... 20
904 The Holy Rose.......... 10
906 The World Went Very Well Then............. 25
969 To Call Her Mine........ 25
1055 Katharine Regina........ 25
1065 Herr Paulus: His Rise, His Greatness, and His Fall...................... 20
1148 The Inner House........ 20
1151 For Faith and Freedom.. 20
1240 The Bell of St. Paul's.... 20
1247 The Lament of Dives.... 20
1378 They Were Married. By Walter Besant and Jas. Rice..................... 10
1418 Armorel of Lyonesse.... 20
1462 Let Nothing You Dismay 25
1530 When the Ship Comes Home. By Besant and Rice...................... 10
1655 The Demoniac........... 20
1861 St. Katherine's by the Tower................... 20
2018 The Revolt of Man...... 25

M. Betham-Edwards.

273 Love and Mirage; or, The Waiting on an Island... 10
579 The Flower of Doom, and Other Stories........... 10
594 Doctor Jacob 20
1023 Next of Kin—Wanted... 20
1407 The Parting of the Ways 20
1500 Disarmed................ 20
1543 For One and the World.. 20
1627 A Romance of the Wire. 20
1845 Forestalled; or, The Life Quest................... 20

Jeanie Gwynne Bettany.

1810 A Laggard in Love...... 20

Bjornstjerne Bjornson.

1385 Arne...................... 10
1388 The Happy Boy......... 10

William Black.

1 Yolande................. 20
18 Shandon Bells........... 20
21 Sunrise: A Story of These Times.................... 20
23 A Princess of Thule..... 20
39 In Silk Attire............. 25
44 Macleod of Dare........ 25
49 That Beautiful Wretch.. 20
50 The Strange Adventures of a Phaeton............ 20
70 White Wings: A Yachting Romance........... 25
78 Madcap Violet........... 20
81 A Daughter of Heth.. .. 20
124 Three Feathers..... 20
125 The Monarch of Mincing Lane..................... 20
126 Kilmeny.................. 20
138 Green Pastures and Piccadilly.................. 25
265 Judith Shakespeare: Her Love Affairs and Other Adventures.. 20
472 The Wise Women of Inverness................... 10
627 White Heather........... 20
898 Romeo and Juliet: A Tale of Two Young Fools... 20
962 Sabina Zembra. 1st half 20
962 Sabina Zembra. 2d half 20
1096 The Strange Adventures of a House-Boat......... 20
1132 In Far Lochaber......... 20
1227 The Penance of John Logan..................... 25
1259 Nanciebel: A Tale of Stratford-on-Avon.. 20
1268 Prince Fortunatus....... 25
1389 Oliver Goldsmith........ 10
1394 The Four Macnicols, and Other Tales............. 10
1426 An Adventure in Thule.. 10
1505 Lady Silverdale's Sweetheart.................... 10
1506 Mr. Pisistratus Brown, M. P.. 10
1725 Stand Fast, Craig-Royston!.................... 20
1892 Donald Ross of Heimra.. 20

R. D. Blackmore.

67 Lorna Doone. 1st half.. 25
67 Lorna Doone. 2d half.. 25
427 The Remarkable History of Sir Thomas Upmore, Bart., M. P............. 20
615 Mary Anerley........... 20
625 Erema; or, My Father's Sin...................... 25

629 Cripps, the Carrier.. ... 20
630 Cradock Nowell. 1st half. 20
630 Cradock Nowell. 2d half 20
631 Christowell. A Dartmoor Tale. 20
632 Clara Vaughan.......... 20
633 The Maid of Sker. 1st half 25
633 The Maid of Sker. 2d half 25
636 Alice Lorraine. 1st half 20
636 Alice Lorraine. 2d half. 20
926 Springhaven. 1st half.. 20
926 Springhaven. 2d half... 20
1267 Kit and Kitty. 1st half.. 20
1267 Kit and Kitty. 2d half.. 20

Isa Blagden.

705 The Woman I Loved, and the Woman Who Loved Me.................... 10

C. Blatherwick.

151 The Ducie Diamonds.... 10

Frederick Boyle.

856 The Good Hater......... 20

Miss M. E. Braddon.

35 Lady Audley's Secret... 25
56 Phantom Fortune........ 20
74 Aurora Floyd........... 20
110 Under the Red Flag..... 10
153 The Golden Calf......... 20
204 Vixen..................... 25
211 The Octoroon........... 10
234 Barbara; or, Splendid Misery.................... 20
263 An Ishmaelite............ 20
315 The Mistletoe Bough. Christmas, 1884. Edited by Miss M. E. Braddon. 20
434 Wyllard's Weird......... 20
478 Diavola; or, Nobody's Daughter. Part I...... 20
478 Diavola; or, Nobody's Daughter. Part II..... 20
480 Married in Haste. Edited by Miss M. E. Braddon.................. 20
487 Put to the Test. Edited by Miss M. E. Braddon.... 20
488 Joshua Haggard's Daughter................ 20
489 Rupert Godwin........... 20
495 Mount Royal............. 25
496 Only a Woman. Edited by Miss M. E. Braddon. 20
497 The Lady's Mile......... 25
498 Only a Clod.............. 20
499 The Cloven Foot........ 20
511 A Strange World....... 20
515 Sir Jasper's Tenant.... 25
524 Strangers and Pilgrims. 20
529 The Doctor's Wife...... 20
542 Fenton's Quest...... ... 20
544 Cut by the County; or, Grace Darnel 10
548 A Fatal Marriage, and The Shadow in the Corner.......................... 10
549 Dudley Carleon; or, The Brother's Secret, and George Caulfield's Journey..................... 10
552 Hostages to Fortune. .. 20
553 Birds of Prey........... 20
554 Charlotte's Inheritance. (Sequel to "Birds of Prey") 20
557 To the Bitter End....... 20
559 Taken at the Flood..... 20
560 Asphodel................... 30
561 Just as I am; or, A Living Lie.................... 20
567 Dead Men's Shoes....... 25
570 John Marchmont's Legacy..................... 30
618 The Mistletoe Bough. Christmas, 1885. Edited by Miss M. E. Braddon. 20
840 One Thing Needful; or, The Penalty of Fate... 25
881 Mohawks. 1st half...... 20
881 Mohawks. 2d half...... 20
890 The Mistletoe Bough. Christmas, 1886. Edited by Miss M. E. Braddon.. 20
943 Weavers and Weft; or, "Love that Hath Us in His Net"............. 20
947 Publicans and Sinners; or, Lucius Davoren. 1st half..................... 20
947 Publicans and Sinners; or, Lucius Davoren. 2d half..................... 20
1036 Like and Unlike......... 20
1098 The Fatal Three......... 20
1211 The Day Will Come..... 20
1411 Whose Was the Hand?.. 25
1664 Dead Sea Fruit.......... 20
1898 The World, Flesh and the Devil.................... 20

Annie Bradshaw.

706 A Crimson Stain......... 10

Charlotte M. Braeme, Author of "Dora Thorne."

19 Her Mother's Sin........ 20
51 Dora Thorne..... 25
54 A Broken Wedding-Ring 25
68 A Queen Amongst Women....................... 10
69 Madolin's Lover 25
73 Redeemed by Love; or, Love's Victory.... 20
76 Wife in Name Only; or, A Broken Heart..... .. 20
79 Wedded and Parted..... 10
92 Lord Lynne's Choice.... 25

148 Thorns and Orange-Blossoms........ 25
190 Romance of a Black Veil 10
220 Which Loved Him Best? 25
237 Repented at Leisure. (Large type edition).... 20
967 Repented at Leisure.... 10
249 "Prince Charlie's Daughter;" or, The Cost of Her Love........ 25
250 Sunshine and Roses; or, Diana's Discipline...... 25
254 The Wife's Secret, and Fair but False.......... 10
283 The Sin of a Lifetime; or, Vivien's Atonement 20
287 At War With Herself.... 10
923 At War With Herself. (Large type edition)... 20
288 From Gloom to Sunlight; or, From Out the Gloom 25
955 From Gloom to Sunlight; or, From Out the Gloom (Large type edition).... 25
291 Love's Warfare.......... 20
292 A Golden Heart......... 20
293 The Shadow of a Sin.... 10
948 The Shadow of a Sin. (Large type edition)... 20
294 The False Vow; or, Hilda; or, Lady Hutton's Ward......... ... 25
928 The False Vow; or, Hilda; or, Lady Hutton's Ward. (Large type edition)................ 25
294 Lady Hutton's Ward; or, Hilda; or, The False Vow.................... 10
928 Lady Hutton's Ward; or, Hilda; or, The False Vow. (Large type edition)................ 20
294 Hilda; or, The False Vow; or, Lady Hutton's Ward.................. 10
928 Hilda; or, The False Vow; or, Lady Hutton's Ward. (Large type edition)................ 20
295 A Woman's War........ 10
952 A Woman's War. (Large type edition)........... 20
296 A Rose in Thorns....... 20
297 Hilary's Folly; or, Her Marriage Vow.......... 25
953 Hilary's Folly; or, Her Marriage Vow. (Large type edition)........... 25
299 The Fatal Lilies, and A Bride from the Sea.... 10
300 A Gilded Sin, and A Bridge of Love......... 10
303 Ingledew House, and More Bitter than Death 10
304 In Cupid's Net.......... 10
305 A Dead Heart, and Lady Gwendoline's Dream... 10
306 A Golden Dawn, and Love for a Day......... 10
307 Two Kisses, and Like no Other Love............ 10
308 Beyond Pardon........... 20
322 A Woman's Love-Story. 20
323 A Willful Maid........... 20
411 A Bitter Atonement..... 20
433 My Sister Kate........... 10
459 A Woman's Temptation. (Large type edition).... 20
951 A Woman's Temptation. 10
460 Under a Shadow........ 20
465 The Earl's Atonement... 20
466 Between Two Loves..... 25
467 A Struggle for a Ring... 20
469 Lady Damer's Secret.... 20
470 Evelyn's Folly........... 20
471 Thrown on the World... 25
475 Between Two Sins; or, Married in Haste....... 10
516 Put Asunder; or, Lady Castlemaine's Divorce. 20
576 Her Martyrdom...... 20
626 A Fair Mystery; or, The Perils of Beauty........ 25
741 The Heiress of Hilldrop; or, The Romance of a Young Girl............ 20
745 For Another's Sin; or, A Struggle for Love...... 25
792 Set in Diamonds......... 25
821 The World Between Them................ 25
822 A Passion Flower........ 25
853 A True Magdalen........ 20
854 A Woman's Error....... 25
922 Marjorie.................. 20
924 'Twixt Smile and Tear... 25
927 Sweet Cymbeline......... 25
929 The Belle of Lynn; or, The Miller's Daughter.. 20
931 Lady Diana's Pride..... 20
949 Claribel's Love Story; or, Love's Hidden Depths.. 20
958 A Haunted Life; or, Her Terrible Sin............ 20
969 The Mystery of Colde Fell; or, Not Proven... 20
973 The Squire's Darling.... 25
975 A Dark Marriage Morn.. 20
978 Her Second Love......... 20
982 The Duke's Secret....... 20
985 On Her Wedding Morn, and The Mystery of the Holly-Tree.............. 25
988 The Shattered Idol, and Letty Leigh............ 20

990 The Earl's Error, and Arnold's Promise....... 25
995 An Unnatural Bondage, and That Beautiful Lady.......... 20
1006 His Wife's Judgment.... 20
1008 A Thorn in Her Heart.. 25
1010 Golden Gates............ 20
1012 A Nameless Sin.......... 20
1014 A Mad Love............ 20
1031 Irene's Vow............ 25
1052 Signa's Sweetheart...... 20
1091 A Modern Cinderella.... 10
1134 Lord Elesmere's Wife.... 25
1155 Lured Away; or, The Story of a Wedding-Ring, and The Heiress of Arne............... 20
1179 Beauty's Marriage....... 10
1185 A Fiery Ordeal.......... 20
1195 Dumaresq's Temptation. 20
1285 Jenny................... 20
1291 The Star of Love........ 20
1328 Lord Lisle's Daughter... 10
1415 Weaker than a Woman. 20
1628 Love Works Wonders... 20
2010 Her Only Sin............ 10
2011 A Fatal Wedding......... 25
2012 A Bright Wedding-Day.. 25
2013 One Against Many...... 25
2014 One False Step.......... 25
2015 Two Fair Women........ 25

Fredrika Bremer.

187 The Midnight Sun....... 10

John Francis Brewer.

1911 The Curse upon Mitre Square.................. 10

Charlotte Bronte.

15 Jane Eyre.............. 25
57 Shirley.................. 25
944 The Professor.... 20

Rhoda Broughton.

86 Belinda................ 20
101 Second Thoughts......... 20
227 Nancy.................. 20
645 Mrs. Smith of Longmains 10
758 "Good-bye, Sweetheart!"............ 20
765 Not Wisely, But Too Well 20
767 Joan.................... 20
768 Red as a Rose is She 20
769 Cometh Up as a Flower. 25
862 Betty's Visions.......... 10
894 Doctor Cupid............ 20
1599 Alas!.................... 20

Louise de Bruneval.

1686 Sœur Louise............. 20

Robert Buchanan.

145 "Storm-Beaten:" God and The Man............ 25
154 Annan Water............ 25
181 The New Abelard 10
268 The Martyrdom of Madeline.................. 25
398 Matt: A Tale of a Caravan............... 10
468 The Shadow of the Sword 25
646 The Master of the Mine. 25
892 That Winter Night; or, Love's Victory......... 10
1074 Stormy Waters.......... 20
1104 The Heir of Linne....... 20
1350 Love Me Forever......... 10
1455 The Moment After...... 25

John Bunyan.

1498 The Pilgrim's Progress.. 20

Captain Fred Burnaby.

380 "Our Radicals".......... 25
375 A Ride to Khiva......... 20
384 On Horseback Through Asia Minor............ 25

John Bloundelle-Burton.

918 The Silent Shore; or, The Mystery of St. James' Park............ 20

Beatrice M. Butt.

1354 Delicia.................... 20
2019 Miss Molly.............. 25

Author of "By Crooked Paths."

430 A Bitter Reckoning..... 10

E. Lasseter Bynner.

1456 Nimport.................. 20
1460 Tritons.................. 20

Lord Byron.

719 Childe Harold's Pilgrimage...................... 10

E. Fairfax Byrrne.

521 Entangled.............. 20
538 A Fair Country Maid.... 20

Mrs. Caddy.

127 Adrian Bright........... 20

Hall Caine.

445 The Shadow of a Crime. 25
520 She's All the World to Me....... 10
1234 The Deemster........... 20
1255 The Bondman........... 20

Mona Caird.

1699 The Wing of Azrael..... 20

LaVergne, TN USA
15 September 2009
157968LV00005B/91/A